THE
U.S.-MEXICAN WAR

CAROL *and* THOMAS CHRISTENSEN

COMPANION TO THE PUBLIC TELEVISION SERIES
THE U.S.–MEXICAN WAR, 1846–1848

BAY
BOOKS
SAN FRANCISCO

THE
U.S.-MEXICAN WAR

This book is published to accompany the PBS series
The U.S.–Mexican War, 1846–1848. This series is a
production of KERA-TV, Dallas/Fort Worth/Denton.

Bay Books is an imprint of Bay Books & Tapes, Inc.,
555 De Haro St., No. 220, San Francisco, CA 94107.
Distributed to the trade by Publishers Group West.

PUBLISHER: James Connolly
EDITORIAL DIRECTOR: Clancy Drake
ART DIRECTOR: Jeffrey O'Rourke
MANAGING EDITOR: Sheryl Fullerton
INTERIOR DESIGN: Paula Schlosser Design
TEXT COMPOSITION: Star Type, Berkeley
PICTURE RESEARCHER: Maureen Spuhler
PROOFREADER: Desne Border

AUTHORS' ACKNOWLEDGMENTS

THANKS TO George Stone and Drs. Sam W. Haynes and Miguel Soto for
repeated readings, corrections, and suggestions, and especially to Dr.
Robert Ryal Miller for his advice and encouragement; to series producer
Sylvia Komatsu for assembling and directing an excellent academic and
production team; to Rob Tranchin for his inspiring scripts; to Andrea
Boardman, Paul Espinosa, Gila Espinoza, Ginny Martin, Therese Powell,
and our other friends at KERA for their generous cooperation.

Special thanks to Pamela Byers for her commitment to creating a
cross-cultural book to mark the 150th anniversary of the war; thanks also
to James Connolly, Clancy Drake, Jeffrey O'Rourke, Courtney Mangus,
and the others at Bay Books for bringing the project to fruition; to
Sheryl Fullerton for her pragmatism and humor; to Zipporah Collins for
her tireless editing; to Maureen Spuhler for her good-natured and professional image research; and to Paula Schlosser, Hilda Chen, and Star
Type for book production.

The publishers gratefully acknowledge permission to use excerpts from the following: "What Happened Here
Before" from *Turtle Island* by Gary Snyder (New Directions, 1974) © by Gary Snyder; *The Mexican War: A Litho-
graphic Record* by Ronnie Tyler (Texas State Historical Association, 1973) © by Ronnie Tyler; *Down the Santa Fe
Trail and into Mexico: The Diary of Susan Shelby Magoffin, 1846–1847* edited by Stella M. Drumm (Yale University
Press, 1962) © by Yale University Press; *Foreigners in Their Native Land* by David J. Weber (University of New
Mexico Press, 1973) © by David J. Weber; *The Buried Mirror* by Carlos Fuentes (Houghton Mifflin, 1992) © by
Carlos Fuentes; *The United States and Mexico, 1821–1848* by George Lockhart Rives (Charles Scribner's Sons,
1913) © by Charles Scribner's Sons; *The Mexican War, 1846–1848* by K. Jack Bauer (Simon & Schuster, 1974) ©
K. Jack Bauer; *Labyrinth of Solitude* by Octavio Paz (Grove/Atlantic, 1985) © by Octavio Paz.

LIBRARY OF CONGRESS CATALOGING-IN-PUBLICATION DATA
Christensen, Thomas, 1948–
    The U.S.–Mexican War / Thomas and Carol Christensen.
        p.   cm,
    Published in conjunction with the four-part television series "The
U.S.–Mexican War".
    Includes bibliographical references (p.   ) and index.
    ISBN 0-912333-44-8 (paperback : alk. paper). -- ISBN 0-912333-57-X
(hardcover : alk. paper)
    1. Mexican War, 1846-1848. I. Christensen, Carol, 1947-
II. U.S.–Mexican War (Television program) III. Title.
E404.C47 1998
973.6'2--dc21   98-24576
                                                                        CIP

ISBN: 0-912333-44-8 (paperback)
ISBN: 0-912333-57-X (hardcover)

Printed in China

10 9 8 7 6 5 4 3 2 1

PRODUCER'S PREFACE

AT THE TURN OF THE twentieth century, one writer observing world events noted, "Frontiers are indeed the razor's edge on which hang suspended the modern issues of war or peace, of life or death to nations." Today we live in a world of constantly changing frontiers: geographical, cultural, political, scientific, spiritual, and economic. It is along these frontiers that we come in contact with one another and in turn become transformed.

Between 1846 and 1848, two neighbors—the United States and Mexico—went to war. It was a defining event for both nations, transforming a continent and forging a new identity for its peoples. By the war's end, Mexico lost nearly half of its territory—the present American Southwest from Texas to California—and the United States became a continental power.

At the time, many Americans saw the United States' victory as fulfillment of their "manifest destiny" and proof that theirs was a "model republic." These days, however, most Americans know little, if anything, about this conflict. In Mexico, the war known as *La Invasión Norteamericana* (the North American Invasion) has never been forgotten and remains a painful scar in Mexico's relationship with the United States.

For the Mexican families and their descendants who have lived on these lands for generations, the United States' conquest is part of their collective memory and marks the birth of the Mexican American people. For Native Americans, who had resisted and endured previous invasions of their homelands, the war's conclusion signaled a new phase of the ongoing struggle to preserve their lands and traditions.

The issues raised during the U.S.–Mexican War are ones we still grapple with today: the contradiction between stated ideals and actual practice; the distinction between a "just" and an "unjust" war; the ways we define citizenship and identity in a multicultural society; and the challenges in building progressive and democratic nations.

At KERA, the public broadcasting station in North Texas, we believe television can lead to a greater understanding of ourselves, our world, and each other. We are deeply grateful to the institutions, foundations,

A Mexican soldier and his brother.

and individuals who share this vision and provided KERA the support to bring this story of the U.S.–Mexican War to the public. These funders are listed on page 246; without their support, *The U.S.–Mexican War* documentary series for PBS and its accompanying educational materials would not have been possible. I would also like to express my appreciation to Sandy Heberer at PBS, Josh Darsa at CPB, Jim Dougherty and Holly Tank at NEH, and David Jackson and John Crain at the Summerlee Foundation for their support since the inception of this project.

A major documentary series such as this one is a collaborative effort requiring the hard work, talents, and dedication of many people. While it is impossible to acknowledge everyone who contributed to *The U.S.–Mexican War* in this space, I want to recognize these individuals: director/editor Ginny Martin; writer/producer Rob Tranchin; senior producer Paul Espinosa; producer Andrea Boardman; cinematographers Ginny Martin and Allen Moore; chief gaffer Jeff Hurst; composers John Bryant and Frank Hames; sound designer David Rosenblad; location sound technician Gerardo Rueda; associate producers Roció Barajas, Gila Espinoza, Rick Leal, Victor Payan, and Therese Powell; principal researcher George Stone; assistant editors Shane Estep, Ken Mandel, Christine McConnell, and Michael Zellner; and unit manager Joe Bellotti.

I would also like to thank Deanna Collingwood for development of ancillaries; Kaye Huffman for development of the website; Bob Perrenot and Chris Rotenberry for design; Sharon Philippart, Dorothy Gentry, Kristi Bare, and Owen Comora Associates for promotion and publicity; Roy Dunn for distribution; Carol and Tom Christensen and the staff at Bay Books for their work on the companion volume; my colleagues Yolette García and Rick Thompson for their encouragement and support. And special thanks go to KERA President/CEO Cheryl Craigie and former President/CEO Richie Meyer for their faith in this project.

Among the many individuals who assisted us in producing *The U.S.–Mexican War* are Steve Abolt, Steven Butler, Leopoldo Martinez Caraza, Antonia Castañeda, Joe Chance, Richard Deertrack, William DePalo, Jr., John S. D. Eisenhower, Ricardo Pérez Escamilla, Donald Frazier, Mark Gardner, Luis Garfias, Israel Cavazos Garza, Enrique Guerra, Carlos Herrera, Laura Herrera, Arturo Inda, Tony Mares, Phillip Martinez, Vicente Martinez, Joe Mirabal, Genaro Padilla, Miguel Ángel González Quiroga, Carlos Recio, Father Juan Romero, Antonio Salazar, and Richard Bruce Winders. Special thanks also go to the members of the living history organizations who participated in the reenactment scenes.

In visualizing the series, we worked with a number of archives in the United States and Mexico, but we owe a special debt of gratitude to Katherine R. Goodwin and Gerald Saxon at the Jenkins Garrett Library of the Special Collections Division at the University of Texas at Arlington. I also want to thank Magdalena Acosta Urquidi and Alejandra Lajous Vargas at Canal Once, our sister station in Mexico City, for their commitment, advice and key production assistance.

In creating *The U.S.–Mexican War* series, we at KERA resolved to present multiple viewpoints. To do so, we planted our feet on both sides of the border and invited a panel of distinguished scholars—historians from the United States and Mexico—to be our guides. These indispensable project advisers include R. David Edmunds, Mario T. García, Deena J. González, Richard Griswold del Castillo, Sam W. Haynes, Robert W. Johannsen, Robert Ryal Miller, David M. Pletcher, Miguel Soto, Ron Tyler, Josefina Zoraida Vázquez, Jesús Velasco-Márquez, and David J. Weber.

During the last six years they have generously shared with us their invaluable knowledge, experience, and wisdom. Together we spent long hours reliving the war, analyzing the events leading up to it, and debating its legacy. At times our discussions were contentious and heated. Our disagreements did not fall simply along national lines. But it was from our differences that we gained the greatest insight—and in many ways ourselves became transformed.

Throughout this long and sometimes arduous process, there was one point upon which we all agreed: the long-neglected story of the U.S.–Mexican War must come to light. Of course, no one documentary or book can tell the definitive story of this war. There are many valid viewpoints on this complex subject, and new research is constantly under way. Our hope is that *The U.S.–Mexican War*—both series and book—will foster a deeper understanding of our common history and encourage further exploration of this important event. History, after all, is never final, as succeeding generations confront for themselves the forces and ideas that shape our lives.

—Sylvia Komatsu, KERA
Executive Producer
The U.S.–Mexican War, 1846–1848

A young U.S. soldier.

CONTENTS

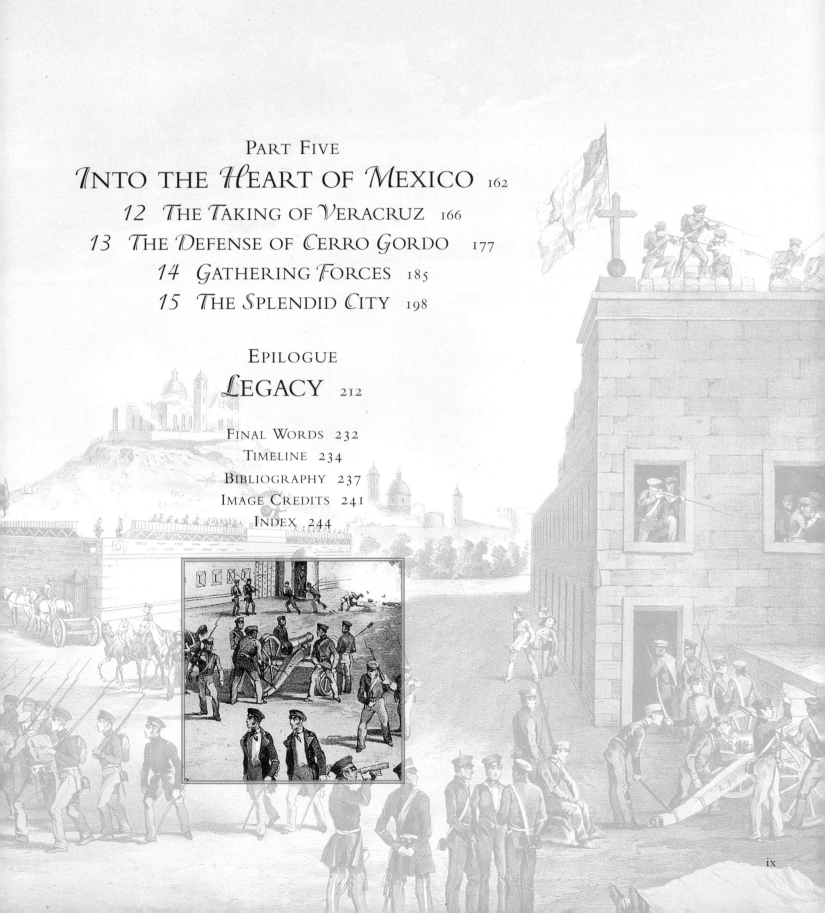

U.S. TROOPS ENTERING MEXICO CITY.

PART ONE

LOOKING BACK

"Los yanquis pueden entrar a México, pero esto no significa que ellos serán conquistadores de la nación mejicana."

"The Yankees may enter Mexico City, but that does not mean that they will be conquerors of the Mexican nation."
—A MEXICAN SOLDIER
IN A LETTER TO HIS WIFE, AUGUST 1847

"We asked, who the land belonged to . . . and who remembers the Treaty of Guadalupe Hidalgo."
—GARY SNYDER, FROM "WHAT HAPPENED HERE BEFORE" IN *Turtle Island*

T HAS BEEN 150 years since the United States and Mexico signed the Treaty of Guadalupe Hidalgo, ending a bitter fight for the North American continent. Within the first year of war, U.S. and Mexican forces met in battles across northern Mexico, from the Gulf to the Pacific Coast. Before the war was over, central Mexico had become the battleground. Fighting ended at the gates of Mexico City, where U.S. troops defeated the Mexican army. While the two nations negotiated the treaty, U.S. soldiers occupied the capital and northern provinces of Mexico, its customhouses, and its ports.

The war changed both nations, redrawing the map of North America. With the annexation of Texas in 1845 and the treaty signing in 1848, the United States acquired a million square miles of territory—land that included the present states of California, Arizona, New Mexico, Nevada, and Utah, and parts of Wyoming, Colorado, and Oklahoma. Mexico lost nearly half of its territory, its northern frontier, an area stretching from the California ports of San Francisco and San Diego to the farms and ranches of New Mexico. The Grand Canyon, the Painted Desert, Yosemite Valley, Pike's Peak—all became part of the United States with a war and the stroke of a pen. Within months, the gold rush—and then the land rush—had begun. Mexico had been torn in two and the United States had become a continental power.

The fight and the 1848 treaty that ended it marked a turning point in relations between the United States and Mexico. The two nations have been living with the legacy of the war for a century and a half—and the feelings aroused by the conflict have been slow to change.

Mexico's "Fury and Tears"

By the final days of fighting in northern and central Mexico, the lives of tens of thousands of Mexicans had been touched by the war. But history is written by the winners, and there are not many Mexican accounts of the conflict—some letters from soldiers, battle plans, records of courts-martial, memoirs of politicians and generals trying to justify their actions,

A New Map

BEFORE THE U.S.–Mexican War, the United States and Mexico were nearly equal in territory, but the two nations had taken very different routes to their claims on the continent.

The first colonies of the independent United States had occupied only a 200-mile strip of land between the Atlantic and the Appalachian Mountains. As population grew beyond the 4,000,000 counted by the first U.S. census in 1790, settlers began moving south and west across the continent, pushing toward the Mississippi River. After purchasing New Orleans and the French territory west of the Mississippi in 1803, the United States continued to grow, purchasing

Florida from Spain in the Adams–Onis Treaty of 1819.

Mexico proclaimed her independence two years later. The new nation's northern boundary, which had been established by the Adams–Onis Treaty, was a line running from the Gulf of Mexico up the Sabine River, northwest to the Red and the Arkansas Rivers, then west across the forty-second parallel to the Pacific. From Spain the young Mexican nation took possession of this huge territory and the problems of administering it. For Mexico's first leaders, says historian Miguel Ángel González, "it was a matter of national honor, not just pride, to maintain the integrity of all of the territory they had inherited from Spain."

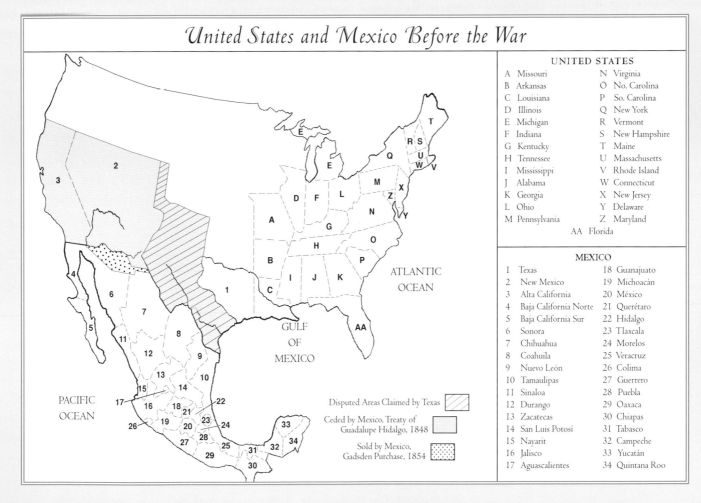

United States and Mexico Before the War

UNITED STATES

A	Missouri	N	Virginia
B	Arkansas	O	No. Carolina
C	Louisiana	P	So. Carolina
D	Illinois	Q	New York
E	Michigan	R	Vermont
F	Indiana	S	New Hampshire
G	Kentucky	T	Maine
H	Tennessee	U	Massachusetts
I	Mississippi	V	Rhode Island
J	Alabama	W	Connecticut
K	Georgia	X	New Jersey
L	Ohio	Y	Delaware
M	Pennsylvania	Z	Maryland
		AA	Florida

MEXICO

1	Texas	18	Guanajuato
2	New Mexico	19	Michoacán
3	Alta California	20	México
4	Baja California Norte	21	Querétaro
5	Baja California Sur	22	Hidalgo
6	Sonora	23	Tlaxcala
7	Chihuahua	24	Morelos
8	Coahuila	25	Veracruz
9	Nuevo León	26	Colima
10	Tamaulipas	27	Guerrero
11	Sinaloa	28	Puebla
12	Durango	29	Oaxaca
13	Zacatecas	30	Chiapas
14	San Luis Potosí	31	Tabasco
15	Nayarit	32	Campeche
16	Jalisco	33	Yucatán
17	Aguascalientes	34	Quintana Roo

Disputed Areas Claimed by Texas

Ceded by Mexico, Treaty of Guadalupe Hidalgo, 1848

Sold by Mexico, Gadsden Purchase, 1854

Until Texas seceded from Mexico in 1836, the international border had followed the line established by the Adams–Onis Treaty in 1819. The United States annexed Texas before the war, and it gained California, Arizona, New Mexico, Nevada, and Utah, and parts of Wyoming, Colorado, and Oklahoma from the war.

satirical pamphlets and broadsides critical of both the United States and Mexico. Fortunately, one group of fifteen Mexican writers set out to write a comprehensive history of the war. The group—intellectuals, soldiers, and politicians, including Guillermo Prieto, Manuel Payno, and Ignacio Ramírez—gathered all their knowledge of the period and all their memories of their nation's suffering.

The result is a powerful work: *Apuntes para la historia de la guerra entre México y los Estados Unidos* (Notes for a History of the War between Mexico and the United States). It details battles and sieges in which thousands of Mexican men, women, and children—soldiers and civilians—were killed or wounded. It tells of U.S. conquerors invading their lands and homes. It describes the *"año infausto,"* the fateful year, 1847, when the capital of their country was occupied

The *Apuntes* was also a purposeful work, intended by its authors to discover the origins of the conflict. They concluded: "The insatiable ambition of the United States, favored by our weakness, caused the war." The authors of the *Apuntes* analyzed this "weakness," identifying forces in Mexican society that soon produced a civil war. From that conflict, Benito Juárez rose to leadership, bringing liberal ideals of national reform and a new national consciousness.

The memory of the war with the United States formed a part of this national identity. "To this day," says Mexican historian Jesús Velasco-Márquez, "Mexicans still feel aggrieved that the United States invaded their country and occupied their capital." The burden of the past, as many modern Mexican writers have pointed out, weighs heavily in Mexico's creation of its future—particularly in its relations with the United States.

U.S. *"Optimism Unbounded"*

The United States was in a jubilant mood after its victory over Mexico. This war was the first "fought in the media" and penny press articles had created strong support for U.S. troops. Songs and plays about heroes, paintings and lithographs of battles, had fanned popular passions during the conflict. After the parades and fireworks that marked its end, it was remembered in thousands of diaries, journals, letters, and sketches.

There were no collaborative histories like the Mexican *Apuntes*. Instead, this first major foreign war was remembered in individual stories, accounts ranging from inspiring descriptions of courage and sacrifice to

"When the war was over, our hearts were filled with a profound sadness at the evils it had loosed, while our minds were enlightened by its lesson: the impossibility of protecting and defending a country torn by poverty and anarchy."

—*Apuntes para la historia de la guerra*

ugly tales of cruelty and savagery. Veterans continued to create portraits—some realistic, some romanticized—of the war for decades.

Ulysses S. Grant served as quartermaster and officer in the Texas and Mexico campaigns. Little more than a decade later, he faced other U.S.–Mexican War veterans in the U.S. Civil War. In his *Memoirs,* he recalled the Mexican War with shame, describing it as "the most unjust war ever waged by a stronger against a weaker nation." During the war, however, most U.S. citizens had blamed Mexico for the conflict that erupted over Texas annexation. The U.S. triumph was seen as proof that the United States was the superior nation and white the superior race.

The war strengthened the Republic, historians exulted. It forged a national identity and revealed "the native germ of the American character." The new territory acquired was seen as proof that the United States had a God-given right to the continent. President Polk boasted that the victory had given his country "a national character abroad." Now, he told Congress, U.S. "power and . . . resources have become known and are respected throughout the world."

"The U.S.–Mexican War," observes historian Sam W. Haynes, "forces Americans to come to grips with some very central questions about who they are as a nation. Clearly, [U.S. President] Polk is responsible for making the United States a transcontinental empire. At the same time, Polk is also responsible for a retreat from the idealism of the 18th century."

"America is the country of the future. . . . It is a country of beginnings, of projects of vast designs and expectations. The bountiful continent is ours, state on state, and territory on territory, to the waves of the Pacific sea."
—RALPH WALDO EMERSON

Forgotten Voices from the Borderland

For years, the voices of the two groups of people affected most directly by the Treaty of Guadalupe Hidalgo were very little heard. Only in recent years have historians begun to search for the stories of the thousands who were living in Mexico's northern territory when the treaty was signed. These included both Native American and Spanish-speaking residents whose homes became part of the United States.

The borderlands that changed hands after the war contained "hundreds of towns and villages that were home to a Spanish-speaking population alien by race and culture to the new government," states historian Ramón Eduardo Ruiz. "Many of the conquered peoples . . . traced their local origins back more than two centuries. But during that time Spain had not simply built a replica of its own society in the Southwest. Like their Mexican brothers to the south, Californios, Nuevo Mexicanos, and Texanos claimed a mestizo heritage, a blend of Spanish and Indian."

After the war, some of these Spanish-speaking southwesterners resettled in lands that still belonged to Mexico. Those who remained in the territories newly claimed by the United States saw their homeland settled by Anglo emigrants. The 80,000 Hispanic residents of the borderlands—called the "Conquered Generation" by U.S. historian Mario T. García—experienced a conflict of cultures that continues to this day.

The Native Americans who lived in California and New Mexico had already seen their lands claimed by the Spanish, their lives changed by Spanish missionaries and settlers. At the end of the U.S.–Mexican War, their nationality and destiny changed again. More than 200,000 Native American people—Hopi, Navajo, Apache, Paiute, Comanche, Miwok, Maidu, Pomo, Yuma, and many others—were living in the area taken over by the United States in 1848. It was the beginning of the most bitter and tragic chapter in the history of their people.

CHAPTER 1

HISTORIES IN CONFLICT

*Mexico City surrendered the day after the U.S. army stormed
Chapultepec, the Mexican military academy protecting the capital.
The story of the Niños Héroes, the "heroic young men"
who gave their lives defending the fortress, has become part
of Mexican legend. The battle is reenacted each year on a
national holiday commemorating their sacrifice.*

Hostilities between the United States and Mexico began on April 25, 1846, and continued until September 14, 1847. But wars begin long before the first shots are fired. Years of cultural, social, and political differences—including sharply contrasting experiences with self-government—shaped the conflict between the neighboring nations.

U.S. Founding Fathers

Washington, Adams, Jefferson, Madison, Monroe: these earliest U.S. leaders crafted the U.S. Constitution and Bill of Rights. Building on such British political institutions as common law and parliamentary procedures, they provided specific guarantees of the rights of individuals against the state. Whatever their differences, these first U.S. presidents shared a commitment to the orderly succession and continuity of government.

As U.S. population and territory grew, rambunctious frontiersmen eventually replaced what they called "the gentry." In 1828, proponents of a new democracy put President Andrew Jackson into office. National power began to shift more dramatically between political parties, but the Constitution was able to evolve and the government to endure.

The Land of the Free

The United States became an independent nation decades earlier than Mexico. When its six-year Revolutionary War ended in 1781, the United States had allies, money, and arms (which Mexico lacked in its first years of freedom). But even after the peace treaty was signed two years later the United States was worried about survival. France, Spain, and Britain all had interests on the North American continent. Enlarging the nation seemed to be one way to counter this European threat.

In 1801, in the first inaugural address given in the new capital in Washington, Thomas Jefferson described

"[In the war] for the first time [the United States and Mexico] came to measure their strength and to sustain the rights of their respective nations—these sons of two distinct races, . . . destroying each other in the new continent as they had in the old."

—*Apuntes para la historia de la guerra*

his vision of a nation vast enough to hold "our descendants to the thousandth and thousandth generation." When he made the Louisiana Purchase a few years later, he doubled U.S. territory. Settlers quickly moved to claim land in the South and West.

There was still considerable resistance to growth, however, especially among northeasterners. But fears of foreign designs on the continent were rekindled when the British attacked the U.S. capital in the War of 1812. In 1828, Jefferson's grandiose vision took on new reality with the election of President Andrew Jackson. "Jacksonian democracy," which was based on Jefferson's agrarian ideals, spurred the next few decades of the U.S. ride into the frontier.

The Mexican Struggle for Liberty

In the "pivotal years" from 1790 to 1825, says U.S. historian John Tutino, the United States and Mexico had contrasting experiences. While the United States "profited from European wars, and wars against their Amerindian neighbors . . . Mexicans fought each other over social justice and independence."

Spain battled long and hard to hold onto its most valuable New World colony. Mexico's independence movement, which began in 1810, was not successful until 1821. Ruled from abroad, Mexican society was dominated by a small group of criollos (New World–born elite of Spanish blood). This European-influenced upper class was at the peak of a social pyramid supported by a vast population of Indians and mestizos.

In 1821, conservative criollo Agustín de Iturbide united this deeply divided society in opposition to Spanish rule. In Mexico's first independent government, Iturbide became emperor of the nation. Not until he was overthrown did Mexico get its first republican constitution, modeled on the U.S. Constitution. But Mexico had limited experience of self-government and long experience of rule by a monarch.

"FATHER OF MEXICO"

IN 1810 MIGUEL HIDALGO, a Catholic priest, led thousands of ragged, barefoot men, women, and children in a revolt against Spain. His plea for sympathy for the poor and suffering of Mexico inspired the long, bloody Mexican struggle for independence, as well as drawing attention to the nation's class and ethnic divisions. Hidalgo and his successor, Father José María Morelos, were captured and executed by the Spanish, but the independence struggle went on.

The Mexican independence movement finally united behind a plan that even the Mexican upper class and conservatives could support. The alliance of rich and poor that finally drove the Spanish from Mexico did not last much longer than the independence celebrations of September 1821. But the fight for social justice went on.

Native Societies

THE UNITED STATES and Mexico had very different native populations. When Europeans arrived on the North American continent, the patterns of conquest of those native societies helped determine the forms taken by New World governments—British and Spanish, and later U.S. and Mexican—as well as their patterns of growth and development in the years before the war.

The Atlantic Seaboard

The small group of European settlers in British North America included British, German, and Dutch Protestants. A dream of religious freedom drew many of the early settlers to the New World. The promise of economic opportunity was a lure for others—although not comparable to the lure of gold in Mexico. The religious dissidents, with their locally governed churches, were slow to form an integrated society.

The colonists encountered native peoples associated in loose federations—among them the Iroquois Nation, which became a model for new ideals of democratic government. The natives had a tradition of fierce independence and were not accustomed to lives of structured subordination. Some Indian tribes were seen as political enemies after they fought against settlers during the French and Indian War and the Revolutionary War.

The early colonists made few concentrated efforts to convert these North American Indians to their own religions. Even after U.S. independence (and after the U.S.–Mexican War), Protestant colonists showed little interest in assimilating native peoples and traditions into their expanding nation. U.S. growth—in contrast

"The Towne of Pomeiooc," from the 1590
A Briefe and True Report of the New Found Land of Virginia *by Thomas Harriot, scientific adviser to the first English colony near Roanoke. The southeastern Algonquian depicted are now extinct.*

to Mexico's—"was not confused by ancient imperial ties," says U.S. historian Daniel J. Boorstin. "The government of each new unit was shaped by and for the new settlers. The main sufferers from this system were the American Indians, who were already there and whom the new settlers treated as mere obstacles to be removed." With the U.S. government developing by what Boorstin calls the "Add-a-State plan," new states had a certain autonomy, since "the 'mother country' headquartered in Washington speedily abandoned efforts to impose its will on remote parts."

The United States established a pattern as its growing population pushed across the continent. The developing nation purchased territory from European interests, who gave up their New World possessions under economic, diplomatic, and military pressures (ranging from claims against French and Spanish debts to the threat of war). Then the United States drove the native population from the land in Indian wars.

The Aztec Empire

Mexico was center of the Aztec or Mexica civilization (the latest of centuries of successive civilizations). This native society had a highly structured political system and an extensive empire. To defeat the Aztecs, the Spanish conquistadores formed alliances with groups of native people who were under Aztec control. Violent conquest was then followed by some degree of cultural integration. "New Spain," the Spanish name for Mexico, replaced the existing Indian political organization; the Catholic Church and the conquistadores appropriated existing

The Great Temple of Tenochtitlán in an artist's reconstruction. Symbolic center of the universe, it is surrounded by a ceremonial district. The original temple was destroyed by the Spanish, who built a church on the site, but archeologists unearthed the ruins in a five-year project starting in 1978.

Aztec social structures. The Aztec capital, Tenochtitlán—the largest capital city in the Old and New Worlds—became the Spanish capital, Mexico City, a New World center of European culture with its own university and printing houses.

Once Spain had claimed New Spain, it issued royal land grants conferring wealth in this huge New World empire. It created a system of customhouses, churches, and missions, extending to the edges of its colony, eventually even building a "Royal Highway" into California. Like the Aztec state, New Spain was centralized, hierarchical, and vulnerable to invasion.

This dual Aztec–Spanish colonial legacy, with "two traditions of absolute power," says Mexican historian

Enrique Krause, "conferred a unique connection with the sacred on Mexico's succession of rulers." Independent Mexico's caudillos (powerful political leaders) took the place of Aztec emperors and Spanish viceroys, continuing "a tradition of centralized, divinely sanctioned power that has lasted—under different forms—almost to the present day."

MEXICO'S NORTHERN FRONTIER

The northern edge of Mexico's territory extended even beyond the boundaries of the Aztec empire. Many of the native peoples in this region were nomadic, moving between Mexico and the United States. Mexican settlers encountered the same problems as U.S. settlers in claiming

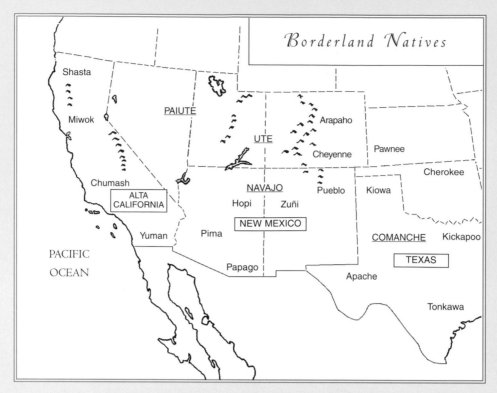

Native American peoples of Mexico's northern territory. The U.S.–Mexican War was not just a two-sided struggle. Native American opposition to both sides influenced the course of events. As David J. Weber points out, "on the eve of war with the United States, autonomous Indian peoples . . . retained control over much of the far northern frontier of Mexico."

the land. Some Indians in the remote provinces of Texas, New Mexico, and Chihuahua especially resisted Mexican control.

U.S. movements against the Indians of the Southeast created more pressure on Mexico's northeast. Less than a decade before the U.S.–Mexican War, for example, the Cherokee people had been relocated from the U.S. Southeast to the Mexican frontier. The Comanche, Apache, and other native peoples whose territories were invaded responded with raids on both U.S. and Mexican settlements. The United States and Mexico sometimes joined forces against Native American occupants of the borderlands both before and after the war.

Indian fighting was not the only battle experience for Mexico's large standing army and frontier garrisons, but Indian wars were the main training ground for a whole generation of U.S. generals, from Sam Houston, who commanded the Texas revolt of 1835–36, to Zachary Taylor, who led the first U.S. troops into combat in the U.S.–Mexican War in 1846.

A Comanche warrior. For decades the Comanche raided an area stretching from Oklahoma to Mexico. During the U.S.–Mexican War, an anonymous writer tried to stir up anti-Indian feeling by claiming that some Comanche chiefs had joined the Mexican army in making attacks on U.S. troops. This image is from the U.S. pamphlet Mexican Treacheries and Cruelties, *published in 1848.*

Mexico City. In the years after the conquest of Mexico, the Spanish did a remarkable job of transforming the Aztec capital of Tenochtitlán into a Spanish city. Frances Calderón de la Barca (whose husband was the Spanish minister to Mexico in the 1840s) wrote: "Here, everything reminds us of the past; of the conquering Spanish who seemed to build for eternity, impressing each work with their solid, grave, and religious character." Mexico's earliest leaders would have to create a new society from this Spanish and Indian legacy.

An Unstable Republic

In the decades after Mexican independence, while the United States was bursting across the continent with expansionist vitality and a vision of Manifest Destiny, Mexico was struggling to create an independent nation from a "dream of New Spain" inherited from the Spanish. The 1824 Constitution promised presidential elections, but the government was often changed by revolts. Numerous "plans" for new governments were used to justify takeovers. Quests for power by military leaders and conflicts between conservatives, liberals, and radicals worked against a stable government.

Fandango in San Antonio. "For three centuries under Spanish colonial rule," says J. Patrick McHenry, "provincial towns such as Oaxaca, Guadalajara, Querétaro, Zacatecas, Mérida—in fact, nearly all major towns in Mexico, cut off as they were from the rest of the country—nurtured a regional pride in their costumes, customs, cuisine, songs and dances." Mexico's sparsely settled areas were famous for their "social fandangos," described by a delighted U.S. observer as "the very poetry of motion."

The nation was weakened by ideological and social differences that divided Mexico "vertically, setting class against class," writes historian J. Patrick McHenry. It was also divided "horizontally into autonomous towns and provinces." During Spanish rule, the system linking outlying areas to the capital city was complicated but clear, with each town's ruler reporting to the Spanish viceroy in Mexico City. After independence, the relation of state to nation became unstable. "The country fell into a loose confederation of states," says McHenry, and its citizens had an ambivalent attitude toward politicians, "particularly those in Mexico City who wished to dominate the country." Rebellions in the provinces often marked changes in the central government.

Economic problems also threatened Mexican society. After the Spanish economic order was overthrown, there was little agreement about use of the country's resources—silver and copper, farmland and ranchland. The young nation was burdened with enormous debt. In fact, bankruptcy threatened almost before the first elected president, Guadalupe Victoria, exchanged his military uniform for the attire of a civilian leader. The nation had been stunned by the loss of a tenth of its young men in the war for independence. Factories, mines, and fields had been abandoned. The economy was stagnant, and investors were scarce.

Crumbling Borders

The new nation drew the eyes of the major European powers and of an expanding United States. "The weakness of Mexico and the rumors of the great wealth that lay hidden and undeveloped in the north of the country invited a race for power on the continent," notes historian David Pletcher. "Britain, France, and Russia all turned their attention to Mexico, and unfortunately not with Mexico's best interests in mind."

Especially attractive were Mexico's northern provinces—Texas, California, and New Mexico. These were sparsely settled, isolated outposts, far from the central government in Mexico City. California ports were coveted by foreign powers after the Mexican government removed Spanish restrictions on trade, substituting a system of free trade with customs duties. A policy of giving liberal land grants to settlers more than twenty-five miles from the ocean made California even more appealing. But the first contest for Mexican territory took place near the Gulf Coast, where Mexico shared an insecure border with the United States. The rebellion that developed there became the first step on the road to the U.S.–Mexican War.

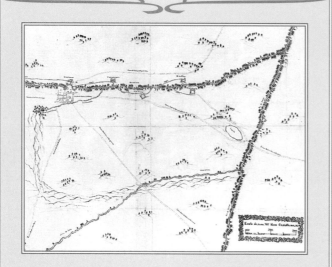

CHAPTER 2

A Fight for Texas

In the first years after independence, Mexico encouraged settlement
in its northern territories to promote national security and to protect
its frontier from raids by the native peoples who had lived there
for generations. Ironically, the Mexican strategy to
safeguard Texas contributed to its loss.

ONLY 2,500 MEXICANS lived in Texas in 1821. More than half of them lived in San Antonio, capital of the province. There were a few scattered missions and a few tiny settlements. The only road beyond San Antonio led to Nacogdoches, near the U.S. border. In 1824 the first Mexican Constitution formed a new state, Coahuila–Texas, joining Spain's northern province of Texas to another former province, Coahuila. San Antonio was not the seat of government for this new combined state, and its interests—and the interests of Texans— were underrepresented in the state legislature.

Despite government encouragement, few of the 6,000,000 people living in Mexico were willing to settle in Texas. But immigrants from the United States —with 11,000,000 people—were eager to settle there, especially in the Gulf Coast area. Faced with the threat of illegal immigration, the Mexican government took steps to encourage legal immigration, especially by European Catholics.

Mexico's Immigration Policy

In 1824, Mexico passed a colonization law offering land, security, and exemption from taxation to foreign settlers. The law required immigrants to Mexico to take up farming or grazing; it encouraged families and required settlers to be "Roman Apostolic Catholics, and of steady habits." Immigration laws also required the use of Spanish for all business transactions and maintained the government's right to "take such precautionary measures as it may deem expedient for the security of the confederation, in respect to the foreigners who may settle within it."

Mexico's settlement policy drew a swarm of speculators to the state capital, Saltillo, where the government was granting these *empresarios* parcels of land. The parcels were to be divided among a specified number of families, each parcel forming a local community with local rights and an elected council. *Empresarios* ran their "colonies," wielding considerable influence and sometimes controlling elections and appointments.

New settlers poured into Texas, first by the hundreds, then by the thousands. Encouraged by the offer of cheap land and minimal taxes, many immigrants recently arrived in the United States from Europe and the British Isles pushed on to settle in Texas. But the overwhelming majority of immigrants to Texas were U.S. citizens.

Anglo Settlers

Soon dozens of colonies of foreigners were scattered across east Texas. Mexican landowners in Texas began to feel that the growth of their province, their own security, and their fortunes depended on the Anglo-American settlers. (Individuals within the "Anglo" cultural group included Irish, Germans, and others, not just those of English descent. Scholars use the term *Anglo* to distinguish these peoples from the Hispanic and Native American populations. David J. Weber writes, "The meeting of Anglo Americans and Mexicans on the Mexican frontier during [the 1820s] contributed to shaping stereotypes in Mexico and the United States which made war between the two nations nearly unavoidable by 1846.")

The Anglo settlers included wealthy *empresarios,* cotton growers, cattle ranchers, pig farmers, and adventurers. Some professed a belief that Texas had been acquired by the United States in the Louisiana Purchase. In favor of self-rule, many Anglo settlers had little loyalty to the Mexican government and ignored the Mexican Constitution and laws. Despite the oaths they signed, few Anglo settlers actually converted to Catholicism—a lapse made simpler by the scarcity of priests on the frontier.

FIRST ANGLO EMPRESARIO IN TEXAS

STEPHEN F. AUSTIN founded the earliest Anglo-American settlement in Texas. Austin's father, Moses, had obtained a land grant from the Spanish governor of Texas, but it was not until December 1821, after Mexican independence, that Stephen settled a group of families on rich land along the Brazos River. Twelve hundred families were eventually attracted to the successful colony.

For years Austin tried to maintain good relations with Mexico. In 1827, he organized a group of Anglos to help the Mexican army suppress the Fredonian revolt. But by 1834 he had written to San Antonio leaders suggesting that they attempt to establish a separate Texas government. Arrested after delivering an Anglo petition to Mexico City, he found an even angrier political situation when he got out of prison eighteen months later. Austin joined the rebels and, in March 1836, voted for the secession of Texas from Mexico.

SLAVERY

ANY ANGLO IMMIGRANTS were from southern states, and when they settled in Texas they brought their slaves with them. Liberals in the Mexican government deplored the presence of slaves in Texas—as would abolitionists in the United States later. Mexicans saw the presence of slaves in Texas as both a moral and an economic issue.

When Manuel de Mier y Teran, a Mexican commissioner, surveyed the Nacogdoches border area in 1827, he observed not only that "the ratio of Mexicans to foreigners is one to ten," with Mexicans forming the lowest class, but also that wealthy Anglos tended to get wealthier when they secured land in Texas. Since the state of Coahuila–Texas had declared that it would "recognize contracts made with servants" in the United States, the Anglo settlers brought "indentured servants" or slaves into Mexico, giving the settlers an ample supply of cheap labor.

When Mexico abolished slavery in 1829, Anglo slaveholding was so entrenched in Texas that slaveholders there received an exemption from the law, which was considered unenforceable unless Mexico could increase its military and settler presence.

Even though Mexican immigration laws were not strictly enforced, a small group of Anglo settlers soon rebelled. In 1827, these Anglos tried to secede from Mexico to set up the independent republic of Fredonia. Defeated almost immediately, the Fredonian revolt nonetheless inspired U.S. newspapers to rally round its "freedom fighters."

Threats to Texas

The Fredonian uprising—and popular U.S. support of it—increased Mexican suspicion of U.S. intentions. Renewed purchase offers by U.S. agents aggravated Mexican distrust of its northern neighbor: U.S. President John Quincy Adams first offered to buy the land between the Sabine and Rio Grande Rivers for $1 million. Then President Andrew Jackson tried to buy the land, this time offering $5 million.

There was growing fear in Mexico that Anglo immigration might lead to U.S. expansion into Texas. General Manuel de Mier y Teran was sent with a commission to "examine" the U.S.–Mexican boundary after the Fredonian revolt. He warned: "Texas is contiguous to the most avid nation in the world. The North Americans have conquered whatever territory adjoins them. . . . In less than half a century, they have become masters of extensive colonies . . . from which they have disappeared the former owners, the Indian tribes." His conclusion: "Either the Government occupies Texas now or it is lost forever."

The government in Mexico City took his advice, strengthening Texas garrisons. Then, in 1830, the Mexican Congress tried to close the Texas border, changing the laws that favored immigration. But the changes came too late: immigrants already settled in Texas ignored the laws—and new settlers continued to arrive, as Mier y Teran said, "with their political constitution in their pockets."

"Texas is Mexico's most valuable possession; I pray God that our neglect will not lead to the loss of such a precious part of our territory."
—COLONEL JUAN NEPOMUCENO ALMONTE, REPORTING TO SANTA ANNA AFTER A VISIT TO TEXAS IN 1834

A Shift in Power

Antonio López de Santa Anna was president of Mexico during a period that saw a major shift in policy. In 1835 a new centralist government increased the power in Mexico City, expanding the authority of the president and the role of the military and the church. A new congress was established, and the Mexican states were reduced to military departments, whose leaders were appointed in the capital. In 1836, the 1824 Constitution was rewritten.

THE CRIOLLOS

URING THE PERIOD in which the fate of Texas was decided—and during the war with the United States—the government of Mexico was in the hands of a small group of upper-class men. Some of them were criollos, New World–born landholders, who had been excluded from political power while Mexico was under Spanish rule. The army had been the path to power for many of them. Criollos had fought alongside the Spanish to suppress the early Indian and mestizo rebellion against Spain. Later, however, they had joined the conservative Agustín de Iturbide to overthrow Spain. When he, in turn, was overthrown, there was little agreement among these leading citizens about how a free Mexico should be governed.

> *To gain power, prominent leaders formed and broke alliances time and again in the years before and during the war.*

SHIFTING ALLIANCES

Mexico's 1824 Constitution created an uneasy balance of power between the provinces and the central government. That balance depended on the strength of traditional institutions, such as the army and the church. (With Catholicism the state religion, the church was able to wield great wealth and influence during several key periods of political crisis.)

To gain power, prominent leaders formed and broke alliances time and again in the years before and during the war—with tremendous impact on Mexican history. These temporary alliances—among men who often had few beliefs in common—created upheavals in a government that was still attempting to define itself. The multiple voices were still struggling toward a Mexican democracy when the United States declared war in 1846.

LUCAS ALAMÁN: MONARCHIST

Devotion to the Catholic Church and to maintaining Mexico as a religious state marked conservative criollos

such as Lucas Alamán. The Mexican Constitution of 1824 was too liberal for these traditionalists. Alamán was behind the revocation of that constitution. A few years later, he published a newspaper advocating restoration of the monarchy. Never president himself, he was an adviser—the power behind the throne—to a succession of conservative rulers, including Anastasio Bustamante and Mariano Paredes y Arrillaga. After 1834, Antonio López de Santa Anna also enjoyed the support of Alamán. As late as 1853, Alamán proposed that Santa Anna establish a military dictatorship.

LORENZO DE ZAVALA: MEXICAN, TEXAN, FIREBRAND

Lorenzo de Zavala was the first to sign the Mexican Constitution of 1824. Allied with Santa Anna, Zavala was part of an 1828 revolt against President Manuel Gómez Pedraza. In 1835, when the government grew more centralized, Santa Anna broke with his former federalist

The aristocratic Lucas Alamán was a man of culture, a scholar, and author of Historia de Méjico. *For years, he insisted privately that Mexico's best hope for a successful government was the restoration of a monarchy. His public advocacy of this plan contributed to a government crisis during the first months of the Mexican war with the United States.*

Lorenzo de Zavala's brief political career had years of impact. In 1828 Zavala raised a mob that attacked the national palace, drove out the elected president, and went on to burn and loot the central market of Mexico City. The riot caused more than 2 million pesos' worth of damage, much of it to foreign property. The international claims against Mexico went unpaid for decades, leading to French and U.S. actions to secure compensation.

Valentín Gómez Farías was an outspoken advocate of liberal and democratic ideals. In a doomed alliance during the U.S.–Mexican War, Gómez Farías ran the government in Mexico City while General Santa Anna raised an army to drive U.S. troops from northern Mexico.

friends, Zavala among them. Zavala went to Texas, where he added to his extensive properties. The next year, when Texas seceded from Mexico, Zavala became vice-president of the independent Republic of Texas. The rebels defeated Santa Anna, and Zavala was reviled as a traitor in his homeland. He died shortly afterward.

VALENTÍN GÓMEZ FARÍAS: ADVOCATE FOR SEPARATION OF CHURCH AND STATE

At the time the liberal Constitution of 1824 was drafted, Valentín Gómez Farías was a moderate congressional leader in favor of mild reforms. During the next decade, he moved to a more radical position in favor of reducing the role of the Catholic Church—and its ally the army—in Mexican society.

During a period of civil disorder in 1833, Gómez Farías was made acting president (filling in for Santa Anna, who had been elected after leading a revolt against conservative President Anastasio Bustamante). Gómez

Farías took the opportunity to secularize the government and society and cut the pay and privileges of the army. When an outbreak of cholera struck Mexico City, it was seen by many as God's wrath, punishment for Gómez Farías's actions.

When Santa Anna returned to Mexico City and replaced Gómez Farías, he was hailed as "liberator of Mexico"—and soon restored the power of church and army.

Gómez Farías and Santa Anna nevertheless formed an alliance again during the U.S.–Mexican War, and the pattern was repeated.

ANTONIO LÓPEZ DE SANTA ANNA— GENERAL AND PRESIDENT

The literary and philosophical figures of the Enlightenment inspired many of the criollos who rose to power in the early years of the Mexican republic, as they had inspired the founders of the U.S. republic. Antonio López de Santa Anna, however, was inspired by Napoleon.

SANTA ANNA.

Antonio López de Santa Anna was described by a contemporary as "in a state of perpetual agitation" so exalted that his "soul doesn't fit in his body." Enormously popular, tall, slender, and dashing, he could gather support for whatever actions he undertook—with the result that he was at the center of decades of political and military struggles.

"From my first years, I was inclined to the glorious career of arms, feeling I had a true vocation for it." Over and over, this "Napoleon of the West" used military power as a springboard to political power. Again and again, he went from leading troops to leading his country, from general to president, from the capital to the battlefield.

Santa Anna's military career began during Mexico's war for independence. Like many criollos, he first fought on the side of the Spanish royalists, not switching sides and joining the rebellion until 1821.

In the first years of independence, Santa Anna appeared to be a liberal. He joined the liberal revolt against Emperor Agustín de Iturbide and supported the Consti-

tution of 1824, which made Mexico a republic. (He later admitted that at the time he did not understand what a republic was.)

In 1829, the Spanish made an ineffective bid to reconquer Mexico. President Vicente Guerrero (against whom Santa Anna had fought during the struggle for independence) put Santa Anna in command of the Mexican defenders. Santa Anna drove the Spanish from the coast and became the "Hero of Tampico."

His popularity—and a liberal revolt in 1832—brought him the presidency the first time. His subsequent turn to conservatism—and the revocation of the 1824 Constitution—provoked revolts all over Mexico, including a successful one in Texas.

For more than a decade, Mexico had been governed under a federalist system: the states were autonomous, allowed to manage their own affairs. Resistance to the new centralism was widespread. By the early months of 1835, protests had begun in several outlying states. Yucatán became an independent state for a time. California threw out the governor sent by Mexico City. The huge state of New Mexico protested long-standing grievances. When there was a revolt in Zacatecas, Santa Anna brutally suppressed it, allowing his soldiers to loot the city.

Rebellion in Texas

Fearing an uprising in Texas, the Mexican government increased the military presence there. Anglo and Hispanic Texans responded by passing a *Declaration of Causes for Taking up Arms against Mexico,* in which they protested the repeal of the 1824 Constitution and the enforcement of the new conservative Constitution. They said their "only recourse" was war. Volunteer soldiers took control of San Antonio, defeating Santa Anna's brother-in-law in a battle that left 150 Mexicans dead or wounded.

Santa Anna pledged to lead the Mexican army to Texas to put down the rebellion. By crushing the rebels, he wanted to send a message to the U.S. government—which he assumed was behind the rebellion. Mexico, Santa Anna swore, would not surrender Texas!

The commander-in-chief of the Texas rebels was Sam Houston, in charge of a few hundred men at garrisons in San Antonio, Gonzales, and Goliad. Stephen Austin had gone to the United States seeking support for the rebellion—money, men, and munitions. With the news that Santa Anna's soldiers were marching to Texas, U.S. volunteers began arriving to reinforce Houston's troops. The volunteers included adventurers hoping for free land after the fight, as well as frontiersmen such as David Crockett, a former Tennessee congressman.

Sam Houston's "call to arms" read: "Citizens of Texas . . . You have realized the horrors of anarchy, and the dictation of military rule. . . . Citizens of Texas, your rights must be defended. The oppressors must be driven from our soil."

The Texas Rebels

Commander-in-chief of the Texas rebels, Sam Houston had been an agent in charge of the forced relocation of the Cherokee people by the U.S. government. He later lived with the Cherokee Nation, after being adopted as a member, and defended the Cherokee against fraud by Indian agents.

Extremists such as William B. Travis had long been agitating for Texas independence. Anglo Texans especially feared the loss of their special tax status and right to hold slaves. With Santa Anna's attempts to reassert control of the province, many Texan voices grew heated: "For what, fellow-citizens, are [the Mexican troops] coming?" asked Texas landowner Robert Williamson. "To compel you into obedience to a new form of government; to compel you to give up your arms; to compel you to give up your slaves, to pay tithes and adoration to the clergy."

When the Texas rebellion began, Commander-in-Chief Sam Houston was joined by Anglos and a few Hispanic Texans. Sam Houston had begun his soldiering career in the War of 1812, fighting with Andrew Jackson against the Creek Indians. Houston was governor of Tennessee before traveling to Texas in 1832. While working as a land agent, he endeavored to negotiate treaties with Indians who were making trade difficult along the border. Although there is no evidence that his Texas activities were as a U.S. agent, in a letter to President Andrew Jackson he expressed his opinion that Texas was ripe for a U.S. takeover. He became the first elected president of the Lone Star Republic.

While rebel troops were battling the Mexican army at the Alamo in San Antonio, rebel leaders were convened for the Texas Convention at Washington-on-Brazos. On March 2, 1836, the delegates voted 33–15 for an independent Texas, with *empresarios* David G. Burnet and Lorenzo de Zavala named acting president and vice-president of the Lone Star Republic. After the vote had been taken, the rebel leaders learned of the tragic conclusion to their troops' first meeting with Santa Anna.

"Civil Wars Are Always Bloody"

To combat the Texas uprising, the Mexican government conscripted new troops, funding the expedition with money market loans at nearly 50 percent interest. The newspaper *El Mosquito Mexicano* reminded readers that civil wars must be "fought without remorse" and announced a special Legion of Honor for Mexican soldiers battling the rebellion.

Santa Anna's book of field commands, *The Campaign against Texas*, described his policy toward Houston's troops: "The foreigners who wage war against the Mexican nation have violated all laws and do not deserve any consideration. . . . No quarter will be given them. . . . They have audaciously declared a war of extermination to the Mexicans and should be treated in the same manner."

"The imagination of the Anglo Americans is stimulated by their own vanity. And in their dreams of grandeur, they look upon us as pygmies, objects deserving of their pity. They consider our possessions as but a fair prize of their greed.

"The loss of Texas will inevitably result in the loss of New Mexico and the Californias. Little by little our territory will be absorbed, until only an insignificant part is left to us. . . . Our national existence, acquired at the cost of so much blood . . . would end like those weak meteors which, from time to time, shine fitfully in the firmament and then disappear."

—JOSÉ MARÍA TORNEL Y MENDIVIL, MEXICAN SECRETARY OF WAR, IN 1836

The Alamo and Goliad

Santa Anna's 1,800 soldiers reached the Alamo, a small former mission held by the Texans, on February 23, 1836. A thirteen-day siege followed, during which the rebels appealed in vain for reinforcements. Finally, Mexican troops stormed the Alamo and killed the almost 200 men inside.

When Houston learned of the massacre, he ordered his troops at Goliad to retreat. The Mexican army overtook the retreating rebels, and the Texans surrendered, believing they would be treated as humanely as they had treated the Mexican prisoners in the earlier battle for San Antonio. Instead, Santa Anna ordered the execution of 340 Texans.

"NO QUARTER"

SANTA ANNA GAVE "no quarter" and was charged with arrogance and brutality after his slaughter of the Texas troops at the Alamo and at Goliad. The brutality of the campaign was meant to force the Texans into submission. Instead, "Remember the Alamo and Goliad" became battle cries of revenge. Houston's rebels retaliated in the massacre at San Jacinto.

San Jacinto

Santa Anna's troops pursued what was left of the rebel army—as well as groups of fleeing frightened colonists—across eastern Texas. But rebel Texans soon assembled at the San Jacinto River, a mile from Santa Anna's camp, which was unprotected by pickets or guards. Sam Houston's army attacked the larger Mexican encampment during the siesta on April 21, 1836, quickly winning a victory. "A three-hour massacre followed, making San Jacinto a war atrocity in its own right," says historian Sam W. Haynes. The Texans killed 630 Mexicans, wounded 200, and captured 730 more.

The Velasco Peace

The day after the Battle of San Jacinto, Houston's troops captured Mexican President Santa Anna. The despised general barely escaped death: many Texans wanted to hang him—"a just vengeance," said more than one. Houston saved Santa Anna's life in exchange for his promise to remove Mexican troops from Texas. (After the war, Santa Anna's second in command, Vicente Filisola, was branded a traitor and courtmartialed for carrying out the order and withdrawing the Mexican army below the Rio Grande.)

Santa Anna persuaded Texas President Burnet that, if he were allowed to return to Mexico City, he would speak on behalf of the new republic. On May 14, 1836, Santa Anna signed two versions of the Treaty of Velasco, one public, one secret. The private version bound Santa Anna to advocate for Texan independence, which the Texans hoped would lead Mexico to recognize Texas as a republic.

When Santa Anna returned to Mexico, however, he denied having recognized Texas independence. "I did promise to try to get a hearing for the Texas Commissioners," he explained, "but this in itself did not bind the government to receive them." Appalled by the results of the Texas campaign, Mexican conservatives had returned the previous president, Anastasio Bustamante, to

MISTAKES AND OVERSIGHTS

A U.S. depiction of Santa Anna's surrender to Sam Houston.

SANTA ANNA DEFENDED his loss to the Texans at San Jacinto by saying, "Mistakes and oversights by some of my subordinates, and the carelessness of others, caused the catastrophe." After that loss, Santa Anna did not return to Mexico until 1837. Then, in disgrace, he retired to his estate near Veracruz, saying that he had abandoned politics forever.

ATROCITIES OF WAR

The new Republic of Texas flew the flag of the Lone Star.

DURING AND AFTER the war, each side accused the other of barbarity in the conduct of its battles.

When the siege of the Alamo began, Texas had not declared its independence. Tradition has it that David Crockett, William Travis, Jim Bowie, and the other rebels inside the San Antonio mission were fighting under a Mexican flag—with 1824 (the date of the suspended Mexican Constitution) in its white field. For the Mexican army, the war was à revolt that had to be subdued by any means. For Travis—and all the Texas rebels after the Alamo—it was a war of independence.

When the Mexicans first approached the Alamo, they were flying a blood-red flag that signaled "no mercy." Mexican sources reported that before the siege, a soldier with a white flag was sent to offer the Texans a chance to surrender. William Travis, in charge of the fort, was said to have fired on the messenger, nearly hitting him. This infuriated the Mexicans.

The Mexican army sounded the *deguello* ("cutthroat") bugle call when they attacked the mission, killing the almost 200 Alamo defenders, who had sworn a pledge to their commander of "no surrender." The attackers suffered even greater losses—630 men killed or wounded—leading a Mexican soldier to observe sadly, "Another victory such as this and we will lose the war." By the time they did lose the war, another 600 Mexican soldiers had been killed after the surrender at San Jacinto.

The executed Texans at the Alamo and Goliad were assailed as pirates by the Mexican press but hailed as martyrs by the U.S. press. Among Mexicans and Texans, the fight for Texas left feelings of hatred and mistrust that would color the U.S.–Mexican War ten years later.

office. His government agreed that Santa Anna—although president when the Velasco agreement was signed—had "offered nothing in the name of the nation."

The Mexican government never accepted the Agreement of Velasco, and so did not accept the independence of Texas. Soon after the Texas rebellion, Mexican troops marched back into the area between the Nueces and the Rio Grande Rivers. This area was still disputed ten years later. It was there that fighting between the United States and Mexico began in 1846.

CHAPTER 3

THE REPUBLIC OF TEXAS

THE FIRST TEXAS CAPITOL.

"Tell our friends all the news, and that we have beaten the enemy. . . . Tell them to come on and let the people plant corn," said victorious Commander-in-Chief Sam Houston. *Like Houston, many of the 50,000 residents of Texas had ties to the United States: four-fifths of the men who voted to secede from Mexico were from slave states. The new Texas Constitution was based on the U.S. Constitution—but it forbade the emancipation of slaves.*

F OR ALMOST TEN YEARS after the Texas revolt, citizens living on the ranches and farms of the Lone Star Republic occupied an uneasy position between Mexico and the United States. Mexico continued to view Texas as a province in revolt. The United States saw Texas as an independent republic but was severely divided about U.S. relations with it.

During those years, there was talk in Mexico of fighting to reclaim the Texas territory, and more than once troops were raised to make the attack. For years, says historian Jesús Velasco-Márquez, among Mexicans "the word *Texas* was used as an excuse to destroy or revive reputations, to increase taxes and waste resources, and to justify all kinds of anti-government movements. But attempts to reincorporate [the territory] failed."

While Texas remained independent, the world watched—and waited for war. From London, Mexico City, Paris, Washington, and Austin, diplomatic notes flew back and forth, as France and Britain made overtures to the Texans. "The Texas question was truly an international question," notes historian David Pletcher. "European loans, trade, and support could have made Texas a permanent buffer state between Mexico and the United States. The actual outcome—annexation—now seems the natural and obvious one in the United States, but it was not obvious at the time."

It was certainly not obvious to Mexico, which repeatedly warned the United States that it would consider U.S. annexation of Texas "equivalent to a declaration of war."

The first Texas currency. The new government of Texas had few resources. It needed money and military aid. As the years dragged on without resolution of its dispute with Mexico, it also needed mediation of its international status.

Jackson's Dilemma

In September 1836, Texans approved their new republic's Constitution, declaring slavery a permanent institution. In the same election, the citizens of Texas voted almost unanimously in favor of petitioning the

"Old Hickory," Andrew Jackson. Jackson's election to the presidency heralded a shift in power to the frontier in the United States. During his military career he had led raids against Indians and smugglers in Spanish Florida, which eventually resulted in U.S. acquisition of the Floridas. When he gained political power, he shifted his strategy, attempting to purchase Mexican territory, both Texas and California.

United States for statehood. Would the United States admit this slave state to the Union?

President Andrew Jackson's second term was drawing to a close. Jackson, who had been trying for years to buy Texas, sent an adviser, Henry Morfit, to assess the new republic. "The present resources of Texas," Morfit reported, "are principally derived from the sympathies of their neighbors and friends in the United States. . . . Perhaps it is the first instance in the history of nations where a state has sustained itself by men and means drawn wholly from a distance. . . . Without foreign aid, the future security [of Texas] must depend more upon the weakness and imbecility of her enemy than upon her own strength."

Jackson decided not to act on the Texas question until the new government "shall have proved" itself. In a December 1836 statement to Congress on Texas, he cautioned: "Beware of a too early movement. . . . Prudence . . . seems to dictate that we should still stand aloof."

Jackson showed unusual restraint. He feared that, if he annexed Texas immediately, the world would perceive the Texas revolt as a U.S. ploy or, "as Mexico had always claimed, a gigantic swindle," in the words of one contemporary commentator. So Jackson merely recognized Texas independence—and left the question of Texas statehood open.

A Divisive Matter

During the next eight years, when the U.S. Congress debated whether to add Texas to the Union, the argument took place across sectional lines. Northeastern commercial interests were opposed to slavery and expansionism; southern and western agrarian interests favored a "negative" or limited government that would allow the exploitation of new regions.

Polarization of these regional interests grew more extreme during the 1830s. Northern states were industrializing while southern states remained agricultural, with plantation owners continuing their reliance on slave labor. This economic division led to deeper political and moral divisions. Increasing sectionalism made compromise increasingly difficult.

Democrats and Whigs, Southerners and Northerners agreed that the slavery issue—and the economic, political, and moral conflicts besetting the land—threatened the Union. Northern Whig politicians saw Texas annexation as nothing but a brazen attempt by the South to upset the Union's balance of power, the slave state–free state balance established by the Missouri Compromise of 1820. They saw Texans as the very image of Jacksonian Democrats: footloose frontiersmen, rambunctious rebels, slaveholders ever hungry for new land.

John C. Calhoun of South Carolina declared that to exclude a state because it permitted slavery could cause the breakup of the Union. But northern Whig congressmen continued to oppose Texas annexation on anti-slavery grounds.

Lone Star Trade and Raids

The "time and events" that President Jackson hoped would create a truly independent Texas in fact worsened the conflicts between Texas and Mexico. While the United States debated the Texas question, Texans and Mexicans launched a series of attacks on each other, both minor and major. Two incidents in particular provoked high feelings.

"Anti-Texass" Abolitionists

Benjamin Lundy, prominent abolitionist, heated up the Texas annexation debate. Historian Nathaniel W. Stephenson relates: "Lundy made several visits to Texas and Mexico and fell in with a notorious Colonel [Juan] Almonte, the bosom friend of Santa Anna, who appears to have filled him with the Mexican view of Texas. Lundy came home convinced that Texas was a den of thieves. He wrote articles for the abolitionist newspapers and published two pamphlets, *The Origin and True Cause of the Texas Insurrection* and *The War in Texas,* in which the violence of his language was matched by the inaccuracy of his knowledge. He looked upon the war as an 'invasion of brigands from the United States' who had the 'avowed purpose of adding five or six more slaveholding States to this Union.'"

YOUNG TEXAS IN REPOSE.

"Young Texas in Repose" was depicted in an 1850s cartoon by abolitionists who still thought that the 1836 revolution was a pro-slavery plot.

Whigs Oppose Expansion

MANY WHIGS "believed that the United States could not succeed as an experiment in self-government if it were too large," says David Pletcher. As a result, they opposed any expansion of U.S. territory, a position that was often fortified by their objections to slavery.

John Quincy Adams had been a staunch expansionist in the early years of the century, as secretary of state under Monroe and then during his own term as president. In his later years as a Mas-

sachusetts congressman, he often spoke out against Texas annexation, leading the opposition against the "nefarious project" of adding a slave-holding territory to the Union.

Fellow Massachusetts Whig Senator Daniel Webster was another powerful foe of annexation. In 1837 he maintained his "entire unwillingness to do anything that shall extend the slavery of the African race on this continent, or add other slave-holding states to the Union."

John Quincy Adams.

Daniel Webster.

The first was an action proposed by Mirabeau Bonaparte Lamar when he was president of the Lone Star Republic. The Texas congress had set the south and west boundary of the republic at the Rio Grande, and Lamar intended to claim that territory by opening a trade route from Texas to New Mexico and Missouri. On June 21, 1841, a *bélicomercantil* (military-merchant) expedition of about 350 Texans, traders, government commissioners, and soldiers was sent on a march to New Mexico. The expedition was supposed to persuade unhappy New Mexico inhabitants to follow the Texans in revolting against Mexico.

George Wilkins Kendall, editor of the New Orleans *Picayune,* accompanied the group, reporting on the ill-fated expedition: "Many of the men who had lost their horses, weak and dispirited from long marches and want of food, had secretly thrown away their arms to lighten themselves upon the road, and, in the meantime, that subordination, without which all efforts are useless, was in a measure lost." New Mexico's governor, Manuel Armijo, captured the desperate Texans, who surrendered without firing a shot. They were marched to prison in Mexico City.

Mexico soon launched retaliatory raids into Texas, capturing San Antonio and taking more prisoners. The 1842 expeditions led by Generals Rafael Vásquez and Adrian Woll reminded Texans just how vulnerable they were. Texas sent answering troops across the Rio Grande in a gesture intended as no more than saber rattling. But the feint drew blood, turning into an international incident. Mexico captured a group of 200 Texans, who had struck off on their own to attack the Mexican town of Mier on Christmas Day in 1842. The prisoners soon escaped, only to be recaptured by other Mexican troops. After threatening to kill them all, the Mexicans received a warning from U.S. Minister Waddy Thompson. He promised that "a much more powerful enemy than Texas" would enter the fight if all the men were killed. Mexican orders were changed: one in ten of the prisoners was executed.

The Decimation of the Mier Prisoners

In the United States, passions excited by George Kendall's sensational coverage of the Santa Fe prisoners were further inflamed when Mexico captured San Antonio. When a group of Texans raiding Mier were captured, and the Mexican government ordered their execution

(pictured here), U.S. anger increased. Mexican newspapers responded with an attack on what they saw as excessive U.S. interest in Mexican affairs. After the capture of San Antonio, Mexico complained that in U.S. newspapers "no other voice was heard but that of war with Mexico and of aid to Texas." Politician José María Gutierrez de Estrada prophetically warned Mexicans: "If we do not change our ways, in less than twenty years we may see the U.S. flag of stars waving above our national palace."

Money Problems

Resentment over the Santa Fe, San Antonio, and Mier incidents aggravated the tension in U.S.–Mexican relations caused by long-standing financial disputes.

During the endless chain of intrigues and coups, riots and revolutions since Mexican independence, Mexicans and foreigners alike had suffered financial losses. Several foreign governments pressed claims for "injuries to persons or property inflicted by the Mexican government or its agents." For years Mexico resisted negotiating these claims. After agreements were finally reached, Mexico could not pay the claims. The country was deeply in debt, its treasury empty.

As early as the Jackson administration, the United States had considered "reprisals" against Mexico for nonpayment of $2 million owed to U.S. citizens. The Democrats, according to Whig John Quincy Adams, were *using* these claims, handling negotiations with the aim of "fretting the people of this Union into a war with Mexico." In 1845, the United States did try to use the claims to pressure Mexico to accept a purchase offer, and this played a part in the failure of the negotiations that were the last hope to avoid war.

Courting the Yellow Rose

President John Tyler's long-standing plan to add Texas to the Union took on a new urgency when the British began courting the Lone Star Republic. Britain had recognized the new nation in 1841, hoping that it would bring about a new balance of power in North America. (France, too, had recognized Texas, but "French relations with both the United States and Mexico were less close and less complicated than Britain's," notes David Pletcher.)

There were rumors that the British intended to offer the republic loans and investments if Texas would abolish slavery, as Britain had done in 1833. Southern politicians were incensed: "Few calamities could befall this country more to be deplored than the establishment of a predominant British influence and the abolition of domestic slavery in Texas," wrote Tyler's secretary of state, Abel Upshur.

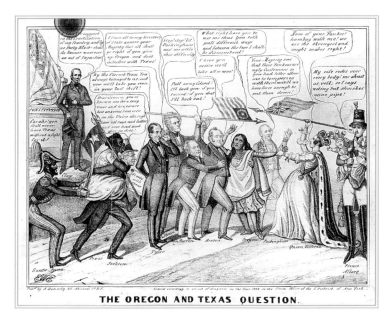

THE OREGON AND TEXAS QUESTION.

Cartoon showing international interest in Texas.

SANTA ANNA: HERO OF VERACRUZ

Long before the U.S.–Mexican War, France went to war with Mexico over the money owed French citizens. French claims—which were for a fraction of the money owed to the United States—led to a conflict that became known as the "Pastry War." A tragicomic encounter with the French navy during this war became General Antonio Santa Anna's path back to power and glory.

The Mexican fight with the French arose when President Anastasio Bustamante was presented with a list of demands by French Minister Baron Deffaudis. He wanted a preferential trade agreement and payment of French claims of property damage pending since Mexican riots in the 1820s. Bustamante refused payment, and the French minister called in the French navy to blockade Veracruz. After a few months, the French sent Bustamante another bill, this time even higher, to cover their blockade expenses. Bustamante balked; the French started shelling. Although Mexico tried to make a joke of the French claims (the war took its name from a small baker's bill that had been exaggerated to a ludicrous sum), the threat was serious.

Santa Anna had sworn, after his ignominious defeat at the Battle of San Jacinto, that he would never again enter public life. He was at his estate near Veracruz when he heard that French troops were coming ashore, and he galloped off to defend the city. After a farcical escape from capture by the French army, Santa Anna was hit by grapeshot as the invaders returned to their ships. The next day, surgeons amputated Santa Anna's right leg below the knee. Santa Anna dictated a fifteen-page deathbed statement, a long good-bye. But he survived, his amputated leg the visible symbol of courage and sacrifice: he was the "Hero of Veracruz."

As Eduardo Galeano puts it, during "a small war against the king of France," Santa Anna lost his leg and regained his popularity. "The mutilated president . . . came back to life and power, as was his habit."

President Bustamante ended up paying twice for the Pastry War, in 1839, when he settled the French claims, and in 1841, when Santa Anna rode triumphantly into strife-torn Mexico City to replace him as president. Santa Anna's reign was the beginning of a tumultuous prewar period.

TROUBLE FOR TEXAS

Santa Anna had never accepted the loss of Texas, and in 1842 he waged two expensive, but brief, campaigns to harass the state. Texas was vulnerable, but Santa Anna was in no position to exploit its weakness, since he also faced rebellion in Yucatán. During this period, both Sam Houston—now serving a second term as Texas president—and Santa Anna were sparring, buying time in hopes that their situations would improve. Both feigned interest in a peaceful settlement, notes historian Justin H. Smith, but negotiations between them were "a comedy." Neither side expected the talks to succeed.

GOBIERNO DE LA REGENERACION HASTA EL 6 DE DICIEMBRE DE 1844.

Cartoon depicting the excesses of Santa Anna's presidency. After visiting Santa Anna at his estate, Frances Calderón de la Barca, the Scottish wife of Spain's minister to Mexico, described the man. He gave the impression, she wrote, of "a philosopher, living in dignified retirement—one who had tried the world, and found that all was vanity—one who had suffered ingratitude, and who, if he were ever persuaded to emerge from his retreat, would only do so, Cincinnatus-like, to benefit his country." But when he came back to power in 1841, she saw his presidency as "the apotheosis of egotism transformed into virtue."

Santa Anna lost his leg and regained his popularity.

EL ULTIMO A DIOS.

(1) ¡Vaya ray pyaria il Antonio!   (5) ¡A Dios mi Dinero!   (4) Soltad el talego   (5) Ni por esas
La Soberania restila en la fuga.   ¡A Dios mi Nacion!   Soltadlo por Dios!   Requiescat inpace

(2) Asi debieran caer siempre de su poder   ¡A Dios mi Gobierno!....   Que fui de la Hacienda
Los malos gobernantes, de cabeza.   ¡Que triste cancion!.   Ministro el mejor

The exiled Santa Anna leaving Mexico.

"DICTADOR RESPLANDECIENTE, GENERALISSIMO, ETERNO ASPIRANTE AL PODER"

While the problem of Texas festered, the Mexican treasury was being drained. Santa Anna bought political support and indulged in extravagant displays of power. In the most grotesque of the gaudy celebrations held during that era, Santa Anna gave his amputated leg a formal burial, with a funeral cortege, hymns, prayers, and speeches.

During this presidency, Santa Anna "proved to be remarkable in collecting money—taxes and more taxes," historians Ruth R. Olivera and Liliane Crété observe. "He imposed 'voluntary' contributions on all householders of the capital, increased import duties by 20 percent, exacted forced loans from the church, and sold mining concessions to the British. But the money was spent for the glory and the pleasure of the dictator, not for the welfare of the general population or the good of the republic. Whenever he tired of life in the capital, he was off again to [his estate] Manga de Clavo and his prized fighting cocks."

EXILE

Finally, in December 1844, Santa Anna was driven from office and in 1845 exiled to Cuba. General Mariano Paredes and his army had put Santa Anna in power in 1841 and then removed him from it three years later. Paredes had gained a dangerous new sense of control over Mexican politics. By the time Santa Anna returned to Mexico and the presidency in 1846, Paredes had led Mexico into war with the United States.

Southern Democrats feared that Britain would secure a "controlling influence" on the continent, establishing Texas as a haven for escaped slaves and threatening U.S. cotton growers. There was already talk of war between Britain and the United States over possession of Oregon; now Upshur raised the specter of widening conflict if the Lone Star Republic made anti-slavery concessions to Britain.

After he appointed South Carolina statesman John C. Calhoun his new secretary of state, Tyler ordered another purchase offer to Mexico. The offer went to Colonel Juan Almonte, the Mexican minister (who rejected it). Early in 1844 Tyler sent the Senate a treaty to annex Texas. But the president had underestimated the resistance to adding a slave state to the Union. Suspicious of any plan favored by Tyler and Calhoun, northern senators saw annexation as a ploy to advance southern interests in a "slavocracy" and cotton economy. Even among expansionists, there was some opposition. The treaty was soundly rejected.

Texas Rides a Dark Horse

While Congress was considering Texas annexation, dark horse Democratic candidate James K. Polk was nominated for president on a platform that called for Texas statehood. Westward expansion, Polk's policy statements stressed, was in the national interest—it was U.S. destiny. The Democratic platform of 1844, says Jesús Velasco-Márquez, "distributed expansionist gains to Southern, Northern, and Western interests." The platform tied "reannexation of Texas" to "the reoccupation of Oregon," thereby appealing to interests in all regions of the country.

Polk's support was not limited to pro-slavery votes, but anti-slavery votes may have cost his opponent the election. A well-known Whig, Henry Clay was indecisive on the Texas question. His unwillingness to promise that Texas would never be admitted as long as it was a slave state probably contributed to his narrow defeat. While the expansionist spirit was still far from unanimous in the United States, it was strong enough to carry Polk, one of its staunchest proponents, into the White House—and Texas into the Union.

SOUTHERN STATESMAN

JOHN C. CALHOUN spoke in favor of Texas annexation as early as the Jackson administration. Historian Frederick Jackson Turner notes: "Fate might have made him a national statesman, but the hot blood of South Carolina, so excessively devoted to slavery and cotton interest . . . compelled Calhoun, as the price of his continued career, to represent, first, the interests of South Carolina, and then those of the South as a whole, in opposition to the rest of the country."

With this election, "the appetite for Texas" began to take on a national appeal. John Quincy Adams called it part of the growing U.S. "Western passion." Annexation was still a bitterly divisive issue, but Democrats from every region of the country favored it. In late February Congress approved President Tyler's controversial joint resolution to annex Texas. In the last week before Polk took office, the outgoing president offered Texas statehood.

James Knox Polk

James K. Polk was president in an age that transformed the United States into a major continental power; he was commander-in-chief in a war that extended its boundaries to the Rio Grande, the Pacific, and the forty-ninth parallel. Yet Polk was little loved by his contemporaries and little noted by history.

The reasons lie in Polk's policies and personality. Polk's "Jacksonian economic agenda," says historian Sam W. Haynes, "which called for a low tariff, firm opposition to internal improvements, and a hard money doctrine, was one that many Democrats were beginning to find ill-suited to the demands of a sophisticated marketplace, and [this] had much to do with his unpopularity."

Not only "dogmatic in his political views," says Haynes, Polk was also "stiffly formal in his personal relations . . . grim, humorless . . . provincial in outlook and tastes." "Seldom," observes historian Thomas Hietala, "had a president achieved so much so quickly; seldom had a president alienated so many men so completely." Hietala describes the puritanical Polk's advent on the Washington political scene:

> Polk dreaded social gatherings, and in one of his first acts as president banished dancing from the White House. He maintained a strained cordiality during his ceremonial duties, but people were a distant second to politics in his affections. In early 1846, Senator [John] Fairfield [of Maine] admitted to his wife, "Tonight the president has his first levee. I had rather be whipped than go, but circumstances render it unavoidable. There will be no dancing and no refreshment of any kind."

POLK'S CAMPAIGN

TODAY POLK'S EXPANSIONISM is seen as an inevitable "westward thrust," but it did not have unanimous support at the time. Running as the Democrat's dark horse candidate, Polk barely won the presidency. The Whigs carried New England, as well as Ohio, Kentucky, Tennessee, and North Carolina. The election revealed a nation with deep political divisions, torn by debates over "Texas and tariffs," slavery and growth. After the war, which further polarized opinions, Ralph Waldo Emerson compared U.S. acquisitions to a dose of arsenic: the nation might swallow the territories, but they would eventually destroy the nation.

A sanctimonious and prim Scotch-Irish Presbyterian, James Knox Polk had a "passion for efficiency and order," says Sam W. Haynes, "and was fond of saying, 'I am the hardest working man in the United States.'" Writes Haynes, "On his 53rd birthday, the president recorded the following melancholy entry in his diary: 'I am solemnly impressed with the vanity and emptiness of worldly honours and worldly enjoyments, and [with the wisdom of] preparing for a future estate.'" He died a few months after the end of his single presidential term.

Polk was the youngest man the United States had ever elected president, forty-nine at his inauguration. Born to an old North Carolina family, he had moved to Tennessee as a boy, later graduating from the University of North Carolina. Polk then developed a successful law practice and married Sarah Childress, whose stern religious principles matched his own. She managed his early political campaigns and was well known in Washington for her intelligence and charm.

The ambitious Polk established himself as a loyal Democrat, first as a member of Congress, then as Speaker of the House, later as governor of Tennessee. Andrew Jackson's protégé, Polk was known as "young Hickory." He dedicated himself to Jackson's vision of continental expansion and "derived great strength from his unshakable faith in Jacksonian precepts, which allowed him to focus his considerable energies on specific, clearly delineated objectives," writes Sam W. Haynes.

Despite his long political career, Polk had little skill in the art of compromise and negotiation. "As a good Jacksonian," says David Pletcher,

MANIFEST DESTINY

IT WAS NOT UNTIL JULY 1845, after Polk took office, that John O'Sullivan, editor of the *Democratic Review,* coined the term *Manifest Destiny.* But the conviction that the United States had a God-given right to the continent was the spirit driving James K. Polk's presidential campaign. Editorials in the *Democratic Review* defined this spirit: "The American claim is by the right of our manifest destiny to overspread and possess the whole continent which Providence has given to us. . . . It is in our Future far more than in our past that our True Title is to be found."

EXPANSIONIST IDEALS

The people of the United States saw their nation as a model republic, "an island of democratic and republican government surrounded by the swirling seas of monarchical oppression and dictatorship and militarism," says historian Robert W. Johannsen. The expansionist spirit expressed by the term *Manifest Destiny* contains a genuine idealism about "the best government," says Johannsen, the conviction that "to extend the boundaries of the United States is to extend the area of freedom."

The 1830s and 1840s were exciting times, with a new sense of boundlessness. U.S. citizens saw no limits to what the individual—and the nation—could achieve. The expansionist principle of "the best use of the land" became the justification for empire building. As O'Sullivan exhorted his readers, "Until every acre of the North American continent is occupied by citizens of the United States, the foundation of the future empire will not have been laid."

The Spirit of Manifest Destiny is represented here in the 19th-century chromolithograph American Progress *by George Crofutt (after the painting by John Gast). The Democrats' conquest of frontiers started with Andrew Jackson, fighting Indians on horseback in Florida, and continued with the "Iron Horse" riding into the West. It was the "age of steam," and new technology gave the United States a new potential to advance across the continent. John O'Sullivan inspired readers of the* Democratic Review *with a vision of a future United States bound together by "a vast skeleton framework of railroads and an infinitely ramified nervous system of magnetic telegraphs." Even before the war with Mexico, the United States had about 5,000 miles of railways and steamboats on rivers and canals. Superior technology and communications gave the United States a great advantage in its conduct of the war.*

*The expansionist principle of "the best use of the land"
became the justification for empire building.*

Washington, D.C., before the war, looking down Pennsylvania Avenue.

NATIONAL LEADERSHIP

The term *Manifest Destiny,* according to historian Thomas Hietala, helped U.S. citizens to view their actions in the 1840s as both "accidental and innocent": it enabled them to rationalize and justify taking the territory they wanted. Hietala titled his 1985 book *Manifest Design* in an attempt to make explicit the intentionality of the expansionist program.

"As American policy makers maneuvered to gain formal title to a continental empire stretching from coast to coast," wrote Hietala, "pioneers moved into several frontier areas to translate settlement into permanent ownership and national possession. Though both of these initiatives were important in the westward expansion of the 1840s, it is the saga of individual pioneers and the romanticization of their frontier experience that has largely formed popular attitudes about westward expansion. The role of national leaders in promoting expansion during the Jacksonian period should not be slighted, however."

Many U.S. leaders spoke—and voted—in favor of expansionism. New York Senator Daniel Dickinson was one of the most articulate. "New territory," he urged, "is spread out for us to subdue and fertilize. New races are presented for us to civilize, educate, and absorb; new triumphs for us to achieve for the cause of freedom."

Thomas Hart Benton. "No statesman from the North Central States had a greater influence upon Congress and the executive policy, during most of the years between 1830 and 1850, than Thomas Hart Benton, of Missouri," writes historian Frederick Jackson Turner. Benton gained a unique perspective on the United States from his state's position at the edge of the Santa Fe Trail. Living on the western frontier, he was "as deeply interested in the Far West as in the Middle West." His conversations with Polk on the conduct of the U.S.–Mexican War were recorded in the president's Diary.

"he brought to the White House the conviction that the president must dominate the government." Although he had not received a majority of the popular vote, Polk viewed his election as a mandate and seemed surprised when Congress did not bow to his will.

Polk's Dual Diplomacy

James Polk had campaigned with a pledge to add Texas to the Union, but Tyler and Congress had offered statehood to Texas before Polk was sworn in as the eleventh president of the United States. On March 4, 1845, Polk delivered an inaugural speech intended for the world:

> Since the Union was formed the number of States has increased from thirteen to twenty-eight. Our population has increased from three to twenty million. . . . Multitudes from the Old World are flocking to our shores. . . . Foreign powers do not seem to appreciate the true character of our Government. . . . To enlarge its limits is to extend the dominions of peace over additional territories and increasing millions.

The speech "opened a Pandora's box of international conflict," says author John S. D. Eisenhower. "The annexation of Texas, his promises regarding California, and a reference [in the inaugural speech] to the United States's 'clear and unquestionable claim' to the Oregon territory put Polk on a collision course with both Mexico and Great Britain."

Although the United States had made no preparations for war, the new president was risking war on two fronts. In the early months of Polk's presidency, says historian David Pletcher, he was "carrying on a dual diplomacy." Forced to confront Britain about the Oregon Territory, Polk kept the Mexican question simmering "on the back burner."

As long as there was danger of war with Britain, Polk moved slowly against Mexico, sending a diplomatic "peace" mission to Mexico City at the same time that he sent 1,500 U.S. soldiers to the Texas border, on the edge of territory that a bellicose Mexico had vowed to reclaim.

CONFRONTING THE *B*RITISH OVER *O*REGON

*P*OLK'S PHILOSOPHY OF diplomacy was based on assuming a position of strength. He advocated facing down the British: "I remarked . . . that the only way to treat John Bull was to look him straight in the eye . . . that if Congress faltered in their course, John Bull would become more arrogant and grasping in his demands." The United States in the 1840s still felt threatened by its old enemy, which seemed to be trying to encircle it—through Texas, California, and Oregon.

John Bull and Uncle Sam.

U.S. troops near Corpus Christi on the Nueces River, fall 1845.

PART TWO

MARCH TO WAR

"Ya sabra usted que se consumo
la agregación de Texas a los Estados Unidos;
no nos queda otro recurso mas que hacer la guerra."

*"You must know by now that the annexation
of Texas by the United States has been completed.
We have no choice but to go to war."*

—TEÓFILO ROMERO TO GENERAL MARIANO PAREDES

When the United States offered Texas statehood in March 1845, Mexico responded by breaking off diplomatic relations and withdrawing its minister from Washington. Mexican governments had declared repeatedly that annexation of Texas would be an act of war. In an effort to avert the conflict, President José Joaquín de Herrera offered to recognize Texas as a separate nation if it chose independence over annexation to the United States. But Texas refused the offer, voting on July 4, 1845, to become the twenty-eighth state in the Union.

President James Polk immediately ordered U.S. armed forces to prepare for hostile action from Mexico. The U.S. navy was put on the alert: The Pacific Squadron was sent to California; the Home Squadron, to the Mexican Gulf. Thousands of soldiers were sent to the Nueces River near Corpus Christi, Texas, ready to enforce U.S. annexation. President Herrera responded in kind, ordering more Mexican troops north to the disputed border region.

Both Polk and Herrera had been in office only a few months, but they seemed to be rushing toward a confrontation. Could the two nations work out a peaceful solution? In the United States, fear of war with Britain was fading as talks on Oregon advanced. The U.S. Congress urged Polk to sidestep war with Mexico, to settle the Texas question through negotiation or purchase.

Discussing U.S. chances of avoiding a costly war, Polk's secretary of state, James Buchanan, was optimistic—and condescending: "The truth is that, although I have no very exalted idea of Mexican intellect, yet I cannot imagine that anyone who could . . . be elected president, could have so small a modicum of sense as to think seriously of going to war with the United States."

Herrera was on the horns of a political dilemma. He was trying to solve Mexico's severe economic and social problems, which he knew would worsen if his country opposed the U.S. annexation of Texas. But the Mexican Congress would not support him in his efforts to head off a fight. Any move toward peace with the United States—even talk of negotiating—put his government at risk of being overthrown.

CHAPTER 4

LAST CHANCE FOR PEACE

THE MEXICAN CHAMBER OF DEPUTIES.

*President José Joaquín de Herrera attempted to convince
Mexicans to accept the loss of Texas, warning that
"war with the United States over Texas is a bottomless
abyss into which our Republic will sink along
with all our hopes for the future."*

José Joaquín de Herrera. Although there was never any real doubt about Herrera's personal integrity, he was condemned as a traitor for his efforts to avoid war with the United States.

*J*OSÉ JOAQUÍN DE HERRERA had been named provisional president late in 1844 when Antonio Santa Anna was deposed in a general revolt. Herrera had been head of the Mexican Council. But this moderate political reformer was not popular enough to unify his politically divided and nearly bankrupt country. When an election was held in 1845, Herrera was opposed by almost a dozen candidates. Although he kept the presidency, he was not able to form a successful government.

Herrera's last-ditch offer to recognize an independent Texas (at the recommendation of British and French diplomats) had not strengthened his position. Mexican factions on all sides had vowed to fight for Texas, insisting that "territorial integrity" and national honor were at stake. A large, noisy segment of the press assured Mexicans that war would teach their northern neighbor a lesson.

An Undiplomatic Mission

Herrera was looking for a way to preserve national honor without going to war. He let the United States know that, if warships were withdrawn from the coast, Mexico *might* receive a U.S. negotiator to talk about "pending issues."

Mexican Foreign Minister Manuel de la Peña y Peña asked Polk to send a conciliatory North American "commissioner" to begin discussions. The Mexican government thought perhaps the United States would offer to pay indemnification for the Mexican loss of Texas. Polk took a characteristically tough stance. He selected John Slidell for the diplomatic mission, naming him "minister extraordinary and plenipotentiary." Even former U.S. Minister to Mexico Joel Poinsett warned that "the Mexican Government would not and dared not receive our Minister Plenipotentiary."

LOVE OR WAR?

*I*N PARIS, MEXICAN Minister Máximo Garro reported King Louis Philippe's views on Texas: "To describe the kind of obstinacy that prevents one from seeing what is evident, we have a word in French that is very easy to translate into Spanish—*infatuation*. This *infatuation* prevents you from recognizing what everybody else sees; that is, that you have lost Texas irrevocably. If I urge you to recognize her independence, it is because I believe that advantages will result to Mexico, in whose happiness I take great interest."

The title was an insult to Mexico: rather than petitioning for the resumption of diplomatic relations, the United States was acting as if the dispute had already been resolved.

Polk's terms for negotiation were as outrageous to Mexicans as the title. He followed the line Tyler and Calhoun had taken in their negotiations with the Mexican minister the previous year. They maintained that, since Texas had been independent for almost a decade and was recognized as such by both France and Britain, its election to join the United States was no affair of Mexico's. Treating U.S. annexation of Texas as a fait accompli, Polk made an aggressive bid to buy even more Mexican territory. He instructed his "peace ambassador" to use unpaid U.S. damage claims to pressure Mexico into accepting a U.S. offer to "purchase for a pecuniary consideration Upper California and New Mexico." Slidell was authorized to pay Herrera's government as much as $25 million for Mexico's northern frontier areas.

Mexico never received *official* word of Slidell's instructions. The mere presence of Polk's representative in the country aroused a storm of protest. Then rumors of the U.S. plan to purchase Mexican territory were published in *La Voz del Pueblo,* a newspaper owned by Valentín Gómez Farías, one of Herrera's federalist foes. Opposition to the government increased. Under attack from all sides, Herrera had no choice but to refuse to receive Slidell, using his designation as minister plenipotentiary as a justification.

"The North American government could never grasp how deeply and passionately most Mexicans felt about the land they considered their patrimony," says historian Josefina Zoraida Vázquez. Mexican President Herrera may have been willing to admit the loss of Texas, agrees Miguel Soto, but he certainly was not ready to sell California and New Mexico. The terms of Polk's peace proposal would have forced even this pacifist president into a war with the United States.

In December 1845, still hoping to open negotiations with the United States, Herrera wrote the governors of all the Mexican departments to ask for their support. His arguments in favor of accepting the loss of Texas

CALIFORNIA AND NEW MEXICO

THE UNITED STATES had long been interested in California. Both Andrew Jackson and Daniel Webster had tried to forward purchase offers. The U.S. navy had made a foray into Monterey, California, in 1842.

Polk's hasty demand for California and New Mexico was inspired by a message from the U.S. consul in Monterey. Consul Thomas Larkin had sent Polk a (false) report that Britain was prepared to support Mexico in its defense of California. Polk feared that Britain was trying to buy land in California. "Polk was not about to allow the British or any other European power a foothold on the continent," says historian Sam W. Haynes. Nor did he want his two enemies to become allies.

The aggressiveness of the purchase demand was "a direct slap at Mexican feelings," says historian David Pletcher. "President Polk held the niceties of diplomacy in contempt." The way he conducted the negotiations, maintains Pletcher, was sure to provoke Mexican resistance.

were reinforced by a description of the destructive consequences of war with the United States:

> In order to start a war, politicians agree that three questions must be examined: 1st, that of justice. 2nd, that of availability of resources. 3rd, that of convenience. . . . If, for launching war, one would only have to consider our justice, any hesitation in this matter would be either a crime or a lack of common sense. But next come the questions of feasibility and convenience for starting and maintaining hostilities with firmness and honor and all the consequences of a war of this nature.
>
> A foreign war against a powerful and advanced nation that possesses an impressive navy and a . . . population that increases every day because of immigrants attracted to its great . . . prosperity, would imply immense sacrifices of men and money—not to assure victory, but simply to avoid defeat. Are such sacrifices possible for the Mexican Republic in her present state of exhaustion, after so many years of error and misadventure?

His warnings fell on deaf ears. Herrera and his supporters were vilified in the newspapers. Texas had become a nightmare for these moderates, struggling to stay in power against a flock of hawkish opponents. Legislator José Fernando Ramírez predicted, "The struggle will be lost [by the first Mexican to say] that terrible word . . . the first person to speak of peace."

By the end of 1845, U.S. observers in Mexico reported that, given the anti-Herrera feeling in the country, a civil war was much likelier than a foreign war. In San Luis Potosí, General Paredes saw an opportunity to seize power. Under orders to march to Texas, Paredes turned his troops around, marched on Mexico City, and forced Herrera to resign. Paredes then rejected Slidell, refusing his "peace offer."

"A Necessary and Glorious War"

General Mariano Paredes y Arrillaga had been waiting for his chance at the presidency. He had led the revolutions of 1841 and 1844 that began and ended Santa Anna's presidency. His influence had led the military to the dangerous belief that it could control the government. President

ON THE EDGE OF WAR

DISPUTED TERRITORY

IN THE EARLY months of Polk's presidency, while the Texas convention debated whether to accept the offer of statehood, General Zachary Taylor had been ordered by the U.S. War Department to prepare to advance to "the Western frontier of Texas." The sixty-one-year-old Taylor was an Indian fighter from Kentucky. He was instructed that, "although a state of war with Mexico, or an invasion of Texas may not arise, it is proper and necessary that your force be fully equal to meet any crisis."

As soon as Texas voted to become a state, U.S. troops were ordered to advance. Taylor reported to Polk in August 1845, "I have settled upon this point west of the Nueces River, as the most favorable for occupation, and have pushed the troops forward as rapidly as our means of transportation would permit." The Texans had recommended the location of the U.S. camp: on the Gulf of Mexico, with troops south of the Nueces River in disputed territory.

U.S. soldiers on either side of the Nueces were in disputed territory, of course, since Mexico did not accept Texas annexation. But the area south of the Nueces, between it and the Rio Grande, or Rio Bravo, was the site of a special disagreement. Although the border had changed repeatedly in the last centuries, many Spanish, Mexican, and U.S. maps during that time showed the southern boundary of Texas at the Nueces River. Mexico had treated the Nueces as a kind of unofficial border during its ten-year dispute with the Republic of Texas.

Some U.S. citizens, however, claimed that the United States had acquired the land as far as the Rio Grande, in the Louisiana Purchase. The Republic of Texas accepted this controversial position and in 1836 drew its border along the Rio Grande, from the river's headwaters in Colorado to the coast far south of the Nueces.

The disputed territory between the Nueces and Rio Grande (Rio Bravo) Rivers.

As early as 1821, the Mexican ambassador in Washington had warned officials at home that the United States intended eventually to draw its southern border at the Rio Grande. "The project will seem delirium to any rational person," he said, "but it certainly exists."

Mexico still considered the claim to this slice of land outrageous. Polk accepted the claim, however, and seemed to intend to back it up: Taylor had instructions to advance "as near the boundary line—the Rio Grande—as prudence will dictate."

While U.S. and Mexican diplomats talked—or failed to talk—U.S. and Mexican armies faced each other across the disputed territory between the Nueces and the Rio Grande.

HALF THE U.S. ARMY

"If Mexico declares war, I believe General Taylor means to march us right on to Matamoros. If he does, it is to be hoped that we will not get a whipping," wrote Lieutenant Napoleon Dana to his wife, Sue. "Here we are at a dead standstill, doing nothing. . . . You have no idea . . . what a military show we have here and how much of the pomp of war with none of the glory. . . . I wish I had all of my glory and was on my way home again, but let us hold on and see what Mr. Polk is going to do."

At the end of July 1845, steamships and sailing vessels carrying U.S. troops started to arrive near the trading post at Corpus Christi. They were joined in September by a larger force, soldiers who had come overland to the largest military encampment since the War of 1812. By the end of the year, General Zachary Taylor had assembled a regiment of dragoons, five infantry regiments, and sixteen artillery companies: 4,000 men, almost half of the U.S. army.

The troops had supplies and equipment but still were ill-equipped for war with the Mexicans. They were on unfamiliar terrain; they had no reliable maps and little knowledge of the region. The arid landscape of northern

Two soldiers in the U.S. army.

Mexico had defeated outsiders before. The Texas militia fighters captured by the Mexican army after their attack on Mier in 1842 had escaped only to become thoroughly lost. Many perished before a party of survivors was recaptured by another group of Mexican soldiers.

Camped in an exposed position, Taylor's soldiers waited for war. They had not trained together before, and they drilled constantly on the sand hills along the Nueces. Day after day, they were on the alert. The Mexican government had said repeatedly that it would fight to prevent Texas annexation. Mexican troops had advanced to the Rio Grande. But weeks stretched into months, and the Mexican attack never came.

THE MEXICAN ARMY OF THE NORTH

"It is calm here right now," wrote General Mariano Arista, *commander of the Mexican Army of the North. "But the Republic of Texas is developing plans to send troops right up to the Rio Grande. We stand ready to launch ourselves against this treacherous and cowardly enemy despite our desperate circumstances."*

Arista knew that the U.S. army had gathered on the Nueces River. Fresh troops and supplies arrived there every month. An invasion seemed likely. Arista's orders were to protect Mexico's northern border. But his troops were far from the capital, and for many weeks they had not been paid or supplied. He wrote to his superiors: "I

Soldier in the Mexican army before the war.

know that nothing can be accomplished without resources, but consider that our country and our military honor are going to hell. . . . Consider my situation in the midst of this, asking the shops to lend us our daily meals, the officers having nothing to eat."

His superiors were part of Arista's problems, according to historian George Lockhart Rives. Power struggles within the Mexican military kept resources from arriving where they were needed:

> Arista . . . probably had less than 3,000 men under him in the late summer and autumn of 1845; but a much larger force, perhaps 8,000 or 10,000 men, who were intended for Texas, were in or within easy reach of San Luis Potosí.

As they had neither shoes nor clothing nor transport, it was difficult to move them through a barren country. The commander at San Luis was General [Mariano] Paredes . . . who [according to one of Polk's agents] had intercepted money and clothing sent by the government for Arista on the frontier.

"It is not possible to make war" with such limited resources, said Arista, "but should we let the North Americans beat us?" Under his command, the Mexican army would not attack unless the U.S. army moved farther into the disputed territory between the Nueces and Rio Grande Rivers. Arista's troops played the same waiting game as Taylor's.

HAWKS AND DOVES

AFTER THE U.S.–Mexican War, the status of the Mexican military waned, so that military takeovers gradually declined. But, in the years before the war, Mexico was cursed with a political system unable to separate military power from civilian government. When General Mariano Paredes became president, he "was convinced that an immediate military solution was necessary, that the Mexicans could not just let go of Texas without a military response," says Miguel Soto. "It was [a question of] restoring honor on the field of battle."

"Historians have insisted upon taking sides with the factions of the period and upon blaming their opponents for the failure [of Mexico to defeat the U.S. offensive]," says Josefina Zoraida Vázquez.

"Gómez Farías, or Paredes y Arrillaga, Santa Anna (the favorite villain), the army, or the church—[those] are the guilty ones." The truth, says Soto, is that "Mexican public opinion and all the various political factions . . . participated in a very hawkish attitude toward the war."

Herrera was the exception. Wilson Shannon, the U.S. ambassador to Mexico during the prewar period, described the difficulty of arranging a peaceful solution. He assured his government that "many intelligent Mexicans privately entertain and express peace-making opinions, [but] there are few who have the boldness to express these opinions publicly, or would be willing to stem the current of popular prejudice by undertaking to carry them out."

Government dinner in Oaxaca. President Herrera appealed to all of the state governors of Mexico in 1845, asking for support for his negotiations with the United States over the Texas question—but to no avail.

UN TIRANO.

General Paredes was part of Mexico's ambitious military class. His power had grown through repeated periods of civil unrest (most recently, he had deposed Santa Anna in the 1844 revolt pictured in this cartoon). Now he raised the threat of civil war by leading his troops to the capital. President Herrera, faced with this threat, chose to resign and hand over the government to the general.

Herrera knew that Paredes was a threat, so he had sent Paredes to San Luis Potosí (where Paredes had compounded the problems of both Herrera and General Arista).

When Paredes returned to the capital and formed a new government, he was supported by members of the military and the aristocracy, including Lucas Alamán and the Spanish minister to Mexico. Some of his supporters had been opposed to war against the United States, but, with Paredes in office, they saw war as a way to strengthen the army and perhaps even achieve their dream of establishing a true monarchy in Mexico.

The new president was in power only seven months, just long enough to lead his country into war. While the United States declared war on Mexico, sending thousands of volunteers to the Rio Grande and dispatching the Army of the West to New Mexico and California, Mexico was struggling to maintain its republican government against a conspiracy determined to destroy it.

General Mariano Paredes y Arrillaga.

CHAPTER 5

HOSTILITIES COMMENCE

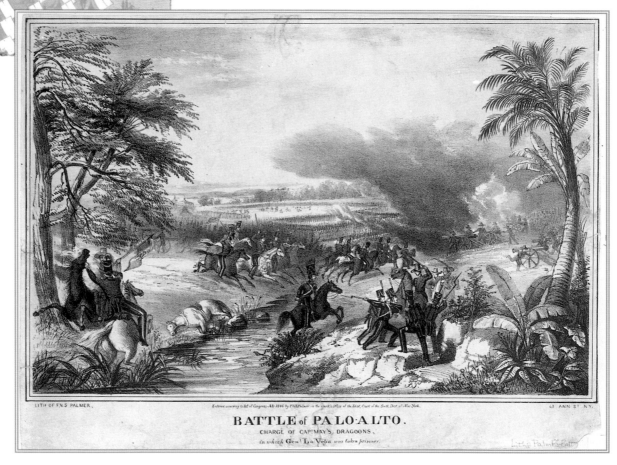

BATTLE of PALO-ALTO.
CHARGE OF CAPT MAY'S DRAGOONS,
in which Gen¹ La Vega was taken prisoner.

Fighting between the U.S. and Mexican armies began in the spring of 1846
after General Zachary Taylor's troops moved to the Rio Grande.
They were soon met by Mexican General Mariano Arista, who announced:
"Discussion is no part of the duty of soldiers; that is the work of diplomatic agents;
ours is to act. . . . Hostilities have commenced, and I do not
hesitate to assure your excellency that arms are hereafter to be used."

By December 1845 Texas had been officially admitted to the United States. That same month, Mexican President José Joaquín de Herrera was deposed. General Mariano Paredes, in his inaugural presidential address of January 1846, vowed to maintain the integrity of Mexico as far as the Sabine River, reiterating Mexico's intention to reclaim Texas—even if it meant war with the United States.

U.S. diplomat John Slidell had already sent a dispatch to Washington describing Mexico's refusal to see him. His message reached President Polk on January 12.

Polk was ready. On January 13, he reinstated the naval blockade of Mexican Gulf ports, and he sent a message commanding General Zachary Taylor to move his troops to the Rio Grande. Polk issued careful instructions: if Mexico makes "any open act of hostility toward us, you will not act merely on the defensive. . . ." To the Mexicans, however, the troop movement itself was an "offensive action," says Mexican General Luis Garfias.

In pushing U.S. troops farther into the disputed territory between the Nueces and Rio Grande Rivers, says Sam W. Haynes, "Polk had two goals": he "wanted to secure what he regarded as the border with Mexico," and he "hoped that the show of force would do what the Slidell mission had failed to do—convince the Mexicans to sell him California and New Mexico." David Pletcher agrees about Polk's motives: Polk wanted to "persuade, threaten, or bluff Mexico into negotiation."

Many Mexican historians—like the Mexican politicians at the time—do not view the U.S. troop movement as an effort to "convince" or "persuade" but rather to force Mexico to give up its territory. In Mexican eyes the United States had not only stolen Texas but also changed the traditional boundary to double the size of the territory taken. Haynes supports the view of Mexican historian Josefina Zoraida Vázquez that the advance of the U.S. army was "an undeniable provocation."

"It is to be hoped that our troops being so close on the borders of Mexico will bring about a speedy settlement of the boundary question. . . .

"I think the chances of a fight . . . are about equal to the chances for peace."
—Ulysses S. Grant, on the U.S. army movement to the Rio Grande

Marching Orders

General Taylor had suggested moving U.S. troops to the Rio Grande as early as October 1845, pointing out that the U.S. camp on the Nueces was "too far from the frontier to impress the government of Mexico with our readiness to vindicate, by force of arms if necessary, our title to the country as far as the Rio Grande."

When Taylor finally received his marching orders from Polk on February 3, his troops had been camped near Corpus Christi for six months. It had been a wet, cold winter, during which many soldiers had fallen ill. When the troops finally began their trip to the Rio Grande on March 8, hundreds had to be left behind.

Almost 3,000 U.S. soldiers marched the 150 to 200 miles, through a landscape described by one soldier as "prairie . . . covered with flowers . . . scattered wood and chaparral." A Hispanic population had occupied this disputed country between the Nueces and the Rio Grande rivers since the eighteenth century. But there were so few settlements that historian George Lockhart Rives describes it as "practically neutral ground, permanently possessed by neither party, and only crossed occasionally by smugglers and Indians."

Now it was being crossed by a huge line of U.S. soldiers. A party of Mexican soldiers watched their progress but did not challenge them.

"OLD ROUGH AND READY"

GENERAL ZACHARY TAYLOR ignored the trappings of military rank, often wearing an old brown coat and wide straw hat against the sun. His men loved him for it, calling him "Old Rough and Ready."

He was respected for his courage, having acquired a reputation for calm under fire during the Seminole War in Florida, when he rode sidesaddle into battle on his horse Whitey, in hit-and-run fighting with small bands of warriors.

Fort Texas

On March 28, the first of General Taylor's soldiers arrived on the north bank of the Rio Grande. Taylor "had several wagon tongues spliced together to form a flagstaff and the Star-Spangled Banner was hoisted," wrote Lieutenant Napoleon Dana about the arrival, "and thus did Uncle Sam take the Rio Grande for his boundary line."

Across the river, Matamoros residents and Mexican soldiers of the Army of the North "were angered by the enemy's insulting act," says *Apuntes para la historia de la guerra.* "For the first time that flag waved proudly before our forces, as if taking possession of what rightfully belonged to us."

The U.S. troops went to work immediately, building an earth-and-wood fort on a wedge of land with the river on two sides. The structure, which they called Fort Texas, was to be supplied from a base established on the coast at Point Isabel, twenty-five miles away.

Fort Texas put U.S. and Mexican guns within striking distance of each other. Taylor contrasted his own "strong bastioned field fort" with the Mexican fortifications, which were "scantily armed with guns of inferior calibre." Still, the Mexican army would have the upper hand if it could cut off U.S. supplies.

Desertions from the U.S. Army

Long before any exchange of fire with Mexican troops, some U.S. soldiers began deserting. After their six months of duty on the Nueces and twenty-day march to the Rio Grande, many of Taylor's men were fed up with soldiering, disgusted with drills and discipline.

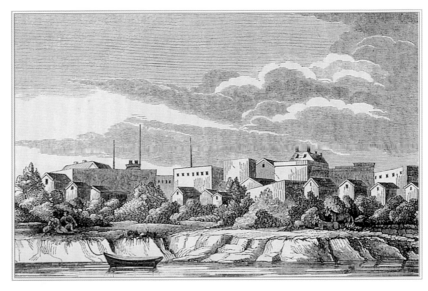

Matamoros was clearly within Mexican territory. Battles fought on the other side of the Rio Grande were within the disputed territory. "Not one member of the Mexican army was ever in U.S. territory," says Mexican historian Jesús Velasco-Márquez.

Some of the soldiers were recent immigrants who complained that the army was full of anti-Catholic and anti-immigrant prejudice. Mexican commanders smuggled pamphlets into the U.S. camp encouraging Catholics to desert and join fellow Catholics in Mexico, where they would be rewarded with land. Mexican handbills sang a siren song to U.S. troops unhappy with army life: "Throw away your arms and run to us."

More than 200 soldiers tried to escape Fort Texas by swimming across the river (at least two were shot by U.S. guards as they made the attempt). During this war, the desertion rate from the U.S. army was higher than in any other foreign war. According to records of the adjutant general's office, at least four thousand men deserted the U.S. army each year of the war (most of them not for religious or political reasons).

"Sergeant, buck him and gag him!"
our officers cry
For each trifling offense which they
happen to spy
Till with bucking and gagging of
Dick, Pat, and Bill
Faith, the Mexicans ranks they
have helped to fill.
—A U.S. ARMY SONG

Opposing Armies

The U.S. Army—Trained Regulars

"Taylor's army was remarkable in the U.S. military experience, because it was made up entirely of regulars," explains writer John S. D. Eisenhower. "These were unusual troops—tough, rigorously disciplined, and reliable in a fight." Almost half the men were recent immigrants—from Ireland, Poland, Germany. They had signed up even before becoming U.S. citizens.

The junior officers in charge of these troops were mostly young graduates from the military academy at West Point, founded in 1802 to train the military to assist in the national goals of expanding and developing the country. The class of 1846 was the academy's largest, 122 men, 53 of whom would fight in Mexico. The West Point graduates, trained in strategy, tactics, and logistics (though without actual military experience), formed the beginnings of a professional U.S. army.

Congress was debating the very existence of the military academy, even as the United States faced the threat of war with Mexico (as well as real or imagined threats from Britain and France). Many felt that a professional army was inappropriate for a democratic nation. By design, the United States lacked the large standing army and traditional military class of the European nations (and Mexico).

This distrust of the professional military led to the common U.S. practice of using political patronage to create instant generals out of ambitious but untrained men. "Officers of the regular army were understandably dis-

Caricature of an Irish soldier.

couraged," notes Otis A. Singletary, "when untrained civilians were given higher rank than their own, and they were quick to criticize the shortcomings of these 'political generals.'"

Conflicts between professional and "citizen" soldiers—both officers and regular troops—grew worse after war was declared and thousands of undisciplined volunteers swarmed to fight in Mexico.

The Mexican Army—Paid with Promises

Before the war, Mexico's standing army was at least three times the size of the U.S. army, with 25,000 to 30,000 men. But the entire army, says Otis A. Singletary, "was vitiated by flaws inherent in the Mexican military system, a system properly belonging to the eighteenth century, when aristocratic officers commanded soldiers from the depressed classes."

Most of the soldiers were conscripts, not enlisted men or volunteers. The Mexican infantry was recruited by a "levy system, in which the government of each state had a 'blood quota' imposed on it," says General Luis Garfias. "Asked to provide a certain number of men, they sent the army their poor, their criminals, their political enemies." A lot of the soldiers were Indians and peasants. Since Mexican law had always prohibited Indians and other *castas* from owning guns, most of the recruits had never fired a gun before they entered the army. Some had never even seen one. Conscripts, who often went without pay for months, were required to provide their own food, either foraging or attempting to purchase it with useless script.

Fautassin en grande tenue.
Nouveau Costume.

The Mexican army was geared to control the local population rather than deal with an external enemy. Lucas Alamán, in his Historia de Méjico, *said that money spent on arming Mexican troops merely enabled them to fight each other and "give the illusion" that the country possessed an army for its defense.*

Their commanders, the large group of officers in Mexico's professional military class, modeled themselves on a European ideal, wearing uniforms like those of the Grand Army of Napoleon. There were almost 200 generals before the war, most of them without a command. Officers lacked leadership experience and "knowledge of obedience and discipline," say Ruth Olivera and Liliane Crété. "Those who entered the army were motivated more by ambition than patriotism; it was a sinecure, a stepping-stone to power." Mexico had established a military academy in 1823 (it found its permanent home at Chapultepec ten years later), but few Mexican officers had formal training in tactics, strategy, or weaponry.

Ever since Mexico's loss of Texas in 1836, there had been talk of reducing the standing army and reforming the conscription system. President Herrera had favored

military reform. When the United States annexed Texas, Herrera wanted to call volunteers to prepare for war. His Congress approved $15 million worth of military loans—but the tiny sum actually collected was not enough to provide the new soldiers with uniforms and supplies.

Departmental governments were asked to provide the army with weapons and ammunition. Mexico had long relied on this regional—not centralized—system to feed, clothe, supply, and transport its huge army. Before and during the war, lack of resources created morale and discipline problems for troops moving from one part of the country to another.

A desperate Herrera insisted in his December 1845 plea to the governors that the success of the war would depend on the "effective will of the Departments." Herrera warned that "soldiers are neither fed nor paid with promises, nor the war . . . supported by pure hopes."

Mariano Arista was a respected and capable general who had a long, distinguished military career. Like U.S. General Zachary Taylor, Arista became president of his country after the war.

First Clashes

As soon as President Paredes learned of General Taylor's advance to the Rio Grande, he declared that the U.S. army had invaded Mexico. "Hostilities . . . have been begun by the United States of America," he announced. To protect "the Mexican territory that the U.S. troops are invading," the president ordered Commander Pedro de Ampudia to Matamoros with reinforcements for the garrison.

On April 11, Ampudia sent Taylor a letter of protest: "Your government . . . has not only insulted but also exasperated the Mexican nation, bearing its conquering banner to the left bank of the Rio Bravo. . . . I require you [within] . . . twenty-four hours, to break up your camp and retire to the other bank of the Nueces River."

Taylor replied that his instructions from President Polk "will not permit" retreat from the Rio Grande, and he ordered the U.S. navy to blockade the mouth of the river—calling it a "simple defensive precaution." This cut off supplies to the Mexican troops in the Matamoros garrison. Again Ampudia protested. Taylor refused to lift the blockade.

On April 23, Paredes announced the beginning of "a defensive war" against the United States. In a speech in Mexico City, he listed three "bitter outrages" by the United States: the Slidell "insult," John C. Frémont's rabble rousing in California, and the moving of Taylor's troops to the Rio Grande. Sending General Mariano Arista, commander of the Army of the North, to Matamoros, Paredes ordered him to "attack the army that is attacking us." With Arista's troops there would be 5,000 Mexican soldiers in Matamoros.

Arista ordered General Anastasio Torrejón to lead a detachment across the Rio Grande. Torrejón and 1,600 cavalry and light infantry forded the river a few miles above Matamoros. Taylor received reports of the troop movement and sent Captain Seth Thornton and two squadrons of dragoons to investigate. On April 25, the scouting party was surprised and attacked by Torrejón's troops at El Rancho de Carricitos, about twenty miles from Fort Texas. Fourteen U.S. soldiers were killed and seven wounded. Thornton and most of his eighty men were taken prisoner.

The next day Torrejón sent a wounded dragoon to Taylor's camp to notify the U.S. commander of the skirmish. Taylor informed Washington on April 26, 1846, "Hostilities may now be considered as commenced." Before the news reached the White House two weeks later, the U.S. and Mexican armies had clashed again, in the first major battles of the war.

Bombardment of the Fort

After the capture of Captain Thornton's men, General Arista made preparations to complete his assault on the U.S. troops. A large detachment of Mexican soldiers was readied to move across the river below Matamoros, where it could join Torrejón's detachment, encircling Fort Texas and cutting it off from the coast.

The U.S. troops at Fort Texas could not survive without the supplies waiting at Point Isabel. On May 1, General Taylor and 2,000 soldiers set off for the coast to pick them up, leaving only 500 soldiers at Fort Texas, with Major Jacob Brown in command.

General Arista took his troops to Palo Alto, planning to block the coast road and prevent Taylor and his troops from returning to Fort Texas. General Pedro de Ampudia stayed in Matamoros to launch an attack on the U.S. troops remaining at the fort.

Using the fixed artillery in Matamoros, Ampudia cannonaded the soldiers at Fort Texas at long range for more than five days. The siege might have succeeded in starving the U.S. soldiers if Taylor's return had been prevented. But the bombardment was more sound than fury, since many of the cannonballs fell short. Taylor later renamed the fort to honor the bravery of Major Brown, one of two U.S. soldiers killed by the shelling.

The Rio Grande and northern Mexico, showing Fort Texas (later named Fort Brown and now Brownsville) opposite Matamoros. The fort depended on the U.S. base in Point Isabel on the coast for vital supplies. Arista's offensive was designed to cut off the coast road, the U.S. supply route.

The Battle of Palo Alto

The sound of the "artillery at the fort could be distinctly heard" all the way to Point Isabel, on the Gulf Coast, where the U.S. troops "lay upon the seashore," said Lieutenant Ulysses S. Grant. Quickly loading their supply train, the 2,000 U.S. soldiers and 200 supply wagons began the twenty-five-mile trip back to Fort Texas.

On the afternoon of May 8, Taylor's men found Arista's army, more than 3,200 men, waiting for them at Palo Alto. The line of Mexican soldiers stretched for a mile across a wide plain covered with razor-sharp grass and spiny cactus.

Arista had chosen this battleground because it favored his mobile attack force, the cavalry, who were armed with lances, carbines, and swords. But the Mexican generals had not surveyed the ground. It was marshy, preventing the cavalry from moving easily. The battle, which began with the roar of cannon fire, quickly turned into an artillery duel. Here the

Anticipating victory, Arista's troops had been eager to engage the U.S. army. A Mexican soldier described the mood before the battle: "Banners floated in the wind, the soldiers stood to their arms, the horses pawed the ground, the band performed inspiring music, and shouts filled the air—'Viva la república!'—the cry of vengeance raised by an offended nation."

The Battle of Palo Alto

Lithographer Carl Nebel was not present at the Battle of Palo Alto. Although he added hills to the background landscape, Nebel "meant his picture to be an accurate document," says historian Ron Tyler. It shows "the First, Sixth, and Tenth American infantries, the Fourth Infantry with two eighteen-pounders (in the center), and Colonel David Twiggs repulsing Anastasio Torrejón with the main body of the Mexican cavalry (on the extreme right). General Taylor astride Old Whitey directs the action from the right foreground. The smoke from the grass fire conceals 150 Mexican cavalrymen, a four-pounder, a corps of sappers, the Second Light Infantry, the Tampico veterans, and the Coast Guards. Behind the Mexican position are thickets." This was the first full-scale battle the U.S. army had fought since the War of 1812. Neither Taylor nor his officers had ever faced a large European-style army such as Mexico boasted.

Lieutenant Napoleon Dana was at Fort Texas, but he recorded other soldiers' impressions of the Battle of Palo Alto: "The battle was a horrid spectacle, corpses mangled most horribly . . . the wounded crying for assistance . . . a woman on the field of battle, with a babe in her lap, unable to weep but wringing her hands and combing the hair of her mangled husband's corpse and kissing his bloody lips . . . all are sights unsuited to my tastes and shocking to my feelings. I do not think . . . that our war will last much longer. The people of Mexico will not stand it."

U.S. troops had the advantage in both equipment and training—the months of drilling at Corpus Christi soon paid off. Mobile U.S. flying artillery units raked Arista's lines with iron shot larger than marbles, tearing the Mexican soldiers to pieces.

The Mexicans were ordered to hold their position and face the slashing rain of shot. This they did, at the cost of many lives. "The American artillery," reported *Apuntes para la historia de la guerra,* "much superior to ours, made terrible ravages in the Mexican ranks. . . . The soldiers finally succumbed, not overwhelmed by combat but decimated in cold blood. The troops, drained by the needless deaths, pleaded to go before the enemy's bayonets and die bravely in close range."

The ferocious artillery fire set the prairie grass ablaze, burning some of the wounded alive. Soon dense smoke covered the battlefield. As evening fell, the Mexicans withdrew and reorganized, while the U.S. soldiers passed the night on the battlefield.

Resaca de la Palma

After the Battle of Palo Alto, the Mexican army retreated about five miles to a new position in a *resaca*—a curved wash or broad dry riverbed—called Resaca de la Palma, beside the road to Matamoros. There was thick chaparral on both sides of the road, forming a natural barrier. Arista chose this site to minimize the devastating force of Taylor's artillery, limiting its use to the narrow road, even though the position also limited Arista's use of the Mexican cavalry, forcing him to rely on his inexperienced infantry.

Supremely confident, convinced of U.S. superiority, Taylor's instinct was to strike the enemy head on and pursue a victory. The survival of his troops depended on returning to Fort Texas and reuniting his forces. So he ignored his officers' vote to suspend the attack and, characteristically, ordered his men to advance. Moving slowly and quietly through tangled, thorny chaparral, the U.S. troops approached the Mexican infantry.

The young Mexican infantry were recent conscripts, says General Luis Garfias, and "they lacked training and discipline. When they were under attack and a unit was overcome, the other units broke up and ran." Nonetheless, the U.S. troops met stubborn resistance until a charge by Captain Charles May's dragoons scattered the Mexican gunners, allowing U.S. artillery and infantry to advance.

After two Mexican cavalry charges and numerous skirmishes, the Mexican troops were driven back to the river. With a U.S. squadron in pursuit, the Mexican soldiers tried to swim across to Matamoros. "The most horrible confusion reigned on the field," says the *Apuntes*. "Terror spread the idea that the enemy was following. . . . [The soldiers] sought some ford that would save them, or threw themselves into the river in their clothes and arms, and almost all were drowned."

By nightfall U.S. troops had returned to Fort Texas. They were already planning to cross the river and enter Matamoros.

DUELING ARTILLERIES

BEFORE THE Battle of Palo Alto, General Taylor had told his men that they would have to rely mostly on their bayonets. But the battle had turned into an artillery duel. The United States had experimental units armed with light guns, bronze six-pounder cannons on wheels, each pulled by six horses. "These 'flying artillery' mounted units were well-trained," says John S. D. Eisenhower. They "could advance their batteries at full gallop, unlimber, fire, remount and whirl off to a new position with astonishing speed."

The mobile guns were a major advance over the fixed heavy iron guns of the Mexican army. The success of an attack by the heavy guns depended on their careful placement by army engineers, mathematicians who calculated the trajectory of a shot. The Mexican cannons did little damage, Ulysses S. Grant reported. The cannonballs "hurt no one because they would strike the ground long before they reached our line, and ricocheted through the tall grass so slowly that the men would see them and open ranks and let them pass." The Mexican guns often used faulty ammunition.

At the end of two days' battle, the U.S. army had suffered fewer than 200 casualties. The Mexican losses were more than three times greater.

Many of the earliest prints of the Battle of Resaca de la Palma were based on newspaper accounts of the U.S. victory and are far from realistic portrayals of the battle's hand-to-hand combat.

Matamoros

Many of the Mexican soldiers blamed General Arista for their losses. At Resaca de la Palma he had been confident that his position was strong and that Taylor would not attack immediately. Describing the battle, José María Roa Bárcena reported: "The troops had had nothing to eat for thirty hours, and there was a lack of leadership, because Arista insisted on believing that the enemy's approach was only reconnaissance. . . . [He] gave no orders nor went out personally to the battlefield to fight as he usually did, until everything was already lost." By the time Arista advanced with his cavalry, the U.S. infantry controlled both sides of the road—and Arista and his cavalry fled with the rest of the defeated troops. Many were "crying out in despair," says the *Apuntes,* "that they were betrayed, that the general was a traitor."

During the night, General Arista and his army left Matamoros. On May 18, Taylor's army crossed the Rio Grande, prepared to storm the town. Matamoros surrendered without resistance. Taylor finally acquired a map of northern Mexico—one left behind by Ampudia. The map became the key to the U.S. invasion. The occupation of Matamoros was the first step of a U.S. drive to Camargo and then Monterrey, Mexico's largest northern city, deep within northern Mexico.

The retreat from Matamoros was chaotic. Heavy artillery, supplies, and equipment had been abandoned. Many injured soldiers had been left behind. "About 400 wounded were abandoned to the generosity of the enemy," noted the authors of *Apuntes para la historia de la guerra*. "Among them there were some who . . . crawled out of hospitals, leaving behind them the red path of their blood. Those miserable ones preferred any kind of pain than to be left behind in a town where they feared they would be treated with cruelty by the victors." Taylor directed his surgeons to try to help the wounded men.

The Mexican army fell back through 150 miles of arid countryside. With soldiers deserting or drowning, dead or wounded, Arista's force had been reduced by over 1,000 men in this first encounter with the enemy. Arista was court-martialed for his defeat. Mexican newspapers stressed that this was only the first encounter.

"All Mexicans have felt the pain and outrage. One loss does not lose the war: Mexico should fight to the end, and, as long as there is one man remaining, he should go and fight the unjust invaders."
—*Semanario Político del Gobierno de Nuevo León,* JUNE 4, 1846

CHAPTER 6

THE UNITED STATES DECLARES WAR

POLK AND HIS CABINET (JAMES MASON, WILLIAM MARCY, CAVE JOHNSON, GEORGE BANCROFT, AND ROBERT WALKER).

*On Saturday, May 9, 1846, President James Polk called
his cabinet together. It was the same day that U.S. and Mexican
troops were engaged in the bloody battle at Resaca de la Palma.
Polk was unaware that fighting had broken out on the frontier,
but he was preparing to ask Congress to declare war.*

THE PREVIOUS DAY Polk had met with John Slidell, who had related the story of his frustrating months in Mexico. As a result of the Mexican treatment of the U.S. minister, diplomatic relations had been severed. The conflict with Britain over the Oregon territory was nearing resolution, and Polk could now afford to be more aggressive with Mexico.

Neither the Slidell mission nor the advance of U.S. troops to the Rio Grande had accomplished Polk's goal of obtaining California and New Mexico. He hoped a declaration of war would finally pressure Mexico into selling its territories.

Polk told his cabinet that the United States "had ample cause of war": the insult to the U.S. diplomat, plus the unpaid claims for damage to U.S. property in Mexico from past political uprisings. His diary records the argument he presented to his cabinet: "I stated that we had heard of no open act of aggression by the Mexican army, but that the danger was imminent."

"The country was excited and impatient on the subject," he said. The time was ripe; the situation called for "definitive measures." Polk was ready to declare war on Mexico without military provocation. A single cabinet minister objected. Polk decided to draft a war message to be discussed at the next cabinet meeting.

That evening, a messenger arrived bearing Zachary Taylor's report of the attack against Thornton's scouting party two weeks earlier. The news of U.S. deaths near the Rio Grande made Polk's task easier. An outraged public was sure to support the war.

Polk's War Message

On May 11, Polk sent to Congress a message recommending war. Hoping to disarm his congressional opponents, Polk's message made a "show of innocence and reluctance," says historian David Pletcher. "His general strategy was to call for troops to defend national territory and honor, to emphasize patriotism and Mexican treachery, and to avoid letting the

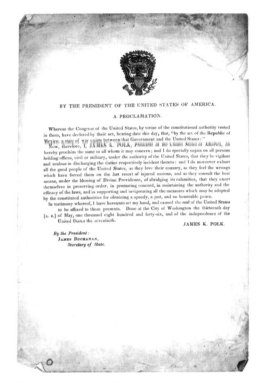

In his message to Congress on May 11, 1846, Polk asserted: "After repeated menaces, Mexico has passed the boundary of the United States, and shed American blood upon the American soil. . . . As war exists, notwithstanding all our efforts to avoid it, and exists by act of Mexico herself, we are called upon by every consideration of duty and patriotism to vindicate the honor, the rights, and the interest of our country."

opposition examine too closely either the dispatches accompanying the war message or the question of how hostilities had begun."

The war message provoked a fierce debate in which many politicians took unexpected positions. Some senators objected to Polk's preamble, which attached blame for the conflict on Mexico, but the controversy had as much to do with divisions in the United States as with sympathy for Mexico. Opponents called the war both unnecessary and unconstitutional. *All* war is unconstitutional, stated Daniel Webster; republics should not fight wars but rather should be dedicated to the arts of peace. *All* wars are founded on pretexts, Webster asserted, including the war Polk had proposed.

John C. Calhoun reminded the president that only Congress was authorized to declare war. He led the opponents, charging that Polk had started the war without congressional approval, since Congress had never voted to send Taylor to the Rio Grande—a clear act of provocation.

Thomas Hart Benton, powerful chairman of the Senate Military Affairs Committee, at first opposed an "aggressive" war. He agreed with Mexico that the Nueces, not the Rio Grande, was the Texas boundary; therefore, Benton stated, the Mexicans had not actually "shed American blood on American soil."

Polk's message had said nothing about California, where the Pacific Squadron had been put on alert. But Sam Houston—the new Texas senator and ardent expansionist, who had played so large a part in adding Texas to the Union—questioned the advisability of going to war to acquire that western state.

Polk's Democrats countered with a demand that the United States support its troops. David Pletcher summarizes their argument: "'Our troops have been attacked by Mexico. We must send them supplies and reinforcements. And if we do that we might as well declare war.' The antiwar element in Congress resisted as long as possible. But eventually they could not define the difference between sending troops and supplies and declaring war."

Congressmen who would not support an "aggressive" war on Mexico did vote men and money for a "defensive" one. In the end, Congress

---

THE FIGHT ON CAPITOL HILL

WHIGS IN CONGRESS were suspicious of Polk; his objective was not "peace with Mexico," said one, "but a piece of Mexico."

Joshua Giddings summarized Whig objections, saying, "This war is waged against an unoffending people, without just or adequate cause, for the purposes of conquest; with the design to extend slavery; in violation of the Constitution. . . . I will not bathe my hands in the blood of the people of Mexico."

But once war had been declared, the Whig opposition passed Polk's appropriation bill "to support the honor of the country and the army," as John Clayton said in casting his vote.

CLAIMING CALIFORNIA

The Bombardment of Guaymas *by William H. Meyers.*

Depiction of the Battle of San Gabriel, near the present-day town of Montebello.

In January 1847, U.S. troops in the Pacific were ordered to take possession of at least one port in Baja California. Several towns were claimed by October, when two U.S. ships sent 500 rounds of cannon fire into Guaymas before it surrendered. Naval contests with Mexican forces trying to reclaim the port damaged every house in Guaymas before the war's end. Gunner William H. Meyers of the Pacific Squadron is responsible for most of the watercolor sketches of the fighting in Alta and Baja California.

U.S. Expedition to New Mexico

El Dorado, Exploded *by Samuel Chamberlain.*

*After the peace treaty was signed, U.S. soldiers from northeastern Mexico made what
Samuel Chamberlain described as an "expedition to New Mexico and California,"
to consolidate U.S. possession of the new territories. Chamberlain's party retraced
Doniphan's steps as far as Chihuahua. They then marched across Sonora and west
on the Gila Trail. There, Chamberlain discovered that El Dorado, city of gold, was really
"a city of sandstone, built by dame nature."*

*"With several Pima for guides, we visited some remarkable ruins...
our guides said that Montezuma built them..."*

Casas Grandes on the Gila *by Samuel Chamberlain.*

*The U.S. expedition traveled past the Grand Canyon and into Pima and Yuma territory,
(where Chamberlain reported seeing ruins "in all directions...the sites of houses or
canals") before many of the mustered-out soldiers joined groups of Mexicans
rushing toward the mines in California.*

MONTERREY, NUEVO LEÓN

Monterrey *(from the Saltillo Road)* by Samuel Chamberlain.

During the war, Samuel Chamberlain served in northeastern Mexico. The seventeen-year-old joined General Wool's troops in San Antonio and then marched to Parras to hold the U.S. line cutting Mexico's Northeast off from the capital. Chamberlain described the street fighting in Monterrey: "For four hours until dark, Hell reigned in this part of the city." He sketched the retreat of the city's civilians, which he called the Mexican army's "camp followers…men, women, and children of every grade, colour, and condition on foot, on donkeys, mules, half-starved little ponys, carrying immense bundles of household goods, with chattering Parrots, Hens, Chickens and Monkeys…"

Heroic Defense of the City of Monterrey *by Julio Michaud y Thomas, from the* Álbum Pintoresco de la República Mexicana.

Surrender of the Black Fort *by Samuel Chamberlain.*

THE SALTILLO LINE

Paso del Linares *by Samuel Chamberlain.*

Chamberlain created this picture of Linares from the stories and sketches of other soldiers. The Monterrey images, too, were products of his imagination. He never saw Linares, nor was he present at the battle for Monterrey. Here he depicts the pass that claimed so many Mexican lives after Arista ordered the retreat from Matamoros. Chamberlain did make the march to Parras, through the Paso el Diablo, the "strange freak of nature…a wild, fearful looking place" that the U.S. troops expected to be defended. But the U.S. "army, with its immense train of wagons," moved through unopposed and quickly occupied the town.

Paso el Diablo *by Samuel Chamberlain.*

Burning of Agua Nueva, and the Enemy in Sight,
Samuel Chamberlain's portrait of the U.S. troops' retreat before the Battle of Buena Vista.

authorized $10 million and 50,000 volunteers to fight against Mexico, empowering the president to "resist foreign invasion." The vote in the House was 174–14, in the Senate 40–2. The numbers did not reveal how deeply Congress was divided.

War Fever

President Polk and his cabinet were right about U.S. popular reaction to the events on the Rio Grande. Congressional passage of the war bill coincided with news of the U.S. victories at Palo Alto and Resaca de la Palma and produced an outbreak of war fever. Robert W. Johannsen notes that the United States was primed for this diversion:

> War news came to a country undergoing unprecedented economic and social change. Rapid commercial and industrial expansion [and] a concern for material advancement were changing people's lives, and with those changes came challenges to the way they looked at themselves and their country. Writers of the time worried that the new commercial spirit was ruining the old republican virtues. . . . A lot of [people] felt that the war was an opportunity to go back to the ideals on which the nation had been founded, to bring back the notion of service and sacrifice, . . . a new age of heroism on behalf of the republic.

The "new age" was marked by a burgeoning population, which most expansionists saw as a sign of growing power and national health. But the tide of immigrants—over 2,000,000 had arrived in twenty-five years—had caused stresses in U.S. cities. In 1844, crowds of native-born artisans and laborers rioted against foreign-born immigrants, mainly Irish, in Philadelphia; the riots turned into armed struggles between Catholics and Protestants. In other cities, too, rioters turned on immigrants, or free black laborers, or the police. In 1845, the potato famine in Ireland spurred more massive immigration to the United States. Crowds of unskilled aliens, desperately poor, wandered the streets of Boston, New York, Philadelphia.

These new conflicts—along with old disputes over the true nature of the republic and its purpose—shook

THE FEVER SPREADS

STATE CONGRESSMAN Abraham Lincoln criticized Polk for provoking a conflict at the Rio Grande. He decried growing violence in the United States, saying, "There is something of an ill omen among us. I mean . . . the growing disposition to substitute the wild and furious passions in lieu of the sober judgments of the courts."

The national mood responded to changes in U.S. society, including inventions of this era—the telegraph and steam-powered trains, boats, and printing presses—that carried news across the country at an ever faster pace. That pace, said critics, often outran reasonable discussion.

NEW HEROES

OR TEN YEARS, people in the United States had been following the story of Texas and Mexico—the Alamo, Goliad, the Santa Fe prisoners, the decimation after Mier. When the United States entered the war, says Robert W. Johannsen, news of the conflict "was hailed with a great deal of excitement. Business was suspended, shops would close, people would be out in the streets celebrating."

PENNY PRESSES

Mass-circulation newspapers, or "penny presses," were the main source of war news. These papers shaped popular perceptions of the war, its battles, and its generals. Reporting the Battle of Palo Alto, the April 25 New Orleans *Picayune* set the tone with a front page article: "The war has begun in earnest. The Enemy is upon our soil!!"

The *Picayune* was foremost among the new penny presses, having two advantages: Its publisher, George Kendall, was an adventurous and enthusiastically pro-war reporter, who followed the troops into Mexico, filing one sensational report after another. And its office in New Orleans was in the U.S. city closest to the front. Most of the troops and supplies going to Mexico were shipped through that port.

Kendall's newspaper supplied war news to much of the United States. From the *Picayune* office, riders carried stacks of papers to Lake Pontchartrain, where they were put aboard fast boats to Mobile, carried by relays of riders to Montgomery, Charleston, Richmond, and Baltimore, and then brought by train and steam packet boat to Washington and up the Eastern seaboard. A recently opened telegraph line relayed war news between Washington and New York in moments.

War News from Mexico, *by Richard Caton Woodville.*

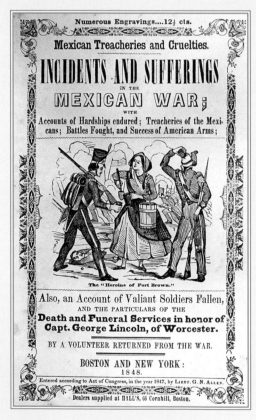

One hero of the bombardment of Fort Texas was a laundress and cook named Sara Borginnis, a large, capable woman whom the soldiers nicknamed "The Great Western" after the world's largest steamship. Borginnis set up a tent in the middle of Fort Texas and doled out food and coffee. She nursed the wounded and fearlessly carried water to the soldiers.

The public thirsted passionately—and sometimes uncritically—for heroes. After the Battle of Palo Alto, Captain Charles May became a national hero for his supposedly brave cavalry charge and capture of General Rómulo Díaz de la Vega, but the charge had actually been bungled, and the general captured almost by accident—by the company bugler.

DAGUERREOTYPES AND LITHOGRAPHS

When news from the battlefield reached the eastern United States, it was transformed into mass-produced patriotic images and sheet music. The U.S.–Mexican War was the first war ever photographed, through the new process of daguerreotype. But, unlike the U.S. Civil War, with its chilling photographic record, "the Mexican War has few such graphic reminders of personal suffering," notes Ron Tyler. There are some daguerreotypes, but "none of them [are] scenes of conflict. The few paintings of the war [with the exception of Samuel Chamberlain's unusual watercolors] are generally grandiose representa-

tions saturated with the spirit of the day—bravery, nobility, and patriotism."

These images of the war, says Tyler, reflect an era "when 'war had novelty and glamour' and politicians entered it with 'enthusiasm.'" Lithographs of war scenes—heroes and battles in an exotic locale—were widely reproduced. Among the most popular shops turning out patriotic lithographs was Nathaniel Currier's studio on Broadway in New York. The idealized Currier style seemed to enable men who had never experienced war to imagine themselves carrying on the glorious tradition of the Founding Fathers of the Republic.

U.S. society. As a result, the war with Mexico, which offered a fresh sense of national identity, was regarded "as the most important episode in the nation's history since the American Revolution," according to Johannsen.

Walt Whitman, young editor of the *Eagle* in Brooklyn, New York, and long a supporter of U.S. expansionism, expressed the nationalistic temper of many: "Let our arms now be carried with a spirit which shall teach the world that, while we are not forward for a quarrel, America knows how to crush, as well as how to expand. What has miserable inefficient Mexico—with her superstition, her burlesque upon freedom, her actual tyranny by the few over the many, what has she to do with the peopling of the new world? With a noble race? Be it ours to achieve that mission." His opinions were echoed in numerous publications.

Against the War

Support for the war was not universal, even in the Mississippi Valley and the West, which had always favored expansion. In New England and the North opponents formed a small but vocal minority. The Massachusetts legislature declared that this was a war of conquest—unconstitutional, criminal, and unworthy of support by honest people. Northern commercial interests often opposed the war on economic grounds. "This unhappy strife hangs like an incubus over the market, paralyzing enterprise and retarding the growth of commercial confidence," said the *Business Reporter*.

"Opposition to the war arose from many sources: antimilitarism, business concern, fear of growing presidential power, contempt for Mexico," says David Pletcher. "But one issue came to dominate." Even though President Polk insisted that he could not see "what connection slavery has with the making of peace with Mexico," most opposition to the war sprang from "the hatred of slavery and the fear that slavery would expand to fill any territory acquired from Mexico," says Pletcher.

The editor of the *Liberator* (an abolitionist newspaper) condemned the war with Mexico as an act "of aggression, of invasion, of conquest, and rapine—marked by . . . perfidy and every other feature of national depravity."

Pro-slavery southern statesman John Calhoun was also filled with dread by the war, fearing that it would have disastrous consequences for the Union he had spent his life trying to preserve. "Mexico," Calhoun said, "is to us the forbidden fruit; the penalty of eating it would be to subject our institutions to political death."

A Flood of Volunteers

When Congress passed the war bill, it granted the president authority to call for 50,000 volunteers. Polk was an ardent believer in the ideal of the "citizen soldier," a volunteer army of gallant young men who would mobilize in times of peril. Many young men shared this dream, and the response to the first call for volunteers, issued on May 15, 1846, was immediate and overwhelming. In Polk's home state of Tennessee, a call for 3,000 volunteers brought 30,000.

Veteran Indian fighters and untrained city men rushed to volunteer. Fire companies, college graduating classes, sports clubs, and fishing clubs joined up together. Immigrants enlisted as soon as they got off the ship from Europe, joining immigrants who had been serving with Taylor since Corpus Christi. Many of the first volunteers were farm boys from the South and West. They streamed down the Mississippi or traveled overland to New Orleans and then shipped out to the Rio Grande. One in nine would never return.

Men wanting to form their own volunteer companies took out big newspapers ads, decorated with eagles, stars, bugles, and banners. Herman Melville reported, "People here [in upstate New York] are all in a state of delirium about the Mexican War. A military ardor pervades all ranks . . . and apprentice boys are running off to the wars by scores. Nothing is talked of but the Halls of the Montezumas."

Occupying Matamoros

In Matamoros, unseasonable rains had brought the Rio Grande to flood, and catfish and gar were seen feeding over the battlefields of Palo Alto and Resaca de la Palma. Volunteers were arriving by the shipload; by the end of June, an army of 12,000 volunteers and regular troops had assembled.

As the U.S. volunteers stumbled off the steamers and schooners into the stifling heat of Matamoros, army regular Lieutenant Napoleon Dana described the new troops: "This afternoon about 600 have arrived, as perfectly used up a set of fellows as you ever saw, completely broken down and disgusted, and I have no doubt, heartily wish themselves home again."

The only known daguerreotype of volunteering soldiers (a group from New Hampshire, late in the war).

Matamoros was the first foreign town most of the volunteers had ever seen, and soldiers reported on it with fascination:

> A hot tropical sun poured down its fierce rays upon our troops . . . and many slept in the open air, surrounded with water; mosquitoes, and innumerable noxious insects of immense size, filled the air, and at night murdered sleep. (T. B. Thorpe)

> The young men dress with much taste and neatness. . . . They generally appear in white, and instead of suspenders they wear around the waist sashes of various colors. (Benjamin Franklin Scribner)

> If you are a lover of nature—unadorned—you can gratify your taste by walking up to Fort Paredes any pleasant evening, and witness the fair ones bathing in the Rio Grande; no offense is taken by looking at them enjoying their aquatic amusements. (William S. Henry)

The volunteers had time on their hands, and drinking and gambling were common. Some of the men attacked and terrorized civilians; the ones most feared by the local population were the Texas Rangers. Many professional soldiers, such as Ulysses S. Grant, expressed disgust at the lack of discipline: "Some of the volunteers and about all the Texans seem to think it perfectly right to impose upon the people of a conquered city . . . and even to murder them where the act can be covered by dark. And how much they seem to enjoy acts of violence too!"

March to Camargo

In July, General Taylor pushed his enlarged army farther into Mexico. The first step was to move about 100 miles upriver to Camargo. Some of the troops traveled by water, jammed into leaky, stinking steamers, which fought the Rio Grande's swollen current chug by chug. Others made the brutal journey overland, through miles of desolate country. Said soldier John R. Kenley: "We marched with a burning sun overhead and burning sand beneath our feet . . . not a drop of rain had fallen . . . and the dust hung over our heads with smothering denseness from which there was no escape."

Food was scarce, and there were shortages of everything else. Taylor now had fewer wagons than when he had left Corpus Christi, yet his army had grown to many times its former size. Thousands of animals were needed to move the supplies and equipment. Teams of oxen were required to pull the heavy artillery pieces.

"In six or eight months if the Mexicans hold out that long, we will be fully as anxious to make peace as they."
—General Zachary Taylor

When Taylor's troops finally arrived in Camargo, the residents must have wondered what they had done to deserve their misfortune. Their town, a sunbaked limestone bowl, had just been ravaged by the floodwaters of the Rio Grande. The flood had contaminated the drinking water and left the town covered in a fine dust. Now the U.S. army, a massive influx by Camargo standards, had invaded.

Camargo proved deadly to the U.S. troops. Men who had left their homes to sacrifice themselves in glorious battle died instead from dysentery and dehydration. Some 1,500 of them perished at Camargo that summer. This was almost as many as would die in battle during the entire war. Some soldiers said the death march was heard so often that the mockingbirds whistled it back to the troops as they passed.

After a month in Camargo's heat and dust, Zachary Taylor wondered whether Washington was prepared for the kind of war it had begun.

U.S. volunteers in Camargo, as Lieutenant Napoleon Dana described it, must certainly have "wish[ed] themselves home again," as they found death from disease instead of glory on the battlefield, and "every day added to the frightfulness of the mortality."

War in an Unknown Land

From Camargo, Taylor intended to march his forces to Monterrey, to attack Mexico's largest northern city, the capital of the state of Nuevo León. But the United States was just discovering the difficulties of carrying on a foreign war, says George Lockhart Rives.

> In the seventy years of national existence only two wars had been fought—both against Great Britain and both on American soil—and the men at the head of affairs were innocent of any knowledge of what was involved in conducting such an enterprise. . . . Not a single step had been taken toward planning a campaign. There was no intelligence department for either the army or navy. The government—as the President noted later with vexation—was without reliable information on the topography of Mexico, the character of the roads. . . . Nobody seems to have known anything even of the seasons. [General Winfield] Scott announced, with the air of disclosing an important [but false] secret, that there was rain in northern Mexico from May to the end of September, and that there was therefore no advantage in undertaking military operations before October. . . . The obvious line of advance along the Rio Grande had never been examined. Nobody in Washington knew what was the depth of that river, or its volume of water at different seasons of the year, or how far it was navigable by river steam-boats."

U.S. newspapers reported the occupation of Camargo.

Polk's war strategy called for the navy to enforce a blockade of Mexico's major ports and harbors, for Zachary Taylor's army to push into northeastern Mexico, and for a second army to march west from Missouri to take New Mexico and California. Of the three U.S. routes, Taylor's through arid northern Mexico was the least known. Taylor had little idea what difficulties he and his troops would face as they moved up the Rio Grande.

The Fussy General

General Winfield Scott, says author John S. D. Eisenhower, "may well have been the most capable soldier this country has ever produced."

The Virginia-born Scott trained in law but was a lifelong military man. Scott had previously distinguished himself in combat in the War of 1812 and the Black Hawk and Seminole Wars.

This very professional but self-taught soldier gave scrupulous attention to every detail in any operation entrusted to him—which endeared him neither to the public nor to his troops, who referred to him as "Old Fuss and Feathers."

This "audacious commander," says Otis Singletary, was also "vain, pompous, impulsive, ambitious," and "too easily caught up in petty disputes." In contrast to "Rough and Ready" Taylor, Scott always appeared in full dress uniform.

Polk and His Generals

President Polk noted ruefully in his diary that, in the first days of the war, General Taylor used a train of hundreds of wagons to move his supplies. No one in the War Department thought of using pack mules to carry supplies and equipment until months afterward.

An active commander-in-chief of the armed forces, Polk studied every aspect of the planning and operation of the war. He was in the awkward position of conducting a war in which his highest-ranking generals were members of the opposition party. Not only were Zachary Taylor and Winfield Scott both Whigs, but they also had political ambitions. Polk, Scott, and Taylor were all suspicious of each other's motives during the course of the war.

In the initial war planning, Polk favored General Taylor, who seemed less of a political threat. As commander of the U.S. forces on the Rio Grande, Zachary Taylor was far from Washington. But, as his success on the battlefield sparked talk of his running for president, Taylor became increasingly suspicious of Polk. Frustrated by what he perceived as a lack of support from the capital, he feared he was the victim of political intrigue: "I might suppose there was an intention among the high functionaries to break me down. . . . The large force now under my command will from design or incompetency of others have to return to their homes without accomplishing anything. . . . The responsibility . . . will be thrown on me."

Taylor lacked the taste for strategy and planning of Winfield Scott, who had political battles of his own. The diminutive President Polk was never comfortable in the presence of this tall, proud general-in-chief.

A Volunteer Army

One of General Winfield Scott's fundamental differences with President James Polk was about Polk's promotion of a volunteer army. Scott—and most other professional soldiers—felt that the plan to rush a huge volunteer army into action against the Mexican army ignored the need for training and discipline in the military.

John S. D. Eisenhower describes U.S. problems with untrained troops: "You would think, in a country [where] so many of the citizens were frontiersmen, that you could pull them together and have an army. But the techniques you use for survival on the frontier include running away when the situation calls for it," which is not what generals want of an army in battle.

Even out of battle, Scott said, regulars have advantages: "A regiment of regulars, in 15 minutes from the evening halt, will have tents pitched and trenched around, arms and ammunition well secured, fires made, kettles boiling, merry as crickets. . . . Volunteers ignore all these points." Volunteers took care of neither themselves nor their equipment, the professional soldiers said. As a result, they were ill or injured more often.

The uniformed soldiers of the regular army looked down on the volunteers as "rabble, as unreliable," says John S. D. Eisenhower. "Volunteers joined up by states, and their primary loyalty was to their state or their volunteer unit. They elected their own officers. They enlisted for three, six, twelve months—or until the end of the war, which most believed would last far less than a year." Some volunteer companies wore uniforms of their own devising. The regular troops disparaged these homemade uniforms as "ragamuffinism."

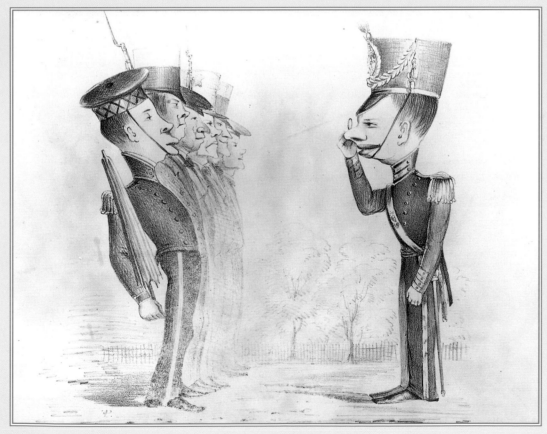

A satire of volunteer troops.

Polk liked neither Scott's personality nor his politics—the widely respected Scott had been considered as a presidential candidate on the Whig ticket in 1844 (when Henry Clay became the nominee).

Although Polk said that "General Scott did not impress me favorably as a military man," Scott was an intelligent and energetic administrator. He was in Washington, making arrangements for supplies and equipment for the expanded army and its assault on Mexico, when he heard from Secretary of War William Marcy that Polk intended to replace him if he did not rush off to fight on the Rio Grande. Scott was already angered at Polk's hasty creation of a volunteer army and his appointment of new Democratic generals. This increased his ire. He wrote the president a hasty letter, saying that he did not wish to place himself where he would receive fire upon his rear from Washington as well as on his front from the Mexicans. Polk retaliated by keeping him in the capital. As a result, the U.S. general with the most battlefield experience lingered for months at a desk job in Washington.

Paredes and the Politics of War

Throughout the war—and the all-important negotiation of the Treaty of Guadalupe Hidalgo—the United States had a single president and commander-in-chief. In the same period Mexico had seven men succeeding each other in the executive office. Even during the U.S. assault on Mexico City, the Mexican defense was plagued by power struggles among generals and politicians.

In the first flush of U.S. enthusiasm for the war, an appropriation bill was passed, and a request for volunteers was answered enthusiastically. By August 1846, the enthusiasm had waned, and the second appropriation bill Polk sent to Congress was filibustered to death. As the war dragged on, opposition to it grew. But no one spoke of removing Polk as commander-in-chief.

By August 1846, Mexican President Mariano Paredes had been driven from office. In his brief presidency, he fought more battles with his countrymen than with the United States. Revolts were widespread, with Mexico's military leading many of the protests against the government.

After the defeat of the Mexican army at Resaca de la Palma, several men were held responsible. Old rivalries among generals were blamed for weakening the defense of the nation. General Arista was court-martialed, but President Paredes, too, was held accountable. Mexicans did not forget

In his brief presidency Paredes fought more battles with his countrymen than with the United States.

that in December 1845 Paredes had refused to join forces with Arista against the enemy troops, instead leading his army against Mexico's constitutionally elected president.

The U.S. occupation of Matamoros had a tragic impact. A Mexican eyewitness to the aftermath of the first battles reported on the sad fate of the war's first civilian refugees: "The worthy inhabitants of this very small population could not resign themselves to the disconsolate idea of living under a foreign yoke. They preferred destroying their little property, to go in search of favor and protection in the arms of their brothers. They left the place where their children had been born, where their fathers had died, and they set fire to their habitations, moved by a patriotism worthy of admiration."

Arista's troops, too, endured hardships as they made their retreat from Matamoros to Linares. Struggling through the forbidding northern Mexican landscape, first they were parched, then flooded by days and nights of rain. The northern Mexican roads were reduced to muddy tracks, almost impassable. "In want of every kind of provisions," wrote Guillermo Prieto, the Mexican troops were "tired, sick, starving, without strength, and without courage," falling back to Linares and then on to Monterrey.

Second Lieutenant Manuel Balbontín of the Mexican artillery described the march in *La Invasión americana, 1846 a 1848.* "At this time, the picked army, which was seen straggling and suffering in its retreat from Matamoros to Linares, counted 1,800 men. Its morale had been assaulted by a shameful discord about its defeats. The rancorous enmities of the officers had found their way among the soldiers. . . . Hasty changes in commands also increased discontent, and the spectacle of the sick, who were dragged after the army and seemed to be victims of neglect and ingratitude, . . . exemplified horribly the pains and prospects Mexican soldiers would face afterward from the persevering skill of General Scott."

Balbontín supported Paredes and at first was optimistic about the president's chances of pulling the army together. Paredes, said Balbontín, "had dedicated himself tenaciously to the organization, discipline, and instruction of the army, with the intention of leading it out to fight the invaders." But great losses of men and equipment had left the Army of the North devastated, and Mexico was in no position to rebuild it. As John Edward Weems observes, "Foreign credit had become ever harder to get, and the Army, which had supported Paredes in his grab for power, quickly showed signs of discontent. The Army supported a man only

IMAGES OF WAR

THE TERRIBLE SUFFERING of the Mexican army was recorded in many accounts of the war written by first-hand observers of the events. Mexican chronicles of the war are full of incidents of personal bravery and sacrifice. But these books are not illustrated.

The surviving Mexican images of the war consist of satires, broadsides, cartoons, and some 1847 *calendarios* (almanacs) illustrating the U.S. occupation of Mexico City. The historian looks in vain for Mexican lithographs of the conflict. No heroic images survive.

Mexican images of the war are "poorly preserved and virtually unknown," notes historian Ron Tyler, even though printmaking had been popular since the sixteenth century in Mexico and was an established art at the time of the war. The best Mexican artists did not "devote serious attention to the war: as one perceptive historian explained when asked about such pictures, 'This is not one of our favorite eras.'"

FIRST MARTYRS OF WAR

U.S. and Mexican records of the first martyrs of the war present a sharp contrast. Among the first heroes heralded by the U.S. public was Samuel Ringgold. A forty-six-year-old major from Baltimore, he was credited in the popular press with invention of the "Flying Artillery," which won the Battle of Palo Alto. The use of mobile artillery was actually a fairly old military strategy, but Ringgold was responsible for its success in this battle. His troops had excellent training and showed remarkable discipline. Major Ringgold was killed in the battle, hit by a cannonball that tore through his legs when his unit put itself in front of U.S. lines.

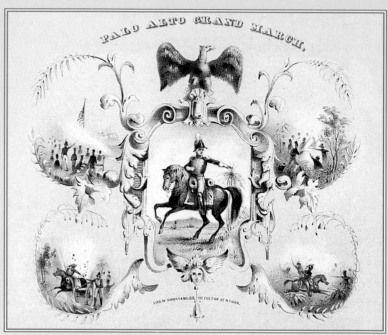

Major Samuel Ringgold was only one of the heroes celebrated after the Battle of Palo Alto.

His last words to his soldiers, "Don't stay with me; you have work to do," were reprinted over and over. His story was celebrated in popular music, such as "The Lament for Major Ringgold," in theatrical productions, and in lithographs (which did not always agree on exactly how he had died).

In contrast, many of the Mexican heroes of this battle are anonymous. A rare exception is the cannoneer Dolores Ramírez, whose story was told in the *Apuntes*. "The unfortunate Captain Dolores Ramírez, who commanded one of the batteries, would not surrender. Fighting with heroic passion, he gave his life—which the Americans offered to spare—and died gallantly beside his cannon."

While Captain Ramírez is remembered, there are no images of his valiant stand, and the visual history of the war is predominantly from the U.S. perspective.

as long as he could meet the military payroll, and in 1846 Mexico that was becoming increasingly difficult. Army upkeep cost 21 million pesos. Revenue brought in only 12 million."

The Fight for Democracy

A few months earlier President Paredes had not had to worry about how to pay his troops. A monarchist conspiracy had raised the money that Paredes used to bring his army to the capital to overthrow José Joaquín de Herrera's government.

Two men in particular had been behind that takeover: the Spanish minister, Salvador Bermúdez de Castro, and conservative politician Lucas Alamán. They were plotting to restore a monarchy in Mexico, headed by a member of the Spanish royal family. The monarchists considered Paredes a transitional leader, who would govern the country until a Spanish ruler could take his place. But Paredes seems to have intended to stay in office. "Paredes played a two-faced game, telling both the monarchists and the republicans that they had his support," says Miguel Soto. But he could not retain control.

The conspirators had encouraged Paredes's warmongering, believing that a conflict with the United States would further their cause. But no sooner had Paredes sent Polk's minister John Slidell back to Washington (making war with the United States inevitable) than Mexico witnessed an outbreak of anti-monarchical and anti-Paredes demonstrations.

As the United States army threatened to push farther into northern Mexico, Indian tribes were raiding parts of Mexico's northwest territory, and Mexicans around the country were attacking the central government. There were revolts against Paredes's government in Sonora, Sinaloa, Puebla, Oaxaca, and Michoacán. Yucatán once again declared its independence.

An insurrection broke out in Guadalajara. As Balbontín reported, "A brigade, commanded by General González Arévalo, . . . was sent to repress it, but had not been fortunate. General Paredes had the bad idea of going himself to quell Guadalajara with all the forces he had in the capital, and if he succeeded, then going to the border to stop the North Americans, who were advancing to Monterrey." In July 1846, while General Taylor was moving U.S. troops from Matamoros up the Rio Grande to Camargo, President Paredes was mobilizing troops to put down the rebellion in Guadalajara.

"Nothing can be expected from an administration that [has] abandoned our frontiers and its valiant defenders, crushed all social guarantees, and respected even more despotic governments."
—A Mexican broadside, July 31, 1846

The Monarchists and Their Foes

The Spanish government stood behind Paredes before and after he seized power, say historians David Pletcher and Miguel Soto. Although the monarchist conspiracy was backed by the Spanish minister, Salvador Bermúdez de Castro, it depended on the traditional Mexican "establishment," says Miguel Soto, "wealthy property owners [and] the Catholic church, both from its upper hierarchy and from the rural priests." According to Bermúdez de Castro, Paredes commanded "the only true army that existed in Mexico," and he had the support of these traditional groups.

A Simple Satire

Paredes attempted to silence the press, but a group of young Mexico City intellectuals began publishing a new journal, *Don Simplicio* (Sir Simpleton). Jesús Velasco-Márquez describes the journal as "extraordinarily satirical . . . full of caricatures of almost all elements of society."

Don Simplicio portrayed President Paredes as "little Santa Anna," the "Idol of the Nation." With critical editorials and cartoons, the newspaper deplored the militarism of the new regime and satirized the nation's return to the "double dominion of the drum and the bell."

Mexico City from the Convent of San Cosmé.

*The Paredes government was a prime target of
Don Simplicio's barbs.*

Guillermo Prieto was one of Mexico's most respected poets and
author of a fine memoir describing the tumultuous period between
1828 and 1853. Earlier young Prieto had been one of the editors
of Don Simplicio. *His writing expressed his anger at the
injustice of his nation's enemy and shame at the inadequacy of
his nation's response. After the war he joined with other
intellectuals, diplomats, journalists, and soldiers to write*
Apuntes para la historia de la guerra.

CROSS AND SWORD

Don Simplicio mocked the alliance Paredes sought to establish between the church and the army with irreverent
songs and poems:

> *Con bonete anda el soldado
> y el clérigo con morrión
> la cruz y la espada unidas
> Gobiernan a la Nación.
> Que viva la bella unión!*

> The priest wears a military cap
> The soldier a biretta
> Sword and cross overlap
> Ruling 'n communion—
> Long live the happy union!

*The fictional Don Simplicio was a cartoon simpleton who
reminded Mexicans that, while they were fighting among
themselves, the country's existence was threatened by
both Spain and the United States.*

The clerical and military alliance with the president
did not last. The conspirators behind Paredes's government had expected Europe to help Mexico in its fight
against the United States. When that aid did not arrive,
Paredes turned to the church. His request for a million-
peso contribution to the war effort cost him clerical support. His military support also faded quickly. Inspired by
former President Antonio López de Santa Anna (in exile
in Cuba), the army rose up against the monarchists' threat
to Mexican self-government.

THE BATTLE OF LA MESA (IN PRESENT-DAY SOUTHERN CALIFORNIA).

PART THREE

WAR FOR THE WEST

"[La batalla de La Mesa] fué el último esfuerzo que los hijos de las Californias hicieron en favor de la libertad e independencia de su patria cuya defensa siempre les hará honor."

"[The Battle of La Mesa] was the last effort made by the sons of California for the liberty and independence of their country, whose defense will always do them honor."
—*APUNTES PARA LA HISTORIA DE LA GUERRA*
(NOTES FOR A HISTORY OF THE WAR)

THE DAY AFTER General Zachary Taylor and his 12,000 troops left Matamoros, launching the U.S. campaign to occupy northeastern Mexico, a dramatic event took place thousands of miles away, in Mexico's northwestern territory. Admiral John Drake Sloat of the U.S. navy's Pacific Squadron landed in Monterey, California, seizing one of Mexico's richest ports. Less than a month earlier, in June 1846, a group of U.S. immigrants to California known as the "Bear Flag" rebels had declared California independent of Mexico. Now the United States was claiming the "Bear Flag Republic" as its own.

"For Mexico's forever-hungry neighbor, Texas was merely an appetizer. The United States had its eyes on New Mexico and California."

—MIGUEL SOTO

Mexico's Northwestern Frontier

The United States had long been interested in Mexico's sparsely settled northwestern territories. The two territories offered access to valuable trade routes: California had excellent ports for Pacific trade; New Mexico had the Santa Fe–Chihuahua Trail, a 1,400-mile route used by merchants carrying goods between Missouri and Chihuahua.

Before war was declared, President James Polk had tried to purchase Mexico's northwestern borderlands. Mexico's refusal to discuss the purchase offer had angered Polk. When war was declared in May 1846, the U.S. president decided to send troops to occupy the coveted territories. He ordered Stephen W. Kearny and the "Army of the West" to set off on an expedition to conquer New Mexico and California.

U.S. ships were already on the alert outside California's ports. The Pacific Squadron of the navy had been ordered to Mexico's west coast in 1845. British and French warships, too, were cruising off the California coast. "When war was declared," says historian Sam W. Haynes, "Secretary of State James Buchanan wanted to assure Britain and France that the United States was not going to war to acquire California or New Mexico. But Polk would not permit it." He preferred to risk war with Britain and France rather than let them gain territory on the continent.

TRADE AND TRAILS

BEFORE THE WAR, overland routes between California and the United States—among them, a trail from the Green River, mapped by U.S. fur trapper Jedediah Smith, and an old Spanish trail from Santa Fe to Los Angeles, severed by the Yuma Indians in 1781 and reopened in 1829—were used by only a few fur traders and settlers.

Most trade with California had been by sea ever since the Spanish claimed the territory in 1542. Most early settlers came by ship, and most early settlement was along the coast. When Spain's claim on the area was threatened by Russian fur traders and English and French explorers, the Spanish government sent missionaries to try to settle the California coast.

Franciscan priests built more than twenty missions in Alta California's coastal region, with Native American workers they recruited with the occasional help of Spanish soldiers. The mission system declined after Mexican independence, but El Camino Real (the

Royal Highway), an almost 500-mile route connecting missions from San Diego to Sonoma, was still the main link among California's coastal settlements in 1846.

Food and water for humans and pack animals were scarce between Missouri and Santa Fe; heavy wagons could travel little more than ten miles a day across the prairie; traders were often attacked by Indians. But New Mexico's population was eager for U.S. manufactured goods, andmerchant caravans soon began to move along the Santa Fe Trail.

As early as 1824, the value of commerce along the Santa Fe Trail had become so obvious that young Missouri Senator Thomas Hart Benton convinced the U.S. government to mark the route. During a period of Indian attacks a few years later, Benton proposed that the United States provide military escort to the traders traveling across the Mexican territory. In 1846, more than $1 million worth of goods passed through Santa Fe, with taxes collected in both directions.

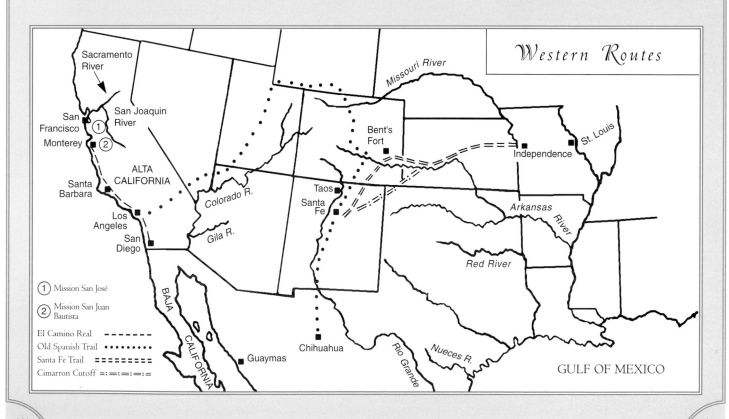

In his *Diary,* Polk maintained "that though we had not gone to war for conquest, yet it was clear that in making peace we would if practicable obtain California and such other portion of the Mexican territory as would be sufficient to indemnify our claimants on Mexico, and to defray the expenses of the war."

Polk "had no intention to undertake a costly war for nothing," writes historian Neal Harlow, who summarizes the president's expedient point of view: "Taking New Mexico and California would best suit the convenience of both parties, Mexico being too weak to retain them and they being contiguous to the United States."

Mexico's hold on its northwestern territories had long been weak. The unstable government of President Mariano Paredes in Mexico City was in no position to control territories that had been asserting their right to manage their own affairs for decades. Paredes was struggling against revolts all over Mexico, as well as the threat of U.S. troops in northeastern Mexico and the menace of a U.S. naval blockade of Gulf ports. Even without these problems, he might have found it difficult to reclaim regions that had been neglected for so many years.

A Naval Contest

FOREIGN TRADE SHIPS showed an increasing interest in California ports during the 1830s. In 1841 the U.S. secretary of the navy recommended that the Pacific Squadron be doubled, to protect U.S. interests and its "considerable settlements" in California. (U.S. citizens in California at the time numbered fewer than 500.)

When war was declared, the United States was more worried about European opposition to its plans to claim California than about Mexican resistance. In a naval contest the superior U.S. Pacific fleet seemed certain to overpower the Mexican navy. The United States had "over thirty vessels actually at sea . . . [with] a brilliant reputation for efficiency," says George Lockhart Rives, while Mexico's fleet consisted of "a few ill-found and ill-manned vessels of small tonnage."

The Mexican navy had boasted two capable warships, the *Montezuma* and the *Guadalupe.* These large British-built steamers, which were in a position to harass U.S. supply ships off Brazos in the Gulf Coast, had given U.S. naval commanders a few anxious moments. But when war broke out, Mexico took the ships out of service, giving them back to their British owners to keep them from capture by the United States.

Yerba Buena (San Francisco) in 1847.

CHAPTER 7

THE FIGHT FOR CALIFORNIA

U.S. PRESENCE AT MONTEREY, CALIFORNIA.

*"Monterey . . . is decidedly the pleasantest and most civilized
looking place in California," said visiting U.S. sailor
Richard Henry Dana in Two Years before the Mast,
the story of an 1835 trip around the Horn.
Eleven years later, another shipload of sailors and
marines landed in Monterey and claimed it for the United States.*

CONSIDERING CALIFORNIA's importance, its conquest was quick and easy. A French attaché visiting in 1840–41 reported that "whatever nation chooses to send there a man-of-war and 200 men" could take California. This is what the United States did on July 7, 1846.

The isolated territory had never had close ties to Mexico City. Like Texas, California resented—and rebelled against—laws passed by the central Mexican government. But there were important differences between California and Texas. Not just the United States, but other foreign governments showed strong interest in California as soon as its ports were opened to trade. Yet only a few hundred foreign settlers (and fewer than 7,000 Mexican citizens) had come to California by 1840—despite a liberal land-grant policy similar to the one in Texas. Immigration—legal and illegal—had increased until shortly before the U.S.–Mexican War, and U.S. immigrants had soon grown rebellious. But earlier revolts against the Mexican central government had been led by Hispanic citizens, who had begun to talk about independence from Mexico before the U.S. takeover.

The Californios Rebel

California's name came from an old Spanish tale of an island rich in gold and jewels. The gold was not discovered until after the United States took possession of the territory. Before that, California's wealth came from land, from cattle raised on huge ranches. "A beautiful country, a warm climate, an abundance of grain and cattle—and nothing else" is how Doña Concepción Argüello described her home state in 1806.

In 1821 there were only a few more than 3,000 Mexican residents in California, most the descendants of the first colonists. These Californios (Hispanic citizens born in the territory) grew increasingly resentful of the central government as their territorial government encountered its own problems. Reforms had weakened the California mission system, and, with independence, military control of the state had eroded.

Beginning in 1833, California mission lands and herds were secularized. In theory, they were to be given to the Christianized Indians who had been working them, but their distribution provoked complaints. Mexico City then made a series of unfortunate moves: It sent 250 colonists to strengthen its control of the region, and it appointed unpopular administrators. Grievances increased and anger intensified.

Rebellion came in 1836. A group of Californios raised armies and overthrew the acting governor. Like the rebels in the Texas revolt of 1835–36, the Californios justified their revolt as a protest against the abolition of Mexico's Constitution of 1824. The rebels—including a few U.S. and English settlers—eventually acknowledged the centralist Constitution. Mexico City rewarded the leaders—among them Juan Bautista Alvarado, José Castro, and Mariano Guadalupe Vallejo—with political power and land grants. Alvarado became governor and Castro military chief. Eight million acres of mission land were divided among 800 influential men.

Second Rebellion by the Californios

Mexican President Antonio Santa Anna aggravated California's problems with the appointment of a new governor in 1842. General Manuel Micheltorena assumed military control with an army of 200 regular soldiers and 300 convict-conscripts, whose lawless behavior angered Californios. The unpopular governor needed support from the foreign population. He made generous land grants, encouraging immigration.

Like the Tejanos in Texas, many Californios welcomed immigrants, observes David J. Weber, and for the same reasons. Residents looked to foreigners to increase trade and "deliver them from economic stagnation." Settlement promised Californios protection from Indian raids. But they had no intention of giving the territory to English or U.S. interests.

A group of Californios revolted against the governor in 1845. Micheltorena was overthrown, but, by the time news reached Mexico

RANCHERO AND GENERAL

BEFORE THE U.S. conquest, California had many ranchers, holders of extensive land grants. After the missions were secularized, these landowners were able to exploit the native labor force that had been settled near the missions to work their lands. Mariano Guadalupe Vallejo was typical of this Hispanic elite.

Vallejo was a member of one of northern California's most prominent families. His ancestors had sailed with Hernán Cortés, and his father had arrived in California as a Spanish soldier. A career soldier like his father, he used his position as an officer to obtain more than 150,000 acres of land grants. On his three ranches north of San Francisco Bay, in the Sonoma region, Vallejo raised cattle and sheep, bred horses, and—unusual for Hispanic landholders—tended orchards and vineyards. (Today Sonoma is in the heart of northern California's wine country.)

With a long military career, General Vallejo was influential in California politics for decades. Although he had served Mexico as commander general of the area, like many Californios he complained of Mexican neglect. Also like other Californios, he was known

Mariano Vallejo headed a huge family, with nine children who survived childhood. He is pictured here with two of his daughters and three of his granddaughters.

for his hospitality to immigrants, despite possible fears of the immigrants' political intentions. In an 1841 letter to his nephew, California Governor Alvarado, Vallejo noted that California was in the position of "consenting to what it cannot prevent"—that there was no stopping the influx of immigrants.

When U.S. immigrants rebelled, Vallejo was among the Californios who paid the highest price. Arrested by the rebels, he was imprisoned for six weeks and not released from his jail cell at Sutter's Fort until U.S. forces had claimed Sonoma. In his memoirs, Vallejo wrote, "I left [Sutter's Fort] half dead, and arrived [in Sonoma] almost without life, but am now much better. . . . The political change has cost a great deal to my person, mind and likewise, property."

The toll on his property continued under the new U.S. government, as his landholdings were reduced again and again by title disputes and squatters.

The Vallejo family's landholdings embraced some 272,000 acres in the Sonoma Valley. By the time Mariano died, he held fewer than 300 acres.

City, President Santa Anna himself had been overthrown. President José Joaquín de Herrera's government approved political appointments for the rebellion leaders: José Castro again was made military commander of the territory, Juan Bautista Alvarado put in charge of the customhouse in Monterey.

Pío Pico, who had mustered a large rebel force from southern California, was appointed governor. At his urging, the capital was moved to Los Angeles. The military force and customhouse, however, remained in the north. Pico controlled legislation; Castro controlled its enforcement. Law was made in the south; order was imposed in the north. California's geography had always created north-south factionalism; this split in government aggravated the problem.

Pico, Castro, Alvarado, and Vallejo (who had supported the 1836 and 1845 rebellions, but had not joined the military campaigns) would be in charge of defending California during the U.S. naval and land-based assaults of the U.S.–Mexican War. They received no help from the central government, led by President Mariano Paredes in 1846, and in fact may have been weakened by their deep ambivalence toward a government that had ignored their pleas for assistance for so long.

Sutter's Fort

Mexican law gave immigrants land only in California's inland valleys. The Sacramento Valley became home to many foreigners, who settled around Sutter's Fort, a successful trading business started in 1839 by a German-Swiss immigrant named John Sutter.

In 1842, John Sutter was described by Sir George Simpson, in *Narrative of a Journey Round the World:* "Trapping, farming, trading, bullying the government, and letting out Indians on hire. . . . If he really has the talent and the courage to make the most of his position, he is not unlikely to render California a second Texas. Even now, the Americans only want a rallying point for carrying into effect their theory, that the English race is destined by 'right divine' to expel the Spaniards from their

Pío Pico

THE PICO FAMILY, one of the most influential in southern California, was the product of a mestizo (Hispanic and Indian) and mulatto (Hispanic and Black) marriage. Before the U.S. takeover of California, class was not as tightly bound to race in this isolated territory as in either Mexico or the United States.

Pío Pico was a powerful player in Los Angeles politics. He raised armies of his fellow rancheros to combat northern interests. Even after Pico fled to Baja California during the U.S. conquest, these rancheros kept their fighting spirit: southern Californians, including Pico's brothers, led the only major resistance to the U.S. military takeover.

The Pathfinder

John Charles Frémont.

Jessie Benton Frémont.

"LET THE TIDE of emigration flow toward California and the American population will soon be sufficiently numerous to play the Texas game," said a New York newspaper. By 1845, hundreds of settlers had made the dangerous overland journey from the United States. Many had been encouraged by romanticized accounts of the exploits of a man known as "The Pathfinder." Reports of John Charles Frémont's western adventures—especially in the paradise of California—did much to popularize westward expansion.

An early settler, Mary Jones, describes the mood of the period in an account she wrote many years later: "Our neighbor got hold of Frémont's *History of California* . . . and brought the book to my husband to read and he was carried away with the idea, too. I said 'O let us not go!' Our neighbors, some of them were old men and women with large families, but it made no difference. We sold our home, and what we could not sell we gave away and in May . . . we joined the camp for California."

The charming Frémont was a bright young mathematician who had been set on his course by the controversial former U.S. ambassador to Mexico, Joel Poinsett. Poinsett got Frémont appointed to the Army Corps of Topographical Engineers, the engineers and surveyors responsible for rapid exploration of the West. Frémont learned geology, botany, and zoology from the scientist who led his first expedition. Marriage to lovely Jessie Benton procured him another patron, her father, Thomas Hart Benton, the influential expansionist senator from Missouri. Jessie was a talented writer whose work on her husband's books helped to make his stories popular. He was also fortunate in traveling with Charles Preuss, a talented cartographer, whose illustrations added much to his journals.

Frémont's reckless temperament seemed to suit the times—though it must have dismayed some of the explorers who accompanied him. In a typical dramatic gesture, he led a party of men to the top of the tallest peak he saw in Wyoming, erroneously claiming it was the highest point in North America. There he planted the Stars and Stripes. The acclaim he won for this exploit may have inspired him to plant flags wherever he went, including northern California.

View of Pike's Peak from 40 miles, from Frémont's report on the expedition.

Sutter's Fort (even before gold was discovered there) was a magnet for new U.S. immigrants arriving overland through the mountains. Located near the Sacramento River, it could be reached by boat from the San Francisco Bay.

ancient seats—a theory that has already begun to develop itself in more ways than one."

There were several hundred U.S. immigrants living near Sutter's Fort, and Simpson described these "American adventurers" and trappers rustling cattle and threatening towns. He noted that when the Californios rebelled in 1836, "American residents, as also some of the American skippers on the coast, supported the revolution, in the hope of its merely transferring California from Mexico to the United States."

Sutter had received his land grant from Governor Alvarado but fought against him in 1845, raising an army to support Governor Micheltorena against the rebellious Californios. Afterward, Sutter wrote to a U.S. immigrant friend that if anyone tried to force him out of California, he would "make a Declaration of Independence and proclaim California for a Republique independent from Mexico." His friend had married one of Mariano Vallejo's sisters, and the letter passed to Vallejo and on to Mexico City. But Santa Anna, again president, was mounting a campaign to reclaim Texas and could spare no troops or funds for California.

The Gavilan Mountain Incident

Captain John C. Frémont led five well-publicized expeditions to the West between 1842 and 1853. In California he was at the center of a rebellious group of U.S. immigrants. His activities incensed Mexican authorities and inspired what came to be known as the Bear Flag Revolt.

In December 1845, Frémont arrived at Sutter's Fort with a small party of heavily armed mountain men. Challenging Frémont's right to lead an army into northern California, the military chief, General José Castro, ordered the men to stay away from California settlements. They refused, and the general demanded that they leave.

The hot-tempered Frémont responded by riding to the nearby Gavilan Mountains and planting the U.S. flag on the highest peak his men

"Compatriots! The act of unfurling the American flag on the hills, the insults and threats offered to our authorities, are worthy of…hatred from Mexicans. Prepare then to defend our independence!"

—GENERAL JOSÉ CASTRO
WARNING CALIFORNIOS
OF THE THREAT FROM
FRÉMONT'S MEN

could climb. For days, Frémont defended this act, riding back and forth above the valley, proclaiming his willingness to die for his country. But in early March he changed his mind and headed north to Oregon.

Californios had been complaining for years that they enjoyed the burdens of Mexican citizenship with few benefits. Mexico City took taxes from California—including tariffs on foreign trade through its ports—without providing such services as schools and roads. California was not supplied with arms and an army, nor could it count on the capital to provide its protection. José Castro had circulated a plan among sympathetic Californios that called for "declaring California independent in 1847–48, as soon as a sufficient number of foreigners should arrive" to help achieve independence. But the foreigners themselves had become a problem.

The Gavilan Mountain incident convinced many Californios that they needed protection from unruly illegal immigrants. "To rely any longer upon Mexico to govern and defend us would be idle and absurd," said Mariano Vallejo. Governor Pío Pico favored forming an alliance with Britain; others favored France. But Vallejo thought California's best hope might lie with the United States. "We possess a noble country," he argued. "I would not have her a mere dependency on a foreign monarchy. . . . We are republicans. . . . Why should we go abroad for protection when [the United States] is our adjoining neighbor? We shall not become subjects but fellow citizens."

Gillespie's Rumors

No one in California—neither Californios nor U.S. settlers—knew that the United States had already declared war on Mexico at the very time the Californios were debating where to seek protection and Frémont's immigrant friends were discussing a revolt. The actions of many of the parties were based on rumors, or hopes, of war.

One source of these rumors was Lieutenant Archibald H. Gillespie of the U.S. marines, who arrived in Monterey aboard a U.S. warship, having hurried across Mexico to join the Pacific Squadron in Mazatlán.

U.S. Consul Thomas Larkin introduced Gillespie to fellow U.S. citizens in San Francisco and Sutter's Fort as a "gentleman of much information." If he was not a spy, as many Californians suspected, then at least he was a U.S. agent carrying secret instructions from Washington.

John Sutter warned General Castro that Gillespie might entice Frémont back to California. His suspicions proved correct. Gillespie followed Frémont to the Oregon border (where he had been fighting Indians) and delivered a message from Polk and some private letters from Senator Benton. Gillespie and Frémont then returned to near Sutter's Fort.

U.S. settlers there were agitated, afraid that California officials would retaliate against them for the trouble that Frémont had caused in the Gavilan Mountains. Frémont encouraged them to take matters into their own hands, and a group of immigrants formed the unruly Bear Flag Party.

General Castro reported his suspicions of Frémont and the U.S. settlers to Governor Pico in Los Angeles. But the rift between northern and southern California had widened. Pico and his soldiers had already begun a march to confront Castro in Monterey. As Californios prepared to fight each other, they learned that U.S. settlers had taken up arms against the Californio garrison in Sonoma.

The Bear Flag Revolt

At dawn on June 14, General Mariano Vallejo, commander of the northern frontier, was awakened by a small but well-armed group of U.S. immigrants pounding on his door. Robert Semple, one of the rebels, recalled: "Almost the whole party was dressed in leather hunting shirts, many of them were greasy; they were about as rough looking a set of men as one could well imagine. . . . Anyone would feel some dread at falling into their hands." Opening the door on what his sister described as a "band of ungrateful horse thieves, trappers, and runaway sailors," Vallejo is reported to have inquired, "To what happy circumstances shall I attribute the visit of so many exalted personages?"

CONSUL LARKIN

THOMAS LARKIN, THE U.S. consul based in Monterey, California, was one of many U.S. agents—commercial, political, or military—active in California. Before the war, Larkin had overestimated the likelihood of a Mexican-British alliance in California. His views had inspired Polk to rush his agent John Slidell into offering to purchase California and New Mexico from Herrera's government.

Suave, congenial, and persuasive, Larkin was the opposite of the rash and impetuous Frémont. Frémont sought the glory of military takeover, while Larkin, the businessman, deftly worked behind the scenes on behalf of U.S. mercantile interests. The commercial and personal alliances that Larkin nurtured between U.S. and Mexican citizens in California eased postwar relations.

The rebels did not seem to have so much a plan as a disorderly intention to seize any arms and ammunition in the town's nearly empty garrison. They placed General Vallejo under arrest. He did not resist, instead giving the men the keys to his storerooms. Fortified with Vallejo's brandy and wine, the rebels were soon engaged in a drunken debate over the wording of a declaration of independence. Proceeding to the plaza, they hoisted a homemade flag, "a piece of linen about the size of a towel," according to Vallejo's sister, decorated with a crudely represented grizzly bear, and read their proclamation of an independent Republic of California.

Frémont's men and others joined the Bear Flaggers in Sonoma, bringing the rebel troops to 130. Frémont ordered Mariano Vallejo and his brother Salvador to be jailed at Sutter's Fort. The explorer later attempted to justify his actions in California. He claimed that "through the Bentons he had been made thoroughly familiar with the government's intentions and had been given discretion to act," says Neal Harlow. But it seems clear that he was never an agent of the U.S. government. In a Senate hearing in 1848, Gillespie revealed Polk's "secret instructions" to Frémont: he had been told only "to watch over the interests of the United States, counteract the influence of foreign agents, [and] conciliate the feelings of the people [Californios]."

The rebels had a few skirmishes with Californios between Sonoma and San Francisco—and Commander Castro did raise some troops in the north to oppose them—but the Bear Flaggers seemed unlikely to be able to expand their revolution.

VALLEJO'S ORDEAL

GENERAL MARIANO VALLEJO and his brother Salvador were arrested in Sonoma during the Bear Flag Revolt. Salvador recalled, "My heart grieved for my brother. . . . When the light of day allowed me to see him lying on a damp floor without coverings or even a pillow on which to rest his head, I cursed the days in which our house had dispensed hospitality to a race of men deaf to the call of gratitude, such perfect strangers to good breeding."

When Vallejo was released six weeks later, he returned to a city under the U.S. flag. Going to Sonoma's central plaza, he made a pile of his Mexican uniforms and burned them.

Possession of Monterey

It was the cautious sixty-five-year-old Admiral John Drake Sloat who brought conquering U.S. forces to California. Sloat had arrived at Mazatlán in western Mexico in November 1845. There he took command of the Pacific Squadron, a fleet of seven well-armed ships that moved between Mexico, South America, and Hawaii. Sloat's instructions were to take possession of San Francisco should Mexico declare war.

It often took months for messages to cross the continent. In the spring of 1846, Sloat had seen Mexican newspaper reports and heard rumors of a battle between U.S. and Mexican troops on the Rio Grande. In June, he learned of the blockade of Veracruz, which he took to mean that the two countries were at war. Sloat sailed quietly into Monterey harbor on July 2. Residents expected a U.S. landing on July 4, but Sloat agonized for days over what to do.

U.S. Consul Thomas Larkin visited the ship with news of the Bear Flag Revolt. Larkin (encouraged by Polk) had hoped to persuade Californios to declare California independent of Mexico, but the revolt upset his plan. With this persuasion, Sloat finally went ashore on July 7. His men, 250 sailors and horse-marines, hoisted the U.S. flag and took possession of Monterey for the United States. There was no resistance.

A few U.S. sailors and marines marched north and claimed San Francisco, without a fight, while others carried the U.S. flag northeast to Sutter's Fort. When the Bear Flag rebels at Sonoma learned that the U.S. navy had landed at Monterey, they replaced their flag with the Stars and Stripes, ending California's short-lived independence.

Frémont and three companies of rebel explorers and settlers made a dramatic entry to Monterey to speak with Sloat. They looked very colorful, like "true trappers . . . [who] had passed years in the wilds," an eyewitness reported. Despite Washington's fears, the British and French were less of a threat to peace than the Bear Flaggers throughout the takeover negotiations. Consul Larkin was convinced that the "moment the stars fall . . . the Bear would take their place."

The unruliness of the Bear Flag forces certainly influenced Californios to accept the more orderly U.S. naval takeover. Sloat's proclamation to the people of Monterey was conciliatory. Despite the "powerful force" he had brought to claim California, he insisted the United States was not "an enemy." He promised a benevolent rule for Californios who chose to remain peaceably in Monterey and fair compensation for those who chose to leave.

Sloat and Larkin launched a campaign to convince Californio officials to accept the U.S. conquest. Larkin wrote to former Governor Juan Bautista Alvarado arguing that conceding to U.S. rule would be no

A Reason for Caution

In 1842 a U.S. naval commander had precipitously raised the U.S. flag in Monterey after rumors of war. Forced to withdraw when the rumors proved false, he had created an embarrassing international incident. Admiral John Drake Sloat did not want to repeat that mistake.

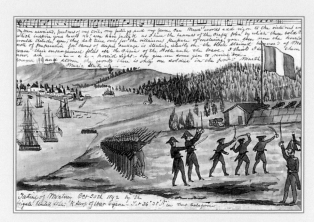

Thomas Ap. Catesby Jones leading the "conquest" of Monterey in 1842.

REACTIONS TO THE U.S. CONQUEST

CALIFORNIOS EXPRESSED mixed feelings about the arrival of the U.S. navy. One resident of Monterey, Doña María de las Angustias de la Guerra Ord, described the conquest: "Californios, especially the women, did not like the takeover at all. But I must confess that California was on the road to the most complete ruin. On one hand, the Indians were out of control . . . with little or nothing being done to curb their depredations. On the other, there were disputes between the people of the north and south and between both against the Mexicans."

Mariano Vallejo was at the anchorage to welcome the U.S. navy back to Yerba Buena (San Francisco) after the capture of Los Angeles. A few years later he had reason for regrets. Before his death Vallejo wrote in his journal: "The language now spoken in our country, the laws that govern us, the faces that we encounter daily, are those of the masters of the land and, of course, antagonistic to our interests and rights, but what does that matter to the conqueror? He wishes his own well-being and not ours!—a thing that I consider only natural in individuals, but which I condemn in a government that has promised to respect and make respected our rights, and to treat us as its own sons. But what does it avail us to complain? The thing has happened, and there is no remedy."

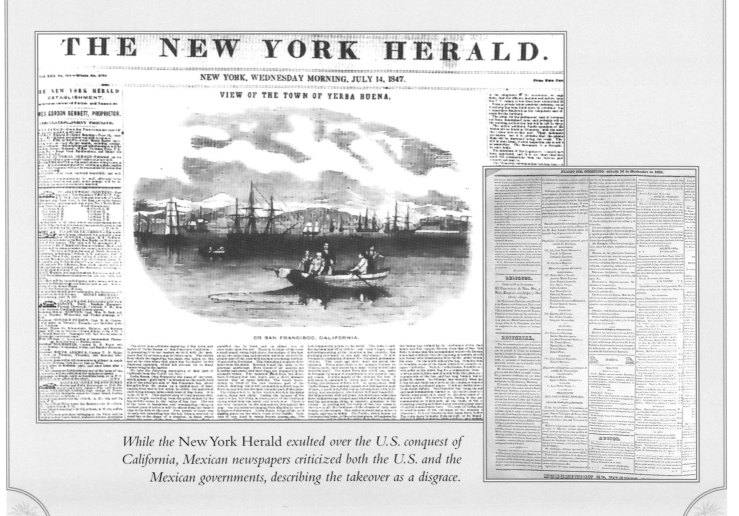

While the New York Herald *exulted over the U.S. conquest of California, Mexican newspapers criticized both the U.S. and the Mexican governments, describing the takeover as a disgrace.*

disgrace to General Castro. Alvarado reminded Larkin that U.S. colonists had been inspired by resentment of foreign rule in 1776; he suggested that Larkin consider the similar feelings of the Hispanics. Sloat wrote to Castro and to Governor Pío Pico asking them to surrender, which they declined to do.

Pico and Castro suddenly allied to face this foreign threat. They planned to meet in central California and march into Los Angeles together. California's governor, legislature, legal tribunal, and military commander would be gathered there. The United States claimed all of California north of Santa Barbara. But southern California remained unconquered.

Takeover of the South

When Commodore Robert F. Stockton arrived in Monterey aboard the *Congress* in mid-July, he had made the nine-month sea journey around Tierra del Fuego (a faster route required overland passage through Mexico or across the Central American isthmus). After the slow journey, he seemed in a hurry to see some action in California.

Stockton took command of land forces immediately, over the objections of John Frémont and Archibald Gillespie. He finally enlisted these two in his enterprise "to improve the estate" of the United States in California. Frémont he appointed major and Gillespie captain of the "California battalion" of U.S. troops. After Admiral Sloat retired on July 23, Stockton took command of naval forces.

Gillespie, Frémont, and a force of about 100 mountain men and horse-marines were put aboard a ship bound for San Diego. They had orders to join Colonel Stephen Kearny's army when it arrived from New Mexico. Anti-Castro feeling was strong in San Diego and Frémont's crew quickly claimed the town. Stockton, who had sailed south with more than 300 sailors and marines, first claimed Santa Barbara and then San Pedro, just south of Los Angeles.

Marching toward Los Angeles, Pico and Castro managed to stay only a day ahead of the U.S. forces. The governor and general may have reconciled, but their forces did not get along. Pico's efforts to raise an army had

THE DUELING COMMODORE

KNOWN AS "Fighting Bob" because of his frequent duels, Robert F. Stockton, a wealthy New Jersey businessman, had volunteered for the Pacific navy, hoping to find some scope for his adventurousness.

After claiming California, Stockton decided that the peaceable occupation of this remote territory was not the way to make his reputation, and he was eager to be off to another theater of war.

Kit Carson, who played a significant role in fighting for California, was described by Samuel W. Cozzens, in his nineteenth-century Explorations & Adventures in Arizona & New Mexico, *as "a Noted Character . . . a little weazen-faced, light-haired, wiry, active frontierman, who wore his hair long, and swore in a horrible jargon of Spanish and English, and who didn't 'fear no Injun a livin'.'" Carson was part of the "American colony" in New Mexico at the time.*

inspired fewer than 100 volunteers, most of whom did not want to fight foreign troops. By the time Stockton's man-of-war appeared on the scene, Castro's troops—which had always been less numerous than the U.S. forces—had been decreased even further by desertion and disease.

Perhaps inspired by Frémont's rabid patriotism, Stockton had made a blustery proclamation of possession when he replaced Sloat in northern California. Washington had sent fairly consistent directives to be conciliatory—since the Californios were reported to be so disenchanted with the Mexican government that they were unlikely to resist a peaceful takeover. But Stockton took a hard line in his communications with Castro, insisting that he would not negotiate unless California declared its independence from Mexico and agreed to "hoist the American flag."

Castro passed Stockton's demand along to the staunchly patriotic Governor Pico. Pico had already warned the central government that California needed help if it were to resist invasion. Castro and Pico agreed that they could put up no defense and addressed their farewells to the populace. They would, they said, go to Mexico to report, in Castro's words, "the iniquitous invasion" by the United States. The legislative deputies agreed that, while they could not fight the U.S. takeover, neither could they consent to it. The assembly disbanded.

Stockton rode into Los Angeles on August 12 followed by 200 marching sailors and marines and a few ox-drawn carts with guns and ammunition. The takeover was quiet except for the military band playing "Hail Columbia." Frémont joined Stockton in Los Angeles. Having missed arresting Castro, he rounded up a few remaining Mexican troops.

Five days later the first official word of the U.S. declaration of war on Mexico arrived in California by ship. Naming himself governor, Stockton established martial law. He started grand plans for a new civil government, calling his scheme "Organic Laws of the Territory" in his correspondence with the president, but referring to it privately, according to Larkin, as the "Organic Law of his Empire." Frémont and Gillespie were promised government positions. Stockton notified President Polk of his success: "My word is at present the law of the land."

His letter to the president was carried east to New Mexico by one of Frémont's party, the legendary scout Kit Carson. Carson met General Stephen Kearny and a small group of his dragoons in the New Mexico desert. He gave them the news that the United States had taken possession of California. Then he turned back to guide them to San Diego.

CHAPTER 8

CLAIMING THE WEST

VIEW OF THE GILA RIVER FROM *NOTES OF A MILITARY RECONNAISSANCE.*

While Stockton's fleet and Frémont's battalion had been advancing upon Los Angeles, in August 1846, General Stephen Kearny and the Army of the West were marching across New Mexico, claiming each town they passed through for the United States.

IN MAY 1846, as soon as war was declared, President Polk had sent orders to Colonel Stephen W. Kearny. Kearny was to lead the Army of the West along the Santa Fe Trail and take possession of New Mexico. Some of the soldiers were to continue along the trade route from Santa Fe to the silver-rich and reportedly rebellious Mexican city of Chihuahua.

Just before Kearny set out with his troops, his orders were changed. The president and his advisers had looked more carefully at their plan for a naval takeover of California. They concluded that the territory was too large to be secured by the navy alone. Kearny was ordered to take a detachment of his best soldiers into southern California.

To Bent's Fort

Kearny mustered 1,600 men to form the Army of the West. It included his own command of 300 dragoons, many of whom had made a 2,000-mile march across the Great Plains the previous summer. Kearny assembled an additional 1,000 volunteers from Missouri, including horse artillery and infantry (he was later joined by a battalion of Mormons emigrating west to avoid religious persecution). He also arranged for supplies and transportation: the quartermaster general in a partial report listed 459 horses, 3,658 mules, 14,904 oxen, and 1,556 wagons, plus light artillery.

The huge pack train left Fort Leavenworth on June 5, 1846. In the next twenty-nine days, the army traveled nearly 550 miles, with Kearny's "long-legged infantry" leading "long files of cavalry," as one soldier described it. Rolling grasslands gave way to arid prairie before the troops reached the Arkansas River. Soon the military caravan was in the heartland of the Plains Indians.

THE PLAINSMAN

THE ARMY OF THE West was led by a fifty-one-year-old career officer from New Jersey, Colonel Stephen W. Kearny. The quiet, disciplined Kearny had spent thirty years on the western plains. Even with that experience, it was a difficult mission. Water and forage were scarce, and more than half the artillery horses died before the troops even reached Bent's Fort.

At the end of July, Kearny's army reached Bent's Fort, the last major outpost within U.S. limits. Bent, St. Varain and Company, the fort's owner, did a profitable business with the Cheyenne, Arapaho, Prairie Apache, Comanche, and Kiowa tribes. Trade with hunters, trappers, and merchant caravans heading in both directions forged New Mexico's growing economic ties to the United States.

Traders and Indians

New Mexico was one of the most populous provinces on Mexico's northern frontier, and its residents were increasingly dependent on cheap U.S. goods. But many New Mexicans did not like U.S. traders. David J. Weber explains why:

> We think of Anglo-American frontiersmen as being hardy souls, wandering out to conquer the wilderness. From the point of view of Mexicans, those very same frontiersmen are not hardy pioneers. Rather they're gun merchants. They're selling guns to Indians. Indians, in order to buy those guns, take Mexican cattle, Mexican horses, sell them to the Anglo-Americans, or exchange them for the guns. If New Mexico had a population of 60,000, 20,000 were Pueblo Indians. New Mexicans were poorly armed and needed to defend themselves against Indians as well as against Anglo-Americans. . . . On the eve of the war, relations with Indians had actually worsened rather than improved.

Outside the safety of a few settlements, such as Santa Fe, Taos, and Albuquerque, New Mexicans lived in constant fear of Comanche, Apache, and Navajo raiding parties. They got little help from Mexico City and were dependent for protection on the adjoining Mexican state of Chihuahua. But in 1846 the Chihuahua legislature admitted that the government could do nothing to keep citizens and roads safe from Indians: "We travel . . . the roads at their whim; we cultivate the land at their wish; we use sparingly things they have left to us until the moment that it strikes their appetite to take them for themselves."

THE BENT BROTHERS

AMONG THE OWNERS of Bent's Fort in present-day Colorado were brothers William and Charles Bent from St. Louis. The influential Bents established personal relations in their trading community. Charles, who managed operations in Santa Fe and Taos, married María Ignacia Jaramillo, cousin to the governor of New Mexico. William married the daughter of a Cheyenne priest. Her name was Mis-stan-stur, but she was known at the fort as Owl Woman.

Charles later became provisional governor of New Mexico and died in a rebellion led by Mexican residents. William, who survived his brother, endured a series of personal tragedies, and finally, in 1849, blew up the fort rather than sell it to the United States.

Bent's Fort.

Santa Fe, guarding the approach to the city. Kearny's troops learned of this and passed an anxious few days. They faced harsh alternatives: either enter a death trap, retreat—with their few remaining rations—along the difficult route by which they had come, or attempt to reach Santa Fe by mountain trails. As they neared the canyon, a passing native laughingly informed them that Armijo and his soldiers had "gone to hell." Armijo had actually fled to Chihuahua.

The September 1846 *Report of the Citizens of New Mexico to the President of Mexico* condemns Armijo for the failure of New Mexican opposition. He had known for months of the coming U.S. attack, the report accuses, and mounted only a token, last-minute defense "at the gateway of the city." The report sadly describes the events at Apache Canyon: "More than 4,000 men . . . presented themselves to His Excellency [Armijo] to aid in the defense of the country. For sixty leagues around this city these masses rushed in at the call of their government, abandoning their families and property [which, left undefended, endured Indian attacks]. . . . Sr. Armijo left this city with his dragoons and the remaining residents. . . . Having camped in the said canyon and having convened the members of the honorable [Departmental] Assembly there, His Excellency invited them to advise him whether to defend the Department or enter into negotiations with the enemy." Not taking advice to fight, Armijo stated that "he would do whatever seemed fitting to him." He sent the volunteers home. Then, "as soon as the citizenry retired, instead of advancing he and the dragoons and artillery retreated. . . . As a result, the troops of the United States occupied this city on August 18 without the slightest resistance. . . . Sr. Armijo" the report concluded, "can say full well: I have lost everything, including honor."

The United States had occupied New Mexico without firing a shot at the enemy. On September 22, Kearny appointed Charles Bent provisional governor. New Mexico's leading families had expected to be given positions in the new government. Many were angry, says historian R. David Edmunds. "Mexican pride was hurt and there were concerns about economic advantages that might have been given to the Bent family."

THE RISE OF MANUEL ARMIJO

U. S. TRADER Josiah Gregg described Governor Armijo as an unpopular enforcer of hated Mexican tax and trade laws, an all-powerful commander-in-chief—but Armijo's army garrison consisted of only 270 men.

John S. D. Eisenhower provides this characterization of Armijo: "A man of imposing size and energy, Armijo was shrewd . . . a businessman [who] sent his own caravans over the Santa Fe Trail to Missouri. Armijo was reportedly born poor and had achieved his political start by his proficiency in avoiding punishment for sheep stealing. Armijo had been governor off and on since 1837, and by 1846 the Armijo family had accumulated most of the lands around Albuquerque, about sixty miles southeast."

THE CONQUEST OF NEW MEXICO

As Kearny passed through New Mexico, he made speeches and posted signs claiming the territory for the United States. When the Army of the West arrived at the village of Las Vegas, for example, Kearny climbed onto a rooftop and addressed the small crowd assembled for the occasion: "People of New Mexico: I have come amongst you . . . to take possession of your country, and extend over it the laws of the United States. We come amongst you as friends, not as enemies, as protectors, not as conquerors. Henceforth I absolve you of all allegiance to the Mexican government." Kearny then forced the mayor and two militia captains to take an oath of allegiance to the United States. He gave New Mexicans a constitution and a set of laws that became known as the Kearny Code. This much-publicized action, which exceeded his orders, was later criticized by President Polk and the War Office. The United States could take possession, they reminded him, only upon the signing of a treaty with Mexico.

Acting Governor Juan Bautista Vigil y Alarid explained to Kearny why there was "no manifestation of joy and enthusiasm in seeing [Santa Fe] occupied by your military forces." For New Mexicans, he said, "the power of the Mexican Republic is dead. And no matter what her condition, she was our mother." Nonetheless, many New Mexicans sought economic ties with the United States that could strengthen their long-held aspirations for independence.

AVISO.

HALLANDOME debidamente antorizado por el Presidente de los Estados Unidos de America, por la presente hago los Siguientes nombramientos para la gobernacion de Nuevo Mejico, Territorio de los Estados Unidos.

Los Empleados asi nombrados seran obedecidos y respetados segun corresponde.

CARLOS BENT Será GOBERNADOR,
Donaciano Vigil " Secretario del Territorio,
Ricardo Dallum " Esherif mayor (alguacil
Francisco P. Blair " Promotor fiscal, [mayor)
Carlos Blumner " " Tesorero
Eugenio Leitensdorfer " Yntendente de cuentas públicas,
Joab Houghton, Antonio José Otero y Carlos Baubien seran Jués de la Suprema Corte de Justicia y cada uno en su Districto sera jues de cir euito.

Dado en Santa Fé capital del terri de Nuevo Mejíco este dia á 22 de de Setiembre 1846, y el 71 ° de la Indepencia de los Estados Unidos·
S. W KEARNY,
General de Brigada
del Egercito de los E. Unidos.

NOTICE.

BEING duly authorized by the President of the United States of America, I hereby make the following appointments for the Government of New Mexico, a territory of the United States.

The officers thus appointed will be obeyed and respected accordingly·

CHARLES BENT to be Governor.
Donaciano Vigil " Sec. of Territory.
Richard Dallam " Marshall.
Francis P Blair " U. S. D. A.'y
Gharles Blummer " Treasurer.
Eugene Leitensdorfer " Aud. of Pub. Acc.
Joal Houghton, Antonio José Otero, Charles Beaubien to be Judges of "the Superior Court."
Given at Santa Fe, the Capitol of the Territory of New Mexico, this 22d day of September 1846 and in the 71st year of the Independence of the United States.

S. W. KEARNY,
Brig. General
U. S. Army.

Kearny's proclamation gave New Mexicans "new rulers [who were] strangers to their manners, language, and habits," in the words of one U.S. soldier.

Wagons in front of the governor's palace in Santa Fe, 1870s.

On September 25, Kearny set out for California with 300 dragoons. Captain Phillip Cooke, who parted company from Kearny to lead the Mormon Battalion in cutting the first wagon trail to San Diego, described Kearny's mission in *The Conquest of New Mexico and California*: "The 'Army of the West' marched from Bent's Fort with only rations calculated to last, by uninterrupted and most rapid marches, until it should arrive at Santa Fe. Is this War? Tested by the rules of the science, this expedition is anomalous, not to say Quixotic. A colonel's command, called an army, marches 800 miles beyond its base, its communication liable to be cut off by the slightest effort of the enemy—mostly through a desert—the whole distance almost totally destitute of resources, to conquer a territory of 250,000 square miles. . . . This is the art of war as practiced in America."

The Santa Fe Rebellion

When Kearny and his dragoons left Santa Fe, he sent a report to President Polk that he had established a civil government and "secured order." A large occupying force remained in Santa Fe: the Missouri volunteers commanded by Colonel Alexander W. Doniphan. Later in the year they left with orders to make treaties with the Indians and then conquer the Mexican province of Chihuahua. The Doniphan troops were replaced by a regiment commanded by Colonel Sterling Price, who became military governor in support of Charles Bent, the civilian governor.

There was unrest in New Mexico even before Doniphan's departure. Bored U.S. troops, overcrowded in Santa Fe, started to attack New Mexican civilians; racial tensions escalated (in their memoirs of the conquest a number of U.S. soldiers made ugly statements expressing contempt for Mexicans). Some New Mexicans regretted not having offered more resistance when the U.S. army took possession of the territory. Now they planned revolts. In December, officials uncovered a plot to overthrow the occupation forces and assassinate Governor Bent. The conspirators were quickly arrested, and the guard was doubled at the governor's palace. Bent believed the danger was over and decided to leave the safety of Santa Fe to spend time with his family in Taos.

On a cold January night in 1847, New Mexican and Pueblo Indian rebels attacked and killed six men thought to be U.S. sympathizers. The rebels then went to Charles Bent's home and kicked in his door. Bent's five-year-old daughter Teresina recalled, "Father told them, 'What wrong have I done to you, when you come to me for help I always helped you and your families.' 'Yes, you did but you have to die now so that no American is going to govern us,' then they commenced to shoot with the arrows and guns."

The men threw the mortally wounded Bent to the floor and scalped him. Sparing the women and children (among them Kit Carson's wife, who was Bent's sister-in-law), the rebels left to join others who were raiding and burning stores owned by U.S. citizens. Terrified families sought refuge at the home of Padre Antonio José Martínez, who called for an end to the violence. Nonetheless, the rebels won support in most of the small towns of northern New Mexico and were preparing to attack Santa Fe.

The Stand at Taos Pueblo

The rebels seemed to be planning "to put to death every American and every Mexican who had accepted office under the American government," said Colonel

INDIAN POLICY

AT THE TIME of the U.S.–Mexican War, the native population of New Mexico was about a third of the total population. Some groups were nomadic and warlike; others, such as the Pueblo, lived in agricultural settlements (but even the Pueblo had more than once risen in revolt against Spanish and Mexican authorities).

"Native American people had often been able to retain autonomy by balancing one political power against another," says historian R. David Edmunds. "But with Kearny's occupation of the Southwest, the balance [was] gone."

Soon after Kearny's arrival in Santa Fe, Pueblo Indians met with him and his staff. Lieutenant William Emory reported: "The chiefs and head men of the Pueblo Indians came to . . . express their great satisfaction at our arrival. Three hundred years of oppression and injustice have failed to extinguish in this race the recollection that they were once the peaceable and inoffensive masters of the country."

Weary of Mexican rule, the Pueblo were still mistrustful of the U.S. army. Although Kearny promised that Indian problems would stop with U.S. control, Navajo and Apache continued their raids on New Mexico's farms and villages.

Taos Pueblo, a Native American city used as a refuge by New Mexican rebels.

Sterling Price later. Price led five companies of U.S. troops intent on putting down the rebellion. On the way to Taos, he defeated first 1,500, then 600 to 700 more rebels. On February 3, his troops reached Taos Pueblo, a 300-year-old adobe city north of the town of Taos, where 700 rebels and their families had taken refuge.

Price ordered an artillery attack that broke through the pueblo's walls. On the second day, U.S. forces attacked the heavily defended Taos church, and dragoons set the roof on fire. The screams of the wounded women and children inside the pueblo echoed into the mountains. Still, the defenders held out. Seven hours later, a U.S. storming party broke into the pueblo. Some of the defenders fled into surrounding fields, where they were chased down and killed. Witnesses said the creek through the pueblo ran red with blood. Price reported 150 Mexican and Pueblo Indian dead. U.S. casualties were seven dead and forty-five wounded.

Afterward, the rebel leaders were brought to trial. One of the judges was a close friend of Charles Bent's; another judge's son had been killed by the defendants. Padre Martínez called the proceedings "frightful" and pleaded with the U.S. consul for justice: "Both the prosecution and the defense attorneys spoke only English; the prisoners were told of their sentence only in that language. . . . I do not mention the quality of the jury, ignorant men tainted with passion."

Fifteen defendants were sentenced to death for murder or treason, and six were hanged as soon as they were convicted. A young adventurer from the United States named Lewis Garrard helped cut the bodies down. "With the execution of those for murder," he wrote, "no fault should be found," but for a man to rise in defense of his native country and be hanged for treason, he thought, was "most damnable."

There was no further challenge to the U.S. occupation of New Mexico.

March to California

While Colonel Sterling Price was dealing with rebellion in New Mexico, General Stephen Kearny and his dragoons were heading for southern California.

Eleven days after leaving Santa Fe in September 1846, Kearny's party met Kit Carson on his way home to Taos. The navy had hoisted the U.S. flag in every port, Carson told them. Believing that the battle for California was over, Kearny sent 200 of his dragoons back to Santa Fe

This is one of many lithographs of the trip between Santa Fe and San Diego made by the engineer and artist Lieutenant James Abert as illustrations for Lieutenant William Emory's Notes of a Military Reconnaissance. *Kearny's men rode past abandoned Indian cities, past the cultivated fields of the Pima and Maricopa tribes, through Apache territory, and across the desert lands of the Mojave Indians.*

and asked Carson to guide the rest of them to California. "Most of us hoped that we might have a little kick up with the good people of California," said one of the dragoons. They were to get their wish.

For weeks, Carson, Kearny, and the hundred or so remaining soldiers dragged themselves across the desert. Kearny's "wilderness worn dragoons, in shabby patched clothing" pulled two cannons through Apache territory across the Gila River, then on to the Colorado, and beyond. At one point they marched ninety miles without finding water. By the time they reached an oak-covered valley in California, they were starving. The hungry army stopped at a ranch, Lieutenant William Emory recorded, and in one meal, seven of his fellow soldiers ate a full-grown sheep.

It was early December; the trip from Missouri to Santa Fe had taken more than two months; the trip from Santa Fe to California had also taken more than two months. Reaching a junction where the road forked to San Diego and Los Angeles, Kearny's troops learned that the rumors they had heard along the way were true. The United States no longer controlled California.

NOTES OF A MILITARY RECONNAISSANCE

MONG THE SMALL body of troops accompanying Kearny to the coast was a detachment led by a topographical engineer, Lieutenant William Emory. Its mission was to survey possible railroad routes (the Atchison, Topeka, and Santa Fe Railroad follows Kearny's route through part of New Mexico) and to lay the groundwork for the westward expansion of the United States.

As the army headed across the continent, Emory observed, measured, and wrote about everything he saw. His record of the trip, *Notes of a Military Reconnaissance,* which included drawings by engineer-artist Lieutenant James Abert, was submitted to Congress after the war. Emory reported:

> The road . . . presents few obstacles for a railway, and if it continues as good to the Pacific, will be one of the routes . . . over which the United States will pass immense quantities of merchandise into what may become, in time, the rich and populous states of Sonora, Durango, and Southern California. . . .
>
> Our road over hill and dale led us through a great variety of vegetation, all totally different from that of the United States. . . . There were cacti in endless variety and gigantic size. . . . On the curve of the river, fringed with large cottonwoods . . . the moon shone

brightly, and all was as still as death, except when a flock of geese or sand-cranes were disturbed in their repose. . . .

> Strolling over the hills alone, I was struck with the fact that not one object in the whole view, animal, vegetable or mineral, had anything in common with the products of any State in the Union, with the single exception of the cottonwood. . . . We are yet 500 miles from the nearest settlement, and no one surveying our cavalry at this moment would form notions favorable to the success of the expedition.

Lieutenant William Emory, known as a keen scientific observer, was also a brave soldier in the battles Kearny's troops fought in California. After the war Emory surveyed the new U.S. boundary, producing a three-volume report on the area's people, places, plants, and animals.

Sketch of Santa Fe by James Abert.

Californio Lancers Revolt

In the weeks after the U.S. takeover, small groups of rebellious Californios had begun to harass the few hundred U.S. troops controlling the state. Resistance to U.S. military rule occurred in northern and southern California.

During this period, John Frémont was governor in the north and Robert Stockton in the south, with Archibald Gillespie his secretary and military commander. Gillespie was a poor administrator, whose actions infuriated the local population. "Neither a judicious leader nor a reliable witness," according to Neal Harlow, Gillespie had a "chronic suspicion of others" and was "in the vanguard of every fray. . . . In Los Angeles he laid down needlessly oppressive regulations. . . . An American, Benito Wilson, reported that, having established very obnoxious regulations, Gillespie upon frivolous pretexts had the most respectable men in the community brought before him for no other purpose than to humiliate them, as they thought."

Californios soon tired of this, and in September 600 lancers joined together in an attack on Gillespie and fifty U.S. soldiers who were camped outside Los Angeles. Leading the successful attack was a soldier, José María Flores, a Castro partisan from northern California, who had arrived with Governor Manuel Micheltorena in 1842.

After Gillespie surrendered, Flores and the Californios forced him and his troops—fewer than seventy soldiers in all—to withdraw from San Pedro. As Gillespie's ship prepared to leave, several hundred mounted Californios prevented Governor Stockton's crew from landing and reclaiming Los Angeles. Stockton and Gillespie had to retreat to San Diego.

The Battle at San Pascual

The Californios had reestablished a government and regained control of most of southern California. Kearny and his exhausted dragoons would have a dangerous trip to the coast. Gillespie and a small party of riflemen, sailors, and guides were sent to assist them. Kearny and this escort were

The Captured Consul

In northern California, Consul Larkin represented U.S. interests. Larkin, considered to be among the most active of the enemies of Mexico, was kidnapped and held captive until the Battle for Los Angeles.

Traveling to southern California with his captors, Larkin witnessed many typical skirmishes: skillful Californio horsemen with old muskets, outnumbering the U.S. troops with their better rifles, would stage false retreats followed by attacks. These would lead to hand-to-hand combat, with casualties on both sides.

Navel Sketches of the War in California — Meyers

Lieutenant William Emory saved Kearny's life in the Battle of San Pascual. The night after the battle, he was among those assigned to bury his comrades. He wrote: "Thus were put to rest together, and forever, a band of brave and heroic men. The long march of 2,000 miles had brought our little command, both officers and men, to know each other well [and] their loss to sink deeply in our memories."

crossing the snowy mountains above San Pascual, when they saw a company of Californio lancers. The horsemen were led by Andrés Pico, brother of former Governor Pío Pico.

In the early hours of December 6, Kearny's group led a surprise attack. Pico did not intend to fight. The Californio lancers retreated and a handful of Kearny's men pursued, sensing an easy victory. But Pico saw the disorder of the U.S. soldiers and ordered his men to turn and fight.

The Californios, said Kearny, "rallied their whole force, and charged with their lances." The *vaqueros* were "well mounted and among the best horsemen in the world." They overpowered the U.S. soldiers, who were scattered into defenseless positions. Twenty-one were killed and seventeen wounded, including Kearny and Gillespie. Six Mexican dead were left on the field, and many dead and wounded were carried off by the expert horsemen.

A series of skirmishes followed. When the wounded Gillespie managed to reach and fire a small cannon, the Californios retired from the field. The U.S. troops counted it a victory, but Emory reported that "their provisions were exhausted . . . their horses dead, their mules on their last legs; and the men, reduced by one-third their number, were ragged and worn." Kearny had ordered the attack to obtain new horses to replace the dragoons' broken-down mules. Now they were worse off than ever. The Californios, too, claimed victory. The next day Pico's lancers surrounded Kearny's men and held them for three days. They might never have reached San Diego if Governor Stockton had not sent reinforcements.

The Fight for Los Angeles

When Kearny's men joined Stockton's in San Diego, Captain Samuel Francis Du Pont of the U.S. ship *Cyane* was hopeful that "things might resume their proper place," with "the army in the interior, the navy on the coast, and some regular troops to replace Frémont's vagabond force." But Stockton, Kearny, and Frémont, commanders of the navy, the army, and the California Battalion, planned a campaign to recapture Los Angeles that was not so orthodox.

In the initial plan, Frémont was to sail to Monterey to obtain cavalry for a land assault on Los Angeles. Kearny had second thoughts. He wrote to Stockton, "I do not think Lieut. Col. Frémont should be left unsupported to fight a battle upon which the fate of California may for a long time depend." Kearny suggested that he and Stockton march from San Diego to Los Angeles to help Frémont, either reinforcing him or creating a diversion that would help him to victory.

As commanders of the army and the navy, Kearny and Stockton had been ordered to cooperate. Despite personal differences, they joined forces for the campaign to retake California's capital. Stockton assembled horses, carts, and wagons. Kearny organized a trade expedition, sending ships to obtain supplies. Together they struggled to turn Stockton's sailors into soldiers, with Kearny drilling them in land combat.

In late December, Kearny and Stockton's combined forces of 600 men set out for Los Angeles to confront rebel leader José María Flores and his troops. On January 8, 1847, they met in the Battle of San Gabriel. Otis A. Singletary writes that U.S. troops "encountered the enemy drawn up on the opposite bank of the San Gabriel River, their artillery commanding the ford from a nearby bluff. Stockton refused to be intimidated by these impressive defenses, and his troops, passing down the ranks the battle cry 'New Orleans,' in memory of Andrew Jackson's smashing

Andrés Pico joined with his brother Pío in the 1844–45 rebellion that led to the transfer of the capital to Los Angeles. Fifteen years later there was more pressure to split the state: in 1859 Pico introduced a resolution to the state assembly to divide California at San Luis Obispo.

THE BATTLE OF BUENA VISTA.

PART FOUR

THE BATTLE FOR NORTHERN MEXICO

"Permitirá la nación que se desmembrase
una parte inmensa de su territorio?
Ah! los destinos de México sólo se
salvarán con la fuerza de su acero,
y con una resolución incontrastable."

*"Will the nation allow an
enormous piece of its territory to be cut away?
Oh! Mexico will be able to save itself only
with the strength of its steel and with an
invincible determination."*
—ANTONIO LÓPEZ DE SANTA ANNA

CHAPTER 9

THE DEFENSE OF MONTERREY

SANTA ANNA DIRECTING MANEUVERS AT SAN LUIS POTOSÍ.

*On July 1, 1846, when Mexican authorities called for a war of defense
against the United States, General Antonio López de Santa Anna
was living on an estate in Havana. Mexicans had reacted to the excesses
of his presidency by sending him into exile in 1845, disgraced and ridiculed.
By late fall of 1846, he was back as commander-in-chief of Mexico's
armed forces, drilling his troops in San Luis Potosí.*

TIME AFTER TIME during his long career, Santa Anna showed remarkable ability to rise like a phoenix from the ashes of political and military defeat. Trying to describe Santa Anna's charisma, a U.S. observer wrote, "According to public opinion, he is a riddle in character; he surely is not in appearance." The observer had seen Santa Anna at the height of his power, "in his coach, surrounded with guards and all the pomp of the military, at the review of eight thousand troops; in church at prayer; in the ball room; in a cockpit betting; in the audience room; at the banquet; and in private interviews of delicate diplomacy, when the political interests of the two nations were at stake. No one can easily forget him." While his nation was at war with the United States, Santa Anna's Mexican friends had not forgotten him.

Polk's Safe Conduct

A stream of messages had flowed between Santa Anna and friends and supporters in Mexico. Or so President Polk was told when he entertained Santa Anna's emissary, Colonel Alexander Atocha, in February 1846. According to Polk's *Diary,* Atocha "represented that Santa Anna was in constant communication with his friends in Mexico, and received by every vessel that left Veracruz hundreds of letters. He intimated that the recent revolution headed by Paredes met Santa Anna's sanction [disapproval], and that Santa Anna might soon be in power again in Mexico."

If Polk would allow Santa Anna to return to Mexico, Atocha hinted, Santa Anna would try to negotiate a treaty ceding Texas, California, and New Mexico to the United States in exchange for $30 million. In Polk's *Diary* entry, Atocha also suggested that Polk move troops and ships to Mexico in a show of force to secure Mexican acceptance of this sale—a move that Polk had already ordered. Although Polk did not open direct communications with Santa Anna at this time, as soon as war was declared, he sent a confidential order to the commander of the Gulf Squadron that Santa Anna be allowed to "pass freely" if he tried to enter Mexico.

Santa Anna was portrayed as the Mexican Artful Dodger in this British cartoon. The British suspected that Santa Anna had been allowed into Mexico to "do President Polk's dirty work." This rhyme from the "Gossip of the Week" in the October 1846 Illustrated London News *gave a clever twist to the British suspicions:*

> *Santa Anna, Santa Anna,*
> *Tell us by what secret juggling*
> *Cam'st thou in by Yankee smuggling*
> *Like a contraband Havannah.*

Santa Anna's Campaign to Return

During the early months of the war, Santa Anna conducted an energetic campaign against President Mariano Paredes. He wrote letters deploring the monarchist policies of Paredes and Lucas Alamán. He announced a change of heart regarding the 1824 Constitution that he had abolished. Its principles, he now stated, had to be respected in order to construct a working government.

His *pronunciamiento* on this subject, distributed to army garrisons throughout the country, inspired at least one of the many army uprisings that tore the country apart in the spring of 1846. That summer, General Mariano Salas and a thousand troops who had been ordered to travel to northern Mexico to fight the U.S. army instead overthrew Paredes's government. Salas used Santa Anna's *pronunciamiento* as the basis for his *Plan of the Citadel,* which became the blueprint for the new government.

Santa Anna immediately set sail from Cuba. His ship was allowed to pass through the U.S. blockade and land in Veracruz. There, Santa Anna rallied a small welcoming crowd: "Mexicans! There was once a day . . . you saluted me with title of Soldier of the People. Allow me to take it again . . . and to devote myself until death to the defense of the liberty and independence of the Republic!"

Alliance with Gómez Farías

Santa Anna formed alliances easily, says Mexican historian Jesús Velasco-Márquez, since politicians and "ideologues could use him to carry out their plans." In the revolution against Paredes, Santa Anna had an unlikely ally: a man who had often been his adversary, Valentín Gómez Farías.

Jailed by Paredes, Gómez Farías had been instigating revolts against the Paredes government when Santa Anna wrote to him suggesting that theirs would be a perfect partnership: "[I can offer] the affection of the army in which I have so many good friends, and you will give me the masses over whom you have so much influence, not because I desire to return to power . . . but to cooperate . . . for the republic's salvation."

On September 15, the eve of Mexico's Independence Day, after a month spent working on their alliance, Santa Anna and Gómez Farías entered the capital together. Gómez Farías gave Santa Anna a copy of the Constitution of 1824 to hold as a symbol of his support for federalist ideals. A skeptical observer commented that it was like giving Santa Anna

Valentín Gómez Farías was a liberal reformer. A religious man, he nonetheless sought to separate church and state in Mexico. To secure those reforms and finance the war effort, he proposed that the government seize and sell church property while his country was at war with the United States. The proposal led to a revolt by supporters of the church, which weakened Mexican defenses just as new U.S. troops were landing on the Mexican coast.

a sack of scorpions. The newspaper *Don Simplicio* printed a "historical romance" about this unlikely partnership, a satire warning that such a marriage of convenience could not last.

Santa Anna was put in charge of organizing his nation's defense. His success depended on his liberal alliances—and on his ability to inspire trust. Undermining that trust were rumors that he had made a deal with Polk to pass through the U.S. blockade. The circumstances surrounding Santa Anna's return to Mexico made even the politicians uneasy, says Mexican historian Josefina Zoraida Vázquez.

Monterrey Prepares for Battle

Between Independence Day, September 16, and September 20, Mexico's northern city of Monterrey celebrated its special holidays, with a fair in the plaza, a market, and amusement rides and games. While the residents celebrated, U.S. troops advanced toward Monterrey. The invaders arrived at the gates on the city's birthday.

Northern Mexico was aware of the threat of Taylor's troops. A month after the Mexican defeat at Resaca de la Palma, every town had been ordered to form a militia, and all men between eighteen and fifty years of age were told to be ready for service. Just a month before the assault, the colonel in charge at Monterrey reported that he commanded 400 men with no training and only 130 guns. Army brigades from Mexico City, Matamoros, and other parts of the country began to arrive and, by late August, 5,000 reinforcing troops had assembled in Monterrey.

In September, interim President Salas named Gómez Farías to head a "council of government" in support of the war effort, and the new administration assigned Monterrey a new military leader and a new governor. Just before the siege, General Pedro de Ampudia arrived to assume command of the city's forces.

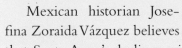

Opportunists Across Borders

A SPECIAL ENVOY from Polk had met with Santa Anna in Havana the month before he crossed the blockade. The envoy apparently told Polk that, if Santa Anna returned to Mexico, he would try to arrange a peaceful settlement with the United States. Santa Anna's old friend, Colonel Juan Almonte, acted as interpreter at the meeting. Santa Anna later insisted that Almonte could testify that the envoy's story was false. Santa Anna had never promised Polk he would work for peace.

James Knox Polk.

Antonio López de Santa Anna.

Mexican historian Josefina Zoraida Vázquez believes that Santa Anna's dealings with Polk simply reflected his determination to pass through the blockade and return to "organize the defense of Mexico . . . and take charge of the government."

U.S. historian David Pletcher says, "When you face Santa Anna with Polk, you are facing one opportunist with another. . . . Polk was using Santa Anna. . . . He was suspicious of Santa Anna, but he felt that he had nothing to lose and everything to gain, if Santa Anna would lead a movement toward negotiations." Polk did not foresee that Santa Anna would rally his people.

Monterrey in 1846

MEXICAN HISTORIAN Israel Cavazos Garza, a native of Nuevo León state (of which Monterrey is the capital), describes the U.S. army's target:

In 1846, Monterrey had no more than 20,000 inhabitants. It was very small, a provincial . . . city, much as it had been during the colonial period. Monterrey was totally isolated from the rest of the country because of the natural barrier of the Sierra Madre. There is only one entrance to the center of the country, through a natural path that opens in the Sierra, which is the same as the present-day route . . . to Saltillo.

During the colonial period everyone was dedicated to agriculture and cattle. In 1820 Monterrey's economy benefited from the opening of two ports, El Refugio [Matamoros] and Tampico. Monterrey became a commercial city. It got another plaza [and] some fountains [but] you could still count its streets with your fingers, four or six streets at most, running east to west. The streets running from north to south were called alleys because they were narrow.

Monterrey was somewhat remote, without means of communication. Very few people [in Monterrey] traveled to Mexico City or Guadalajara. But despite the lack of communication, people became informed of the international situation. Near the border, through contact with people from San Antonio and Louisiana, people [in Monterrey] found out [that the U.S. Congress had declared war], and there was serious concern.

In September, Monterrey celebrated the fiesta of the Immaculate Conception Virgin, Mary Purísima, Patroness of the City. This coincided with the celebration of Independence Day. And the year 1846 was special: the city was celebrating the 250th anniversary of its founding on September 20, 1596.

U.S. Captain Daniel Whiting, a West Point graduate trained in topographical drawing, created this image of central Monterrey, a colonial city made of stone, surrounded by fortifications, and guarded by heavy cannon on the flanking hillsides.

Monterrey had abundant natural defenses. Mountains and a shallow river shielded its southern edge. Two hills, Independence and Federation, guarded the approach from the northwest; both were well defended with troops and guns. To the northeast was a high-walled, well-armed, unassailable fortress called the Citadel. Taylor's soldiers, who had to pass beneath it to make their assault, dubbed it the Black Fort. Three other forts protected the southeastern access. And the city itself was fortified: its stone walls were pierced for shooting rifles, its roofs equipped with gun parapets.

Ampudia set up headquarters in an ammunition-filled cathedral off the central plaza of the city, while Mexican army technicians worked to improve the fortifications protecting the city.

Pedro de Ampudia, the commander at Monterrey, had a reputation for cruelty. The forty-one-year-old general had served under Mariano Arista in Matamoros. But Arista, who had a hacienda in Monterrey, was considered a "northerner," one of their own, by the population, while the Cuban-born Ampudia was seen as an outsider and was even accused of not fighting hard enough in the shelling of Fort Texas.

The U.S. Attack

In their month-long advance on Monterrey, the 6,640 U.S. troops left Mexico's hot, dusty lowlands to climb toward the Sierra Madre. "It is a grand and beautiful sight," said one soldier, "dark and blue, the peaks towering high up towards the skies." Its "picturesque beauty," said another, exceeded his "most romantic dreams." But the mountains also formed a natural defense for the south of Monterrey, which was itself a well-armed fortress prepared to repel the U.S. attack.

On September 19, Taylor camped three miles outside the city, at a shady grove watered with several springs and surrounded by corn and pasturelands. There he and his generals went over their battle plan. The capable General William Worth would lead some of the troops on a wide circuit to the city's southwest side. First, they would close off the road to Saltillo, then capture Federation and Independence Hills. To distract attention, Taylor would launch a diversionary attack on the other side of the city, where the troops would be within range of the fearsome Citadel. It was, in the words of John S. D. Eisenhower, "almost a classical tactical problem," which Taylor approached in "a time-honored military way."

Worth led half of Taylor's men, among them the fiercely anti-Mexican Texas Rangers under Colonel Jack Hays and Captain Ben McCulloch. As they crossed the Saltillo road, they met a group of lancers from Jalisco, led by Lieutenant Colonel Mariano Moret. After repeated charges killed most of the Mexicans, Moret, torn and bloody, charged once more, before retreating. Later, a Texas Ranger would say, "I have never called a Mexican a coward since." The U.S. troops succeeded in cutting off the road to Saltillo and with it any hope of Mexican reinforcements or supplies.

Worth's troops then forded the river and attacked the smaller hill, Federation, with its two gun emplacements. The Texans raced the regulars up the slope. The 500 Mexican defenders fought courageously, but they could not stem the attack. Their artillery had not been lowered sufficiently to hit troops scrambling up toward them.

The Diversion Turns Deadly

As General Worth's troops were fighting their way to victory, the diversionary attack of Taylor's troops on the northeastern side of the city was running into problems. Intended as a feint to keep Mexican troops in the Citadel from joining the fight against Worth in the west, the attack was executed poorly and proved costly.

Colonel John Garland led his men too close to the Mexican guns. When they were between the Citadel and one of Monterrey's outlying forts, a murderous crossfire of cannonballs from these two and musket shot from within the city walls showered the troops. Horses and men lay on top of one another, gasping, soaked with foam and blood.

Taylor ordered up more divisions to support Garland. The advancing reinforcements were cut to pieces. As U.S. war correspondent Thomas Thorpe described the scene, "The wind of passing balls and bombs continually fanned their faces. . . . A twelve-pound shot literally passed through the closed ranks of the Tennessee regiment, throwing fragments of human beings into the air, and drenching the living with gore."

It was the Tennessee regiment that finally moved closer to the eastern edge of the city. The Tennessee soldiers, a volunteer division, captured a well-defended bridge and a tannery that had been converted into a fortress, forcing the Mexican troops to retreat toward the city center. But 394 U.S. soldiers had been killed or wounded in the "diversionary" fighting.

Worth's Struggle at the Hills

Once General Worth's troops held Federation Hill, their next objective was Independence Hill. It had a gun emplacement at the top and a heavily fortified ruin called the Bishop's Palace halfway down. Taylor's troops—and General Ampudia—watched the day's battle from a distance, occasionally launching shells toward each other.

José Sotero Noriega, a doctor with the Mexican army, described the mood before the battle: "As night fell, we faced an enemy proud of its victories, in the midst of our own fears: a night when our most tender memories of home and independence were revived. The military bands announced the solemn hour in which our birth as a nation was announced. All bowed to the sentiment of patriotism; they forgot all else, and longed for the fight, for revenge and for glory."

He went on to describe the day's Mexican triumph: "Our soldiers, confused and in a frenzy, charged. And over the turf they gained, over the bodies of our enemies, [over] the haze of tainted blood, rose to the heavens the triumphant shout of 'Viva Mexico!'" But doctors on both sides were busy after the battle. That night surgeons had the grisly duty of amputating legs and arms.

The storming of the Bishop's Palace, a formidable abandoned residence on a stony hillside west of Monterrey.

At 3:00 A.M., in a cold, driving rain, Worth's troops began clawing their way up the slippery hillside, dragging a twelve-pound howitzer. At dawn, the shooting began, as more than 1,000 U.S. soldiers rose up shouting from the rocks and crevices. "Up the hill we went with a rush," Lieutenant Dana recalled, "the Texans ahead like devils. Nothing could stop us." The Mexican troops aimed their fusillade too high, and the U.S. troops quickly stormed their parapet at the top of the hill, forcing them to retreat. The U.S. gunners then turned to launch a howitzer attack onto the roofless Bishop's Palace halfway down the hill.

When the Mexicans inside the palace surged out to meet them, U.S. infantry on two sides of the ridge drove them back. The soldiers remaining inside the palace could not fire on the advancing U.S. troops without hitting their own men. The retreating Mexican soldiers were caught between the firing from the palace and the U.S. troops, who took after the Mexican soldiers, and, according to Lieutenant Dana, "pursued so hotly that they entered pell-mell with the enemy into the Palace before [the soldiers inside] could close their doors. . . . The Mexican tricolor flag was hauled down and soon the Star-Spangled Banner waved." The Mexican troops streaming from the palace retreated to Monterrey.

From the Bishop's Palace, Worth's troops turned the Mexican guns on the city below. Now the palace's "immense strength, . . . admirably . . . fortified by the enemy," as Dana noted, could be used to U.S. advantage.

Breaching the City

During the night General Ampudia ordered his troops to abandon most of the outer defenses ringing the mountain capital. Those who had fought well against Taylor's and Garland's attacks were recalled, over

The third day's fighting at Monterrey.

protest, from the perimeter ditches and forts defending the southeastern approach to the city. With Mexican troops concentrated in the center, cannon fire from the Citadel did not keep Taylor's troops from advancing for long. By midmorning they had entered Monterrey.

When Worth heard firing in the city, he moved his troops into the fray. U.S. troops now penetrated the city from opposite sides, Taylor's from the north and east and Worth's from the west, fighting toward the center. Monterrey's houses were made of stone, and each became a small fortress, with sandbagged parapets protecting gunners on the flat roofs. Shells, shrapnel, and grapeshot rained death down into the narrow streets, as Mexican defenders fired from rooftops and windows.

A U.S. soldier reported that, despite the firing, "General Taylor was walking about perfectly regardless of danger. . . . By every chance [he] should have been shot." Some of his men "reminded [Taylor] how much he was exposing himself, to which he replied, 'Take that axe and knock in that door!' "

Despite U.S. artillery and troops swarming into the city, Mexican soldiers continued to fight. The attackers broke down doors, punched holes in walls to insert shells, and entered houses to capture Mexican gunners on the roofs. House-to-house, hand-to-hand fighting went on

CARNAGE AND *HEROISM*

THERE WERE HUNDREDS of dead and wounded in the fight for Monterrey. Not all of the civilian population had left the city; many of the poor and those without resources suffered during the battle to defend their homes. Historian Israel Cavazos reports that, although most of the city's children and elderly had been sent away before the battle began, many women stayed to fight alongside their husbands, fathers, and brothers.

Mexican chroniclers mention María Josefa Zozaya, who climbed to the roof of her home near the center of the city to bring water and bandages to the soldiers fighting there. Guillermo Prieto wrote the poem "Triste y Dolorido Romance de Monterrey" in her honor. Another Mexican heroine was María de Jesús Dosamantes, who apparently followed her soldier-husband from San Luis Potosí. In Monterrey, she reported to General Ampudia for orders dressed as a man and went through the line of fire.

U.S. soldiers recorded acts of heroism and mercy by the citizens of Monterrey as well. One soldier wrote that, during the day's fighting in the city streets, "I saw a Mexican female carrying water and food to the wounded men of both armies. I saw her lift the head of one poor fellow, give him water, and then take her handkerchief from her own head and bind up his wounds. . . . I heard the crack of one or two guns and she, poor good creature fell. . . . She was dead! I turned my eyes to heaven and thought, 'Oh God, and this is war!' " That woman became known as the Maid of Monterrey in U.S. commemorations of the battle:

> She cast a look of anguish
> On dying and on dead;
> Her lap she made the pillow
> Of those who groaned and bled . . .
> And when the dying soldier
> For one bright gleam did pray,
> He blessed the señorita,
> The Maid of Monterrey.

U.S. printmakers, songwriters, and playwrights commemorated the battle in a grand and romantic fashion, but for the families of the Mexican and U.S. dead, with over 400 killed or wounded on each side, grief blotted out romance.

U.S. journalist Thomas Thorpe, spared by the carnage at Monterrey, imagined the sorrow that would be felt for an anonymous soldier who had perished in the brutal invasion: "The poor private died unnoticed and unknown, yet by some quiet hearthstone, far from the tumult of cities, tears will be shed for his fall; the stern old father will nerve himself to his loss, by the thought that the sacrifice was made for his country, while the aged mother's heart bleeds with a wound time cannot heal."

all day, as U.S. soldiers pressed relentlessly toward the center of the city. By nightfall, they had nearly reached the plaza. Taylor ordered his troops from the city, but continued firing shells at Ampudia's headquarters throughout the night.

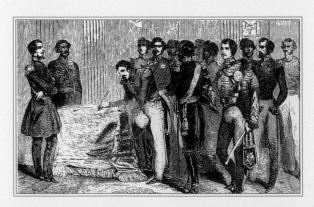
Truce

Threatened by the explosion of the huge stockpile of ammunition in the cathedral, General Ampudia sent an aide to General Taylor with a white flag of truce. Taylor demanded complete surrender, but the Mexican general was a good negotiator. Ampudia insisted that a joint commission establish the terms under which the city would be turned over to the U.S. occupiers. He persuaded Taylor to agree to an eight-week armistice.

John S. D. Eisenhower cites Taylor's exhausted state as justification for this decision: supplies, provisions, and ammunition were low; there were many wounded; and the Mexicans still held the Citadel, which they evacuated only after the armistice was signed.

Having lost the city, Ampudia was able to save his army, which was allowed to leave with its personal arms plus a six-gun battery. On September 25, Mexican troops surrendered the Citadel. Over the next few days the entire force withdrew from Monterrey.

The Mexican Army Reassembles

On September 28, as Ampudia's troops were moving out of Monterrey, Santa Anna was leaving Mexico City with two brigades, marching to Monterrey's defense. The news that Monterrey had fallen did not reach him until he was a few days away from San Luis Potosí. By October 8 he had set up headquarters in that city and was sending out orders for army garrisons from all over northeastern Mexico to join forces to confront Taylor's army.

Among his first orders was for Ampudia and his troops to abandon the strategic garrison of Saltillo, where they were stationed after their defeat in Monterrey, and withdraw to San Luis Potosí, a fortnight's march to the south. This decision made it possible for Taylor and the U.S. army to walk into Saltillo virtually unopposed as soon as the armistice was over. Santa Anna also ordered up the 4,000-man garrison from the northern port of Tampico, so that it too was virtually unprotected against U.S. conquest.

Santa Anna fortified San Luis Potosí with defenses and used it as a training ground for the soldiers who assembled there. From the neighboring states of Zacatecas, Guanajuato, Jalisco, and Tamaulipas almost 20,000 men had assembled by the end of the year.

"Santa Anna was an energetic general," says Josefina Zoraida Vázquez, "with a genius for forming an army without resources, often putting up his own money, or collecting it however he could." He managed to press factories into service to manufacture uniforms and ammunition and to repair guns. But he needed to quarter and feed a huge number of soldiers.

Funding the Army

In his autobiography Santa Anna described the challenge he faced as his troops "began to prepare for the battle. Only one thing bothered me," he wrote. "I was constantly puzzled as to how to meet the necessary expenses. Previously, the General Treasury of the nation had supplied the commissary of the army with the basic necessities for each soldier. Now there was no money to supply these needed essentials, and each day our needs increased. The government answered my entreaties with false hopes and evasions. The soldiers grew more anxious with each passing day. 'No one wants to send even bread and meat to the army,' they grumbled."

Although Santa Anna complained about the government's inability to provide funds for him, he had deliberately distanced himself from the problems of the administration, leaving Mexico City after barely two

DRILLING THE TROOPS

SOLDIER MANUEL BALBONTÍN, in *La Invasión Americana* in 1883, described the complaints of an officer who witnessed Santa Anna's drills:

The infantry was exercised by brigades under the command of the respective officers; but I never saw any general maneuvers even by divisions. The cavalry was drilled only by regiments. The artillery hardly ever maneuvered and never fired a blank shot. The general in command was never present on the field of maneuvers, so that he was unable to appreciate the respective qualities of the various bodies under his command. On Sundays the troops went to mass, marched through the city, and returned to their quarters. If any meetings of the principal commanding officers were held to discuss the operations of the campaign, it was not known, nor was it known whether any plan of campaign had been formed. In none of the corps were there schools of officers as there should have been.

Mexican soldier, in the romanticized rendering of Claudio Linati, whose watercolors and lithographs in Costumes de Mexique *portray men and women from every level of Mexican society.*

PATRIOTISM AND NATIONALISM

Santa Anna complained that "the leaders of the army did their best to train the rough men who volunteered, but they could do little to inspire them with patriotism for the glorious country they were honored to serve."

Manuel Balbontín reported the impressions of an officer in the army at San Luis Potosí: while "the state of San Luis has distinguished itself by its patriotism and services in this war . . . nevertheless one failed to note throughout the republic the patriotic fire, the enthusiasm of a people that rises en masse to defend its homes. The aspect of the city was tranquil; and if the presence of our troops had not given it a certain martial appearance there would have been nothing to recall the fact that the nation was sustaining a just war against invading foreigners."

To the poorest Mexicans, some historians have suggested, one government may have seemed as bad as another—none eased their struggle to survive. Even many of the more well-to-do Mexicans had not yet developed a deep sense of national identity. Instead, their attachments were to the church, the family, and the local and state governments.

Fray Gregorio, Carmelite, and worshipper, depicted by Italian artist Claudio Linati.

weeks there. In the capital, meanwhile, every government effort to raise money to pay for the war led to a crisis.

After Mexico City learned of the defeat at Monterrey, President Salas had attempted to levy a new property tax. There were riots at the mere announcement of the new tax, even though no provision had been made to collect the money. In November, when the armistice with Taylor's troops was over, the government proposed even more unpopular funding measures: an assessment on the clergy and certain wealthy individuals. Before any money was raised by this method, the Salas government was overthrown.

In December 1846, Santa Anna was appointed president of his country once again. He remained in San Luis Potosí, drilling his troops. As president, he had often been able to count on the support of the Catholic Church and Mexico's wealthy conservatives. He had once said he would rather cut off his hand than appropriate church property. But he needed money for the war. Vice-President Gómez Farías was entrusted with fundraising. He asked Congress to authorize $15 million to support Santa Anna's army. When church leaders discovered that the money would be raised by auctioning church property, they fought back. They raised the threat of excommunication for anyone guilty of "consenting to any execrable fraud and usurpation" of church property. In the capital, and throughout Mexico, the liberal government's efforts to seize church property produced not revenue but revolt.

CHAPTER 10

DIVIDED ARMIES

U.S. VOLUNTEER INFANTRY IN SALTILLO.

After the fall of Monterrey, there was not another battle in northeastern Mexico until early in 1847. When the November armistice ended, Taylor moved his troops from Monterrey to nearby Saltillo, the key to a U.S. defensive line. Santa Anna and his troops were two weeks' march away in San Luis Potosí. Politicians in both countries had thought that the war would be over quickly, but there was no end in sight.

*P*RESIDENT POLK had been furious when he received news of the armistice in Mexico. Publicly at least, Polk could hardly voice his bitterness over what he considered a lost opportunity, but privately he criticized his commander's judgment. "If General Taylor had captured the Mexican army and deprived them of their arms," he said, "it would have probably ended the war with Mexico." He quickly sent orders that the armistice should not be extended.

Lieutenant John James Peck of New York, stationed with Taylor's forces in northeastern Mexico, recorded in November that "An officer left on the 6th for San Luis Potosí to announce to Santa Anna the renewal of the war. Where it shall end no one can tell. I think it will continue for a long time. President Polk is in for it."

Whig Gains in Washington

Before the war was six months old, President Polk's political problems had begun to mount. Early in August he had asked Congress to appropriate $2 million to pay Mexico for territory if a peace treaty was signed. Expansionist Pennsylvania Congressman David Wilmot, a former supporter of Polk's, tried to amend the appropriations bill to prohibit slavery in any territory to be annexed in the war. Although the House approved the amended bill, it provoked weeks of debate over slavery and U.S. policy toward Mexico. This gave Whigs such as John Quincy Adams another chance to express their opposition to the war. The bill was filibustered in the Senate, and Congress adjourned without passing it.

In the November congressional elections, the Whigs gained a small majority in the House. The Democratic president's policies would now meet even greater resistance. Polk's cabinet began discussions of war appropriations. Securing the forces and funds necessary to end the war was very much on Polk's mind.

Thomas Hart Benton, Democratic senator from Missouri, came to talk to the president. According to Polk's *Diary,* Benton "expressed the opinion that a blow should be struck at once. . . . He said ours is a go-ahead people, and that our only policy to obtain a peace or save ourselves was to press the war boldly." Benton proposed that "the City of Veracruz should be taken at once . . . and that after this was done there should be a rapid crushing movement made from Veracruz on the City of Mexico."

There was discussion about who might direct such an important action. Benton modestly put forward his own name to be lieutenant general, the highest-ranking position he thought Congress might create to suit his unique "talents and resources." For Polk, who doubted that Congress would go along with the creation of this new position, the choice boiled down to one of two politically unsatisfactory candidates: Zachary Taylor and Winfield Scott.

Polk did not want Taylor to lead the campaign on Mexico City. Taylor, a Whig, had become tremendously popular through press coverage of his successes in northern Mexico. The Whigs talked of drafting Taylor to run for president. Disturbed by this, Polk complained in his *Diary,* "General Taylor is very hostile to the administration. . . . He is evidently a weak man and has been made giddy with the idea of the presidency. . . . I am now convinced that he is a narrow-minded, bigoted partisan . . . wholly unqualified for the position he now holds."

The obvious alternative was Scott, another Whig. "I have strong objections to General Scott," wrote Polk in his diary. "Nothing but stern necessity and a sense of public duty could induce me to place him at the head of so important an expedition." Despite these misgivings, the president gave him the command.

The "grateful" and "delighted" Scott was eager to see combat. The plan of attack he created for eastern Mexico called for him to take half of Taylor's troops and lead them against Mexico City. Santa Anna would be forced to fight on two fronts.

The Saltillo Line

General Taylor received two "instructions" from Washington: Do not extend the armistice, and do not extend the U.S. position. Polk and the War Department wanted Taylor to concentrate his troops in Monterrey.

A MORE AGGRESSIVE STRATEGY

GENERAL WINFIELD SCOTT responded with misgivings to news of General Taylor's Monterrey armistice and his plans to establish a defensive line in northeastern Mexico: "I suppose that the war must go forward, and not be allowed to degenerate into a *war like a peace,* which would be as bad, or worse, than a *peace like a war,* involving an indefinite period of time and waste of money."

By the end of 1846, there was some talk of settling for a *peace like a war* with Mexico, by using Taylor's defensive line to protect the U.S. annexation of Texas. Such a policy, however, would do nothing to address the fate of California and New Mexico. To obtain those territories, Scott developed plans for a new offensive on the Mexican capital.

The Capture of Chihuahua

President Polk's war plan had called for General Wool to advance upon Mexico's wealthy northwestern city of Chihuahua. Instead, Wool joined Taylor to fight Santa Anna.

When the attack on Chihuahua finally came, it was led by an unlikely commander, a member of Stephen Kearny's volunteer forces in New Mexico: Colonel Alexander W. Doniphan. Sent from New Mexico in December 1846 to reinforce Wool's expedition, Doniphan conducted his own "Grand March," more than 2,000 miles through northern Mexico to Chihuahua, and then on to the Gulf Coast. His tour of duty took him from Fort Leavenworth to Matamoros, then home; more than 5,500 miles.

DONIPHAN'S EXPEDITION

General Kearny left Doniphan in charge of U.S. troops in Santa Fe when he set off for California. Doniphan was relieved of that command by the arrival of a regiment from Missouri, but he had additional orders. First, Doniphan was to march into Navajo territory and secure the Indians' goodwill and promise of good conduct. This he did, signing a treaty with the Navajo and negotiating a peace between the Navajo and the Zuni by early December.

The rest of his order was to "report to Brigadier-General Wool" in Chihuahua. That Mexican provincial capital was more than 500 miles away, at the end of the trade route from Missouri. Doniphan set off with fewer than 1,000 men on a march to El Paso (now Ciudad Juárez) and then on to Chihuahua. After crossing a ninety-mile desert, the soldiers met about 1,000 Mexican troops at Brazito. Doniphan's men succeeded in driving them off and capturing a Mexican howitzer.

Currier & Ives portrayal of the Battle of Sacramento.

*After crossing a ninety-mile desert, the soldiers met about
1,000 Mexican troops at Brazito.*

THE BATTLE OF SACRAMENTO

Doniphan's volunteers waited in El Paso for reinforcing artillery to arrive from Santa Fe and then set off with a caravan of wagons and merchants traveling to Chihuahua on business. As they approached Chihuahua, they defeated 2,000 Mexican troops at the Battle of Sacramento. A line of wagons, artillery, and U.S. troops advanced upon the Mexican position and drove the Mexican troops from the field. The U.S. volunteers then entered Chihuahua without encountering any more resistance.

Doniphan's expedition was irregular in having civilian caravans attached it. It was also unusual in carrying out a line of action that, as Doniphan wrote to Taylor, could have been "ticklish," since his troops were "out of the reach of help." Although hardly decisive in the course of the war, Doniphan's march caught the imagination of the U.S. public. George R. Gibson wrote in his *Diary of the Mexican War:*

> [The Battle of Sacramento] was one of the most important which occurred during the war in its results and effects. It was the means of keeping down the disturbances which had broken out in New Mexico a short time previous, and secured peace in our newly acquired possessions in that quarter. It made the Indian tribes look upon us as a race far superior to the Mexicans, and overawed them. It prevented a large amount of property in the hands of the traders from falling into their hands; property which was sufficient to have supported the whole Mexican Army for several months, and at that particular time would have been of the utmost value to Santa Anna and the government.

Plus, Gibson adds, Doniphan's volunteers captured the "Black Flag" that the Mexicans had flown against them at Brazito.

Celebration of Doniphan's Grand March.

OCCUPATION OF CHIHUAHUA

Doniphan's party occupied Chihuahua for months. Susan Magoffin, who was at Bent's Fort when Kearny arrived there and then followed him into Santa Fe, covered many of the same routes as the U.S. armies, eventually visiting the "Black Fort" in Monterrey, and then Saltillo, after "some very hard traveling." But first she passed through El Paso and went on to Chihuahua. Arriving there on April 4, she

> found Col. Doniphan's command occupying the city, and a beautiful sight they have made of it in some respects. Instead of seeing it in its original beauty . . . I saw it filled with Missouri volunteers who though good to fight are not careful at all how much they soil the property of a friend much less an enemy. The good citizens of Chi. had never dreamed I dare say that their loved homes would be turned into quarters for common soldiers, their fine houses many of them turned into stables, the rooves made kitchens of, their public *pila* [drinking fountain] used as a bathing trough, the fine trees of their beautiful *alamador* [*alameda*—public walk] barked and forever spoiled, and a hundred other deprivations equal to any of these, but yet all has been done.

When Doniphan's army left Chihuahua, they set off on another long march, this time to northeastern Mexico. They reported to General Wool after the Battle of Buena Vista, before continuing on to the mouth of the Rio Grande and shipping home to the United States. Chihuahua was recaptured by Colonel Sterling Price, in one of the last actions of the war. Price, who had relieved Doniphan in Santa Fe, made an even faster march than Doniphan had, to attack the town in 1848 while the peace treaty was being approved.

General John Wool and his staff at Saltillo, the key to Taylor's line. General William Worth had his headquarters in the center of the town. Both his 1,200 troops and the reserve in Monterrey were supplied by the fertile region.

But Taylor had other ideas. As soon as the armistice ended in mid-November, he advanced his troops to Saltillo, capital of the state of Coahuila.

Saltillo was a town of only 10,000, extending twelve or fourteen blocks around a central cathedral, but it lay in a strategic location. Taylor saw that it controlled "the only practicable route for artillery across the mountains." By occupying Saltillo, he could establish small outposts of U.S. troops to defend a line from Parras to Tampico.

Several factors contributed to the initial success of this plan. Santa Anna's call for almost all the Mexican troops from the northern states to assemble in San Luis Potosí had left nearly empty garrisons in the towns along the U.S. route. Taylor's troops were able to march virtually unopposed into town after town. The U.S. navy captured one end of Taylor's line for him, taking the gulf port of Tampico without firing a shot (this garrison, too, had been deserted).

General John Ellis Wool captured Parras for Taylor. Wool had been commanded by President Polk to take more than 3,000 troops, with at least six cannons, from San Antonio to Chihuahua. While waiting out the armistice, he learned that the only route to Chihuahua would lead him back toward the U.S. troops in Saltillo, so he joined Taylor. After taking Parras without firing a shot, Wool's troops held one end of the Saltillo line.

The Violence Continues

While U.S. troops occupied northern Mexico, during the armistice and even afterward, General Taylor continued to hope that the United States might be able to gain a victory in northern Mexico without further fighting. He hoped that treating the local population well would win their support. That seems to have been the U.S. policy, says historian Miguel Ángel González, but "this policy was unsuccessful."

Taylor found it difficult to control a large army on foreign soil. Less than two weeks into the armistice after the Battle of Monterrey, the new governor of Nuevo León was complaining to Taylor about the occupying forces' treatment of civilians in Monterrey. He accused the volunteers of killing civilians "without mercy or reasonable motive."

The Texas Rangers were "brave and gallant" in war, according to Taylor, but some were savage in peace. Many of the volunteers, especially those from Texas and the South, had vivid memories of the Alamo, Goliad, and the "hellish outrages" that had occurred during the independence of Texas. To avenge "the atrocities that the Mexican army had committed at that time," says González, these soldiers "carried on their own campaign of terror against the Mexican population."

In the final months of 1846, the U.S. army held a huge territory—from Chihuahua to El Paso to Saltillo to Matamoros to Tampico. With Mexican troops concentrated in San Luis Potosí, the only actions against the U.S. troops were guerrilla attacks. Mexican guerrilla fighters resisted the U.S. occupation by launching raids on supply trains and small parties of soldiers. Soldiers who had been traveling alone were sometimes found dead, mutilated beyond recognition, the victims of guerrillas or bandits.

Mexican family during the war years. "When the North Americans arrived in Saltillo at the end of 1846," notes Carlos Recio, "the citizens received them coldly. Everyone closed their doors and put black ribbons, or bows, of mourning on them in honor of the Mexican soldiers who had died at Monterrey." But, as the U.S. occupation of northern Mexico continued, the population could not avoid dealing with the invaders. Some Mexican families eventually established relations with the U.S. troops but suffered reprisals from their countrymen. The occupation had a tragic impact on the population that lasted long after the war.

U.S. Lieutenant Samuel Chamberlain described the "carnage and devastation" along the Saltillo line, saying "the guerrillas, if possible, were guilty of worse acts than the Rangers," and there were "many revolting acts committed by volunteers and Rangers." U.S. troops often treated Mexicans with contempt, calling them "greasers," reported Chamberlain. Southern soldiers, "looking upon the 'greasers' as belonging to the same social class as their own Negro slaves . . . plundered and ill-treated them. . . . We were obliged to patrol the country for miles around camp to protect the wretched inhabitants and arrest these heroes."

Mexican civilians often were set upon by both Mexican and U.S. soldiers who sought their provisions and forage. González explains, "Many of the people living in the small towns, ranches, haciendas, and farms suffered attacks by the Mexican guerrilla fighters because they thought the people were aiding the North American army. And, at times, the North Americans attacked them, burned and razed their buildings, because they thought the people were helping the guerrilla forces. It was a situation from which the countryfolk could not escape. Many of the haciendas were totally destroyed."

Dividing the Command

During the months after the armistice, Taylor was an active leader, moving between the outposts along the Saltillo line, at one point even leading a division to Victoria before giving up the position as untenable. Supplies were short, and Taylor complained to Washington that "the task of finding and beating the enemy is among the least difficult we encounter."

Taylor moved so frequently that letters and dispatches often did not catch up with him. But he did receive the warning General Winfield Scott sent him late in 1846. Scott wrote to inform him of a plan to land troops in Veracruz and attack Mexico City. He notified Taylor that, to carry out this campaign, he "would be obliged to take . . . most of the gallant

CHAMBERLAIN'S CONFESSION

SAMUEL CHAMBERLAIN, a U.S. soldier from New Hampshire, joined General Wool's troops in a spirit of adventure. His record of the war, *My Confession,* provides a highly romanticized picture of troop travels and battles in northeastern Mexico (and Mexico City, although Chamberlain never fought there), with Chamberlain devoting his attention not just to battles but also to "fun and frolic," fandangos and festivities, nights of "wild fun and unlicensed debauchery, wine and *aguardiente,* cheap and abundant, the women fine shaped, with black flashing eyes, and very accommodating!"

Lieutenant Chamberlain witnessed one of the most violent of civilian attacks in northern Mexico, the "Rackensacker massacre." Among the wildest of Taylor's troops were Arkansas frontiersmen, called "Rackensackers." On February 9, a Rackensacker accused of "insulting" a Mexican woman was killed by civilians. The next day, a group of volunteers went seeking revenge on the murderers. Chamberlain was among those sent to investigate the sound of gunfire in the hills near Agua Nueva.

> Overhead circled a cloud of Zapilotes or Vultures, that would occasionally dart down on something on the ground ahead. . . . Soon shouts and curses, cries of women and children reached our ears, coming apparently from a cave at the end of the ravine. Climbing over rocks we reached the entrance, and as soon as we

Chamberlain's original handwritten account of the U.S.–Mexican War was illustrated with almost 100 paintings depicting battles and life in camp and town, including several fights over women.

could see in the comparative darkness a horrid sight was before us. The cave was full of our volunteers yelling like fiends, while on the rocky floor lay over twenty Mexicans, dead and dying in pools of blood. Women and children were clinging to the knees of the murderers and shrieking for mercy.

An investigating commission reported five Mexicans dead or wounded in revenge for the guerrilla killing the day before. The volunteer companies were ordered to the Rio Grande for expulsion from the army. But before they could leave, U.S. scouts reported a large Mexican army movement. The Rackensackers stayed to fight the Mexican army.

The Rackensacker massacre.

Exodus

To make his planned assault on Veracruz and the Mexican capital, General Scott took almost 5,000 of Taylor's most experienced troops. Early in 1847, they and their supply trains were aboard steamships or on the march to join their new general on the Mexican coast.

Among the officers called to leave Taylor's army and join Scott were George B. McClellan, Gustavus W. Smith, and Napoleon Dana.

The Charm and Excitement of a March

Lieutenant George B. McClellan (who would command the Union Army of the Potomac in the U.S. Civil War) was in Camargo when Scott's order to move to the coast arrived.

McClellan described Scott's new troops on the early morning march to Victoria in his *Mexican War Diary:* "I know nothing more pleasant than this moonlight marching, everything is so beautiful and quiet"—except for "a little more yelling than usual among the Volunteers." He had seen the volunteers earlier "marching by the flank, yet the road was not wide enough to hold them and it was with the greatest difficulty that you could get by—all hollowing, cursing, yelling like so many incarnate fiends—no attention or respect paid to the commands of their officers, whom they would curse as quickly as they would look at them."

McClellan, with thousands of companions, was on his way to Tampico, which he found to be a "delightful place," and from there to General Scott's staging area on the Isle of Lobos, "a small island formed by a coral reef—about 18 or 20 miles from the [Mexican] shore, forming under its lee a safe but not very pleasant anchorage."

George B. McClellan in military dress with his family before departing for the war.

While the Whigs and others at home in the United States were growing weary of the war, McClellan wrote to his mother, "You have no idea of the charm and excitement of a march—I could live such a life for years and years without becoming tired of it."

The Military Engineer

McClellan's superior, Gustavus W. Smith, requested McClellan, who had just graduated from West Point, for his elite engineering corps. Smith says, in *Company A Engineers in Mexico,* "I had taught McClellan during his last year in the Academy, and felt assured that he would be in full harmony with me in the duties we would be called upon to perform." Smith's description of the engineers' march to join Scott's forces, however, is not "in full harmony" with McClellan's:

The first day [out from Victoria] we had three bad boggy brooks to cross besides a great deal of cutting to do with axes in order to open the road and many bad ravines and gullies to render passable. To make a bridge across a boggy stream, with no other material than the short, knotty, hard, and crooked chaparral bush, was no easy matter. The first day's march was about 10 miles—we encamped about sunset after a very hard day's work.

In order to shorten the route and save the forces one day's march, we were, for several days, working on a mule path cutoff from the main road. . . . The mule path was infamous. No wagon had ever traveled that road. [After four days'] tremendous hard work, [the road was improved] very decidedly. . . .

We arrived at Tampico on the twenty-third. The distance from Victoria to Tampico is 120 miles; whole distance from Matamoros to Tampico, by way of Victoria, is 354 miles.

McClellan (who would command the Union Army of the Potomac in the U.S. Civil War) was in Camargo when Scott's order to move to the coast arrived.

Although the service was arduous, the men came through it in good health, and were all the better soldiers for the practical schooling acquired in that 350 miles of road making. After this experience, ordinary marches and drills were to them very light matters.

A CLOSE SHAVE

Lieutenant Napoleon Dana had served with "Old Rough and Ready" Taylor since Corpus Christi. He had fought with the general from Matamoros to Monterrey and was sorry to leave him: "that noble old man, that hero of the north, our brave old General Taylor, has stricken the enemy so in his quarter that they shrink from him as he advances. He is a noble specimen of a soldier and a gallant general. That honest old man, we believe him the greatest general our country has produced, and there is nothing the army will not do for that old chief. I believe he can call around him now if he were so inclined a host of brave spirits from all sections of our country who would follow him to anything and guard him to the last. It is useless for such insignificant pygmies as J. K. Polk to beat their brains out against such men as he!"

After being ordered to join old "Fuss and Feathers" Scott, Dana wrote to his wife: "We have parted from our brave old chief and seen him for the last time during this war. I have no doubt the lion-hearted old fellow felt the separation as keenly as any of us. . . . As we are going to

Dana, his wife Susan, and daughter Mary, probably taken in 1848 upon his return from Mexico.

join General Scott, we will expect to have to pay more attention to the regulations of dress, hair, whiskers, and so forth. . . . I shaved off my beard . . . this afternoon."

Soon Dana would join the assault on Veracruz: "Our quartermasters are all busy making their preparations for the passage by sea to Veracruz. They are all occupied now in making slings for the horses. Those animals which have been shipped from New Orleans were nearly all of them lost through the mismanagement of the quartermaster's department. . . .

"On board brig *Othello* at anchor off Lobos, February 28. We have been anchored here for two days, rolling and pitching and tossing about. . . . We have all been more or less seasick, and if the sea had not been so bad I would have had a long letter, but I could not write as it is. There are over fifty vessels anchored here, all loaded with troops. All the regulars are here, besides some three thousand volunteers. We are all afloat and will not go on shore, not even General Scott, who holds his headquarters on board the *Massachusetts*."

After the landing at Veracruz, Dana was wounded at the Battle of Cerro Gordo near the Mexican coast. He was left for dead on a hillside for two days before being brought back to camp by a burial party. Fortunately he recovered and was soon on his way home.

officers and men (regulars and volunteers) whom you have so long and nobly commanded."

When Scott arrived in northeastern Mexico to take command of the troops, Taylor purposely avoided him. Scott, who was desperately concerned about any delay in his planned invasion of Veracruz, finally gave up on finding Taylor on the road and simply ordered the troops to leave for the Gulf campaign. In a breach of army etiquette, he informed Taylor of his decision by letter.

Only about 6,000 men, mainly inexperienced volunteers, were left under Taylor's command in northeastern Mexico. Half of his force, including his best regular troops, had been taken. Taylor was so upset that an aide observed him mistakenly spooning mustard into his coffee instead of sugar. Taylor protested "against [both] the amount of force to be removed and the manner in which it was done." He noted that, when he had prepared his strategy, "such a decimation of my army had never crossed my mind."

Survival

Scott's letter warned Taylor that the transfer of so many of his troops would "reduce [him], for a time, to stand on the defensive." Taylor replied angrily, "The idea of a further advance with the remaining force is too preposterous to be entertained for a moment."

Taylor had to concentrate on survival. Even at full strength, his lines had been thin. Now he was dangerously exposed, with less protection for the weak points on his line. One vulnerable spot was the supply route from Camargo to Monterrey. Another was the town of La Encarnación, at the turn to Parras on the road to Saltillo.

Taylor was instructed to pull his remaining troops in closer to Monterrey. There would be no more Saltillo line stretched across the Sierra Madre. Rumors of Mexican troop movement caused Taylor's subordinates in Saltillo and Parras to pull their troops closer. But, before the U.S. soldiers realized it, Santa Anna and the entire Mexican Army of the North had advanced to a camp only sixty miles from Taylor's troops. The battle for northeastern Mexico was imminent.

Taylor had no choice: with his reduced forces he would be facing Santa Anna and the large Mexican Army of the North.

CHAPTER 11

THE BATTLE OF BUENA VISTA

MEXICAN SOLDIERS MOVING THROUGH A PASS IN THE SIERRA MADRE.

*In only four months, Santa Anna had assembled a huge army.
But many Mexicans questioned why he had not yet begun to fight the
invaders. As* Apuntes para la historia de la guerra *records, they
accused him publicly of cowardice or worse. These charges so exasperated
Santa Anna that he was forced to order the army to march even though
it had none of the supplies upon which it depended."*

WHEN SANTA ANNA learned from captured documents that Taylor had lost almost half of his troops to Scott, he decided to begin his fight. On the cold wintry morning of January 27, 1847, his army began to move north from San Luis Potosí. Over the next six days, 20,000 troops left in stages, accompanied by an unknown number of women and family members. It was 240 miles to Saltillo through harsh and desolate country. For the soldiers and their families the march to battle would be a struggle for survival.

In the month since Santa Anna had been elected president of his country yet again, his vice-president in Mexico City had succeeded in passing an act to finance the war effort. Santa Anna's troops had cheered the news. Santa Anna approved Gómez Farías's plan to auction church property until he learned of the reaction to it among "those devoted to the clergy." They had "formed a conspiracy for the overthrow of [Santa Anna's new] government," the *Apuntes* reported.

The day before his troops began the long trip to the battlefield at Buena Vista, Santa Anna wrote to Mexico City complaining that the auction measure had aroused too much opposition and that another fund-raising scheme should be found. His contribution was the seizure of ninety-eight solid bars from Spanish-owned silver mines.

The March to Battle

Santa Anna did not precisely "lead" his troops to battle, according to a group of U.S. soldiers captured at La Encarnación who witnessed the Mexican troop movement. The first troops to leave San Luis Potosí were engineers, infantry, and a company of U.S. deserters known as the San Patricio Battalion. Santa Anna left San Luis Potosí six days later, according to the Encarnación prisoners, "seated in a chariot of war drawn by eight mules and surrounded by his staff elegantly and gorgeously equipped, and followed by a number of women and a train of pack-mules, among which were said to be five loaded with fighting cock." As one contemporaneous account had it, Santa Anna was known for going to war with "every thing compatible with a camp which could contribute to comfort and luxury," including "silver tea urns, . . . cut glass tumblers and decanters, the latter with stoppers mounted with gold." The infantry, in contrast, had neither tents nor wagons.

By February 13, Santa Anna and his army had traveled about a hundred miles. Second Lieutenant Manuel Balbontín had made this same journey in the heat of summer to fight Taylor's army in Monterrey. In *La Invasión Americana,* he described the winter trip: "It is very cold. Windy and snowing. Last night some of the soldiers and the women died from exposure. The troops were so hungry and numb that they refused to march." By the end of the three-week march, the army had been reduced to about 15,000. Some had been left in garrisons along the way, but as many as 1,000 soldiers had deserted or died.

The Mexican soldiers marched half the night as they neared Agua Nueva, where they expected to find Taylor's troops. When he saw that Agua Nueva had been abandoned, Santa Anna ordered his army on. "Without giving them time to get a drink of water or fill their canteens," said Balbontín, "he compelled the troops to continue their advance at the double quick. He sent the whole cavalry galloping ahead."

Retreat from Agua Nueva

Taylor had repeatedly insisted to the War Department that he would maintain his troops' forward position at Agua Nueva. But Agua Nueva was not a favorable site for either side.

Santa Anna's troops, who had already marched more than 200 miles through a cruel landscape, made their last day's approach to Agua Nueva through 35 miles of desert. If the U.S. troops had still been there, they would have blocked the Mexican soldiers' access to the water supply. Said one Mexican commentator: "It is certainly very [unwise] that voluntarily, either because he did not carefully examine the country or because of uncalculating haste, [Santa Anna] should have risked the fate of our arms and the fate of the republic upon the illusory idea of taking a strong position with soldiers who must have marched twelve leagues without

THE SOLDADERAS

"**H**OW DOES SANTA ANNA feed his troops?" asks General Luis Garfias. "The women feed them. At this time, *'soldaderas'* [camp followers] were active in Mexico. They traveled along with the soldiers, fed them, cooked for them, made their uniforms. They even cared for them when they were sick or wounded. These women traveled on foot, often carrying babies on their backs, carrying small grills for cooking, accompanying the soldiers. And many times they died, too—hungry, sick, and abandoned."

Linati portrait of "Indigenous Servant."

water, and who, in order to drink, [would have to defeat the enemy] at the point of a bayonet." The Mexican army's chance of victory was not improved by Santa Anna's subsequent decision to advance without rest toward Taylor's position.

The U.S. troops were just ahead of the Mexicans. Taylor had received increasingly reliable reports from his scouts about the size and movements of the advancing army. But he had continued to drill his soldiers in Agua Nueva. He did not fortify the town, which had a good, but not particularly defensible, position. With the Mexican army a day away, Taylor's troops finally retreated, burning the buildings and grain supply as they fled. According to Manuel Balbontín, Taylor's men left in such haste that the Mexicans advancing past the town found "pieces of harness, and four or five wagons abandoned at different places."

The Battlefield at Buena Vista

As the exhausted Mexican troops soon discovered, Taylor was at Buena Vista, about five miles south of Saltillo, where he waited for Santa Anna's approach, said Manuel Balbontín, "with the utmost tranquillity."

Taylor had assigned General John Wool to select the field of battle, and Wool established the U.S. troops near the hacienda of Buena Vista, at the Angostura pass. It was a wise choice. On one side were mountains and hills, cutting off any military action. On the other side was a series of arroyos, or ravines, which hampered the Mexican infantry and prevented its strong cavalry from charging. The U.S. army dominated the landscape and was well entrenched.

Samuel Chamberlain described the battlefield:

Our Squadron moved onto the Angostura pass, since known as Buena Vista. Under the cliffs at the pass the Surgeon and his assistants were busy preparing amputating tables. We rode up on the plateau, where we had a good view of the whole ground. . . . Some five miles away to our front, clouds of dust rolled up telling us the enemy were moving on our position. Our troops came on to the ground with drums beating and columns flying; line of battle was formed with our right resting on the pass, the left extending to the foot of the mountain.

The Mexican troops dazzled many of the U.S. soldiers watching their approach. These were among the finest of the lancers and horse artillery. Chamberlain called them "a beautiful array, firm and steady as if on parade." Santa Anna's army continued to arrive throughout the

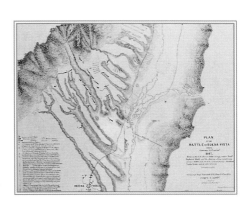

The deeply cut landscape of Buena Vista, with numerous hills and ravines, and one narrow stream providing the only water supply, gave the U.S. forces a strong position. "It was defensible . . . against a much larger force," says writer John S. D. Eisenhower. Maps of battle sites like this one were prepared by the engineers of each army. These engineers (such as Robert E. Lee) were among the most highly educated soldiers. They were trained in survey techniques, mapping, and preparing fortifications, and their maps were invaluable in developing strategy.

NO SURRENDER TO DISCRETION

BEFORE THE BATTLE began, General Santa Anna gave General Taylor one last chance to surrender, Chamberlain recounted:

About 3 P.M. a large force of enemy, estimated at about three thousand strong, moved towards our left, and began to ascend the mountain, and thus flank our position, while an officer with a flag of truce left their ranks and galloped towards us. The officer reported himself to General Taylor as Pedro Vander Linden, a Belgian surgeon in the Mexican service and bearer of a letter from Santa Anna. The letter interpreted was as follows.

"To His Excellency, General Z. Taylor, Commanding the Army of the United States of the North.

"Illustrious Sir.

"You are surrounded by twenty thousand men, and cannot in any human probability avoid suffering a rout, and being cut to pieces with your troops; but as you deserve consideration and particular esteem, I wish to save you from a catastrophe, and for that purpose give you this notice, in order that you may surrender at discretion, under the assurance that you will be treated with the consideration belonging to the Mexican character; to which end you will be granted an hour's time to make up your mind. . . .

"With this view, I assure you of my particular consideration.

"Ant. Lopez de Santa Anna."

General Taylor, on getting the purport of Santa Anna, replied, "Tell Santa Anna to go to hell!" and turning to his Chief of Staff said, "Major Bliss, put that in Spanish, and send it back by this d—d Dutchman."

The reply of the wrathy old General, reduced to writing by Major Bliss read as follows:

"In reply to your note of this date summoning me to surrender my forces at discretion, I beg leave to say that I decline acceding to your request."

U.S. artists depicted Taylor's refusal of Santa Anna's surrender offer as a battlefield meeting, although none actually occurred.

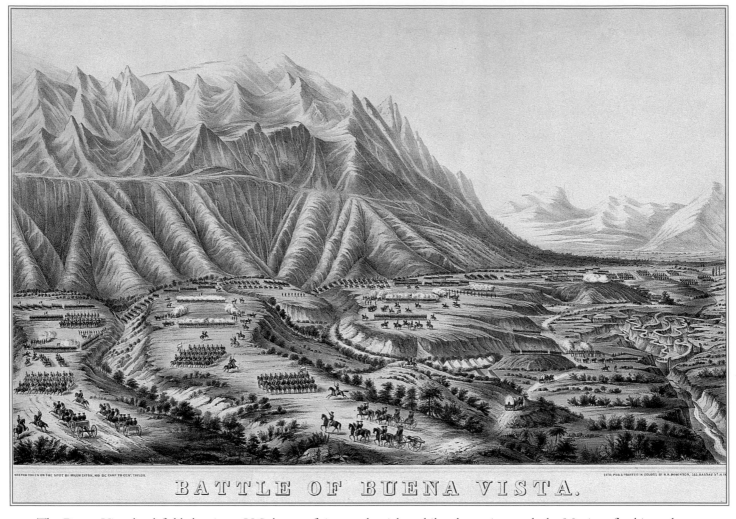

BATTLE OF BUENA VISTA.

The Buena Vista battlefield showing a U.S. battery firing on the right, while other units attack the Mexican flanking columns.

afternoon of February 22, with the mass of the Mexican troops presenting a far sorrier appearance after their 240-mile march.

Santa Anna launched some of his troops in an attack on the eastern hills in midafternoon. Manuel Balbontín reported: "When General Taylor saw our light infantry mounting the hill on the right, he immediately ordered his riflemen to stop them. This started an energetic exchange of fire that lasted the rest of the afternoon. By the time darkness set in, our soldiers remained in control of the high ground." Most of the troops from both sides simply watched the afternoon's inconclusive fighting. During a night of light rain, both commanders reinforced their positions on the mountainsides.

The Second Day

The next day was clear and cold. The U.S. troops listened to reveille as it sounded along the Mexican lines and watched as "a procession of ecclesiastical dignitaries with all the gorgeous paraphernalia of the Catholic church advanced along the lines, preceded by the bands playing a solemn anthem," Samuel Chamberlain reported. As the priests blessed the Mexican troops, the U.S. soldiers could see how seriously they were outnumbered—more than three to one.

The Mexican army was assembled in three columns, each with supporting cavalry. General Ignacio de Mora y Villamil was in command of one column, General Pedro de Ampudia in command of light troops attacking the slopes, General Manuel María Lombardini and General Ramon Pacheco in charge of the main body of infantry. General Manuel Micheltorena, one-time governor of California, was Santa Anna's chief of staff and commanded a battery. Santa Anna, too, commanded a reserve of troops.

Taylor had left General John Wool in charge of the U.S. troops while he led a few units to Saltillo to defend his supply center there. Captain John M. Washington's artillery battery was placed in charge of guarding the pass. He was supported by infantry and cavalry units at the pass and on the plateau. Riflemen and cavalrymen were deployed along the mountainsides.

At dawn Santa Anna began a series of attacks. One Mexican column advanced up the Saltillo Road toward the pass where they were held off by the artillery unit there. Lombardini's troops charged against the U.S. troops on the plateau, the weakest section of the U.S. position. There the volunteers of the Second Indiana Regiment bore the full brunt of the main attack by 7,000 Mexican lancers and infantry. The Second Indiana's commander became confused and ordered a retreat. The inexperienced troops panicked, leaving an artillery unit under Captain John Paul Jones O'Brien without support. Most of O'Brien's artillerymen were killed or wounded, and in the retreat he lost one of his guns.

U.S. soldier at Buena Vista.

Wool sent reinforcing troops and artillery to defend the weakened line, but the U.S. left had been turned. With the U.S. defensive position shattered, the Mexican army had the advantage, and Mexican columns kept up a continuous

After a day's rest, the devastated Mexican troops began the difficult march back along the route down which they had rushed toward battle only a few days before. The desert between Agua Nueva and La Encarnación took a terrible toll. "The troops who formed the rear guard soon overtook and passed the convoy of wounded, producing an inevitable confusion," said Manuel Balbontín. "The setting of the moon was another cause of disorder; and the poor wounded were victims of a thousand inhuman acts. The vanguard began arriving at La Encarnación at one in the morning, and as at Agua Nueva, each man lay down how and where he could. This night too was a *noche triste*" (the night Cortés was forced to evacuate Mexico City with great losses to the Spanish and their Indian allies).

Santa Anna's battle report explains that he withdrew his troops from Buena Vista because his soldiers were exhausted, since they had gone without food and water for two days. But Mexican commentators have found Santa Anna's action hard to understand. Most Mexican military historians believe that Mexico was close to victory. General Luis Garfias insists, "This was a battle that could have been won if [Santa Anna] had made better decisions." The Mexican army could have driven Taylor's troops out of northeastern Mexico.

U.S. military historian K. Jack Bauer disagrees. Although Santa Anna's Buena Vista campaign was relatively sophisticated, Bauer says, he "was not a good battlefield general. Neither he nor his troops were capable of responding rapidly to changing tactical situations." Taylor's strategy of letting his subordinates react to battlefield conditions, he feels, might well have led to victory if the battle had continued.

Taylor's troops followed Santa Anna's a few days later—down a road "literally strewed with the dead and dying"—and reclaimed Agua Nueva and La Encarnatión. Taylor's army of almost 4,600 men had suffered 272 dead and 387 wounded. Santa Anna's army of about 15,000 suffered 591 dead and 1,048 wounded. Mexican losses continued along the trip back to San Luis Potosí, amounting to at least another 3,000 men, counting many who deserted.

War and Politics

Some of the stories of soldiers fighting at Buena Vista had long-term effects on U.S. politics. Two received exceptional publicity:

Jefferson Davis was a colonel with the Mississippi regiment of volunteers. His battlefield strategy of forming an inverted V with another regiment made him a hero, assuring him a brilliant political career. He went on to become President of the Confederacy.

Henry Clay Jr. carried a set of pistols from his father, the Kentucky senator who had run for president against James Polk, into battle at Buena Vista. Badly wounded, Clay ordered his men to leave him behind, giving them one of the guns. "Tell him," Clay said before he died, "that I used them to the last." His father became an outspoken critic of the war.

Aftermath of Buena Vista

The first reports of the battle reaching the United States gave the victory to Mexico. Later, in early April, news came that the U.S. had reoccupied its former positions in northeastern Mexico. Even then, Polk was critical of Taylor's conduct of the campaign, noting in his *Diary* that "Gen'l Taylor is a hard fighter, but has none other of the qualities of a great General." Taylor's strategy was characterized by Polk as "blundering into difficulties," his tactics as leading to unnecessarily "severe loss." The U.S. public, however, hailed Taylor as a hero. Whig newspapers immediately proposed that he run for president.

The first reports of the battle reaching Mexico City also gave the victory to the Mexican troops. The Mexican public was overjoyed. Cathedral bells in the cities and towns called people to special masses of thanksgiving. But soon the ravaged remnants of the army began to arrive back in San Luis Potosí with their tales, reported in the *Apuntes,* of "men abandoned in a desert, steeped in their own blood, shivering with cold, parched with thirst" while "coyotes and dogs await[ed] the moment when they might begin their frightful banquet."

Although Santa Anna's losses were large, he continued to claim a victory. His withdrawal from the battlefield at Buena Vista was bitterly criticized. Theories about it are varied. Still debated is Santa Anna's own explanation for the retreat: "Duty called," he wrote in his autobiography, *The Eagle.* "A special messenger was dispatched from the government" during the Battle of Buena Vista, he claimed, and "the government ordered our troops back to defend the capital and to restore law and order." The war was shifting to central Mexico.

The U.S. and Mexican armies clash on the road to Mexico City.

PART FIVE

Into the Heart of Mexico

"Lo que el ejército de los Estados Unidos venía a hacer era . . . a incendiar nuestras ciudades, a saquear nuestros templos, a violar a nuestras mujeres e hijas, a asesinar a nuestros hijos e inmolar a nuestros defensores en nuestra misma presencia, a las puertas de nuestras casas y esas escenas de destrucción y de muerte . . . harán que encuentren por todas partes mil vengadores."

"What the United States army is coming here to do is . . . to burn our cities, loot our temples, rape our wives and daughters, kill our sons, and sacrifice our defenders right in our presence, at the doors of our homes; these scenes of death and destruction . . . will find a thousand avengers on every side."

—El Republicano, *April 1, 1847*

Commodore David Conner used steamers to pull several ships over the bar into the river at Tampico in November, when the eight-week armistice ended. Because Santa Anna had ordered all garrisons to report to San Luis Potosí, the navy captured the town without firing a shot. The spy Ann Chase, wife of Tampico's U.S. foreign consul, obtained information, supplied misinformation, and was credited with the easy U.S. victory. She became known in the United States as the "Heroine of Tampico."

EXICO WOULD NEVER surrender, President Polk had decided, unless the United States attacked its capital. General Winfield Scott planned a "double invasion"—a defensive line in the northeast and an assault on central Mexico. Santa Anna had two options: "Mexico must either divide her forces and increase our chance of success on both lines," said Polk, "or double her forces on one, and leave the other comparatively open."

U.S. forces, too, were divided. While Taylor's troops held the line against the Army of the North, Scott's forces were preparing to march to Mexico City. Both the Scott and the Taylor campaigns depended on naval support. Taylor needed ships to deliver men and supplies to Point Isabel and Camargo. Scott needed them for the planned attack on Veracruz.

Although the U.S. army was not large for a country of its size, the navy had recently been strengthened to protect its national borders and international trade. The United States had a fairly sizable force in place in the Gulf: some two-thirds of U.S. trade was said to pass through the area, and these commercial vessels could be converted to military use.

Even before Scott's attack was ordered, the navy had been blockading Veracruz, cutting it off from trade through summer heat and winter storm. The naval contribution to the war effort was little appreciated, said officer Raphael Semmes. He described his duty aboard a blockading ship in *Service Afloat and Ashore during the Mexican War:*

> While the people illuminated their cities and lighted bonfires in the country, in celebration of the victories of the army, the toils and hardships of the navy were not only forgotten, but this branch of the service was loaded with obloquy for not performing impossibilities. With the exception of Veracruz, there was no town in the whole Gulf coast of Mexico, within effective cannon range of which, a sloop-of-war could approach. The maritime towns of the enemy were more effectually defended by reefs, sandbars, and shallows than were the inland towns by redoubts and intrenchments.

Despite these difficulties, by the fall of 1846 the Gulf Squadron under Commodore David Conner had managed to occupy some ports, including Tampico and a string of shallow Gulf harbors. The navy also sailed up the Tabasco River to attack several small towns. Commodore Matthew Perry's first effort to capture the Tabasco capital led only to seizure of a few merchant ships. In a second attempt, in June 1847, more than 1,000 U.S. sailors and marines went upriver, landed, occupied the town, and destroyed its defenses. Plagued by disease and guerrilla attacks, Perry withdrew, to maintain what he described as "quiet possession of the mouth of the river, which, with the occupation of Laguna, completely shuts the Tobascans from the sea."

The most significant naval action, however, was Scott's operation at Veracruz. Leaving the coast undefended, Santa Anna led his troops to battle against Taylor in northeastern Mexico. Why did he— the "Hero of Veracruz" and the "Hero of Tampico"— ignore the Gulf towns where he had had such successes in the past? Santa Anna later denied that his decision to march on Taylor's troops at Buena Vista was based on an intercepted dispatch from Scott. He maintained that he knew neither that Taylor's troops had been halved nor that Scott intended to attack the port city guarding the National Highway to the capital. Most historians dispute that claim.

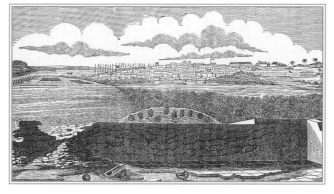

After capturing Tampico, the U.S. navy occupied its fort at the mouth of the Pánuco River. Tampico was the end of Taylor's northeastern defensive line, and Taylor's troops staffed the garrison. Many of Scott's troops passed through Tampico on their way to his Isle of Lobos staging area. It thus became the connecting point between the operations of the two U.S. forces.

Santa Anna's actions have inspired many theories: Perhaps he believed that a crushing defeat of Taylor would devastate the United States and turn the public against Polk's war. Or he thought that he could defeat Taylor and then march his troops to the coast to cut off Scott's supply line. Or that the winter storms and summer fevers, coupled with the fortifications at Veracruz, would turn back Scott's force.

Mexico did not divide its forces to confront the double invasion by the United States. Instead, the Mexican troops were forced to fight first Taylor and then Scott, rushing from northeastern to central Mexico in the spring of 1847. And President Santa Anna was forced to fight not just U.S. troops but also an uprising in Mexico City, which threatened the government. While the capital was torn with revolt, Scott was launching his assault on the Mexican coast.

CHAPTER 12

THE TAKING OF VERACRUZ

MEXICANS IN THE CASTILLO DE SAN JUAN DE ULÚA AND VERACRUZ WATCH THE U.S. LANDING.

Early in 1847, as winter drew to an end, the 15,000 residents of Veracruz anxiously awaited a U.S. attack. For months all Gulf Coast ports, from Tampico almost to Villahermosa, had been sealed by a U.S. naval blockade. Throughout the winter, an army of 12,000 U.S. troops had been massing on the Isle of Lobos, between Tampico and Veracruz.

GENERAL JUAN MORALES, in charge of the Veracruz garrison, did not think he had enough men to defend the city. He pleaded with Mexico City for additional troops. But the few not fighting with Santa Anna against Taylor at Buena Vista were fighting one another in the streets of the capital. Veracruz, with its undermanned garrison and weakened civilian population, stood alone to defend Mexico from the U.S. soldiers poised to begin their advance along the National Highway to Mexico City.

In the Footsteps of Cortés

Veracruz had long been the point of entry into the heart of Mexico: Cortés and his soldiers and priests first landed north of Veracruz in 1519, seemingly fulfilling ancient Aztec prophesies of avengers who would arrive by sea from the east. After establishing La Villa Rica de la Vera Cruz, the first mainland settlement created by Europeans, Cortés burned his ships and set off on a fateful march to the Aztec capital, Tenochtitlán, acquiring Indian allies as he went.

Since that time Veracruz had turned back numerous attacks—by the English, Spanish, and French. In the sixteenth century, the Spanish brought African slaves into Mexico and took native wealth out of Mexico through its harbor. Frequently raided by privateers, the city fought off John Hawkins and Francis Drake in 1568. Later, walls and forts were built to protect the city; a fortress (the Castillo de San Juan de Ulúa) was built to defend the harbor. During the War of Independence, the Spanish turned the fort's heavy guns on the city. Before the Spanish flag was finally lowered, Veracruz had been almost leveled. In 1829, the Spanish attacked the coast again. They were defeated with help from the central government. Nine years later, Veracruz was bombarded by the French.

After two centuries of naval bombardments, the city's defenses were strong but by no means unassailable. Within its fortifications, General Juan Morales and his garrison—3,300 troops in the city and 1,600 in the fort—waited for the U.S. attack.

FORTRESS CITY

SPANISH FORTIFICATIONS protected Veracruz. Across the bay from Veracruz, the Spanish had constructed the island fortress Castillo de San Juan de Ulúa, with 135 guns trained to repel pirates attacking from the sea. High walls surrounded the city. The waterfront was protected by a reinforced granite seawall that joined landwalls at the water's edge. Nine small forts topped these walls, with 100 pieces of heavy artillery, as well as guns and garrisons. Guns and walls were in some disrepair by 1847, but Veracruz also had natural defenses: reefs and bars in the harbor that kept out large warships with long-range guns.

Bound for the Shores of Mexico

"Hi oh, hi oh
We are now bound for
the shores of Mexico
and there Uncle Sam's
soldiers we will land,
hi oh, hi oh."
—U.S. ARMY SONG

On the eve of the assault on the Mexican coast, as U.S. troops waited for General Scott's orders, Navy Lieutenant Raphael Semmes looked across the water to Veracruz and dreamed of history and destiny: "What if Cortés had been able to look down upon our gallant fleet, interspersed with that most wonderful and most potent of all modern machines, the steamship, and arrayed in the stars and stripes of an unknown flag! Time, with his scythe and hour-glass, had brought another and a newer race, to sweep away the moldering institutions of a worn out people, and replace them with a fresher and more vigorous civilization."

"Time, with his scythe and hour-glass," had indeed brought vigorous new military technology and organization to the shores of Mexico.

Gathering the Forces

To invade Mexico, the United States had to land a large army and provide it with a supply base that would allow it to travel more than 250 miles inland, through fever-ridden coastal swamps, to the cities of Jalapa and Puebla, and over a mountain rim to the historic capital city with its natural defenses. Between November 1846 and March 1847, General Scott planned every detail of the expedition, supervising all the preparations.

To assemble his troops Scott had sailed from New York to New Orleans, across the Gulf of Mexico to the Rio Grande delta, and upriver to Camargo, where he ordered half of Taylor's troops to the coast. Some of the requisitioned troops traveled by steamboat down the Rio Grande and then to Tampico. Others marched overland to Tampico with their supply and baggage wagons.

The troops were ferried the short distance from Tampico to Lobos, an island with a large sheltered harbor behind the line of the U.S. Gulf blockade. Volunteers arriving by ship from the United States joined them on Lobos. By early March, Scott had amassed a force of some 12,000 men, with volunteers still arriving from New Orleans.

Ships were requisitioned from all over the Eastern seaboard. After numerous delays caused by bad weather and poor communications, the fleet finally assembled at the Isle of Lobos. The invasion plan called for army transport ships, navy warships, small gunboats, and special double-ended surfboats. The surfboats had been built in Philadelphia, at the exorbitant price of $795 each, to carry his troops ashore. Munitions needed included mortars, twenty-four-pound siege guns, muskets, bayonets, and ammunition, as well as tremendous logistical support, supplies, and transportation—wagons, horses, and oxen.

The massive U.S. armada traveled with several military bands. Troop movements were accompanied by a blare of brass, shouts, rousing tunes, and a chorus of voices "bound for the shores of Mexico."

The U.S. Gulf Squadron gathered at the Isle of Lobos.

Preparing the Assault

In the first months of 1847, U.S. warships began to move closer to Veracruz, converging on Antón Lizardo, an anchorage a few miles south of the city. The first week of March, army transport carriers began to arrive "ship after ship, crowded with enthusiastic soldiers."

Scott did not think he could defeat Veracruz from the sea, but he needed naval forces to carry out his strategy. He planned an amphibious landing, followed by a land attack. Scott would bring his troops ashore, pull his guns up close to the city walls, and lay siege to the city's weaker inland side. His plan called for 50 ships of 500 to 750 tons each and 140 surfboats—enough to transport 5,000 men in the first landing wave alone (only 65 surfboats arrived in time, however).

Even with the best planning, the huge amphibious landing was a fearful prospect. Under cover of protective fire from U.S. ships, groups of forty soldiers were to be carried toward land on the slow surfboats and then wade ashore. This would be their most vulnerable moment.

Scott feared that Mexican forces were hidden on the beach. There were rumors of cavalry lying in ambush in the windswept dunes and sand hills outside the city. After the messenger carrying plans to Taylor had been captured by the Mexicans, Scott thought Santa Anna might assemble a force to cut down the U.S. soldiers as they came ashore. He did not know that Santa Anna had only recently returned to Mexico City from the battlefield at Buena Vista.

Ashore

On March 9, 1847, the walls of the city of Veracruz were lined with spectators. Among them were General Juan Morales and his garrison, 3,360 men stationed in the forts along the city's ramparts, guns trained toward the attacking U.S. ships, prepared to defend the coast of Mexico.

It was the first clear, calm day after a series of late winter storms. Early in the morning, tall navy warships, began to move closer to the city, towing landing boats. Soon dozens of ships, their decks and rigging thick with U.S. soldiers, were waiting ninety yards off Collado Beach, behind a line of U.S. gunboats.

At 3:30 in the afternoon Scott ordered the navy to load the surfboats. Each of these specially designed landing craft held at least forty soldiers. At 5:30 a cannon was fired. It was the signal for the first wave of troops, General William Worth's regulars, to move toward land. The soldiers, as Captain Kirby Smith reported, started "leaping from the boats as their keels grated on the sand, wading the short distance that remained," advancing "in order of battle"—onto an empty beach. The landing was uncontested.

Before midnight more than 9,000 U.S. soldiers had come ashore. In the next three days, they moved around the walls to encircle the city, cutting off its food and water supplies and the possibility that reinforcements would come to its aid.

More storms delayed the landing of the equipment needed to set up U.S. mortar batteries: horses, wagons, heavy cannons. It was more than a week before troops moved within range of the Veracruz guns. The

---

RECONNAISSANCE

GENERAL WINFIELD SCOTT personally planned the assault on Veracruz to the smallest detail. Its success depended on his ability to work closely with the navy. While his troops lay at Antón Lizardo, he; Commodore David Conner, commander of the U.S. Gulf fleet; and most of the command staff set out on a reconnaissance mission around the Veracruz harbor aboard the steamship *Petrita*. Scott wanted one final check on a detail of his plan of attack, but the trip almost turned deadly. The reconnaissance ship at one point drew several shells from the Fortress of San Juan de Ulúa, which splashed in the water nearby. George Meade, a member of Scott's party, wrote that "one shell, hitting the vessel . . . might have been the means of breaking up the expedition." The harbor tour confirmed Scott's prior approval of the site selected by Commodore Conner: the dunes of Collado Beach, beyond the city's cannon range.

Military historians have criticized the decision not to attack the U.S. troops as they landed. If the Mexican army had defended the beach, the battle for Veracruz might have cost many more U.S. lives.

Nathaniel Currier print of U.S. artillery mounts on the beach engaged in the siege of Veracruz.

Mexican garrison fired on the soldiers, keeping up a steady barrage as they prepared cannon emplacements around the city.

On March 22, Scott had his batteries in place in four separate attack sites. They included ten-inch mortars, twenty-four-pound siege guns, and eight-inch howitzers. He sent an ultimatum to General Morales demanding surrender and offering safe conduct to civilians in the city. Morales refused. Soon after, the first U.S. shell arched over the walls of Veracruz and exploded on the streets below.

Shells, Then Cannonballs

Once the first U.S. shots were launched, Mexican soldiers in the forts along the city walls returned the fire furiously. Gun emplacements on both sides were "soon completely hidden by smoke." But at nightfall, when Mexican firing slowed, U.S. shells continued to explode, "like bright red stars" against the dark sky. For all the terror the shells inflicted on Veracruz residents, they had relatively little effect on the city walls, which had hardly been damaged by the night of March 23. Scott again sought naval assistance, and Commodore Matthew Perry, who had just replaced Commodore Conner, ordered six huge naval cannons brought ashore, to be manned by naval gunners. If the army's twenty-four-pound siege guns were inadequate, these three-ton naval guns—three firing thirty-two pounds of solid shot, three firing sixty-four-pound shells—might make an impact.

"The shells thrown from our battery were constant and regular discharges, so beautiful in their flight and so destructive in their fall. It was awful! My heart bled for the inhabitants. The soldiers I did not care so much for, but it was terrible to think of the women and children."

—Captain Robert E. Lee

A Devastating Attack

THE EXCHANGE OF FIRE in the siege of Veracruz inflicted death and destruction within the city walls but caused few casualties among the U.S. forces, according to Alfred Hoyt Bill, author of a popular history of the war.

The Mexican guns worked fast and well, but with poor luck. They blew holes in the sand big enough to bury a horse. They riddled the stone wall of the cemetery that stood near the naval battery, smashed the mortuary chapel, dug up graves, and strewed the ground about it with bones and skulls. They ripped the sandbags and rawhide facings of the embrasures. But when their shells fell inside a battery, they either failed to burst or, bursting, killed and wounded few and did little damage. Inside the city, on the other hand, the huge American projectiles plunged through supposedly bombproof roofs, burst, and gutted the interiors and set them blazing. One, smashing through the roof of a church, killed the women and children at prayer before the altar. The ground quaked. Bells rang without human hand to swing them. And sometimes, between the explosions, the American outposts near the walls could hear shrieks and wailing. Civilians took refuge in deep mercantile storage vaults or camped in the only safe area above ground, the mole between the city and castle. Great smoke clouds arose above castle and city, merged, and hung there like a thundercloud, reddened by the bursting shells and the glare of the Congreve rockets. When the moon rose, it shed a ghastly radiance over the scene.

CIVILIAN CASUALTIES

Once Scott and his troops had surrounded Veracruz, they could have starved the city and waited for it to surrender. But Scott wanted a swift victory. He knew that, as the stormy winter ended, each day increased the threat of *vómito*—yellow fever. One of the worst diseases to afflict his men, it took a greater toll than grapeshot and cannonballs. So he ordered the bombing of the city.

Some 6,700 shells were launched into the city of Veracruz during four days of bombardment. Some of the shells drove Mexican soldiers from their artillery posts. One landed inside a Mexican fort, setting off an explosion that killed almost all of the soldiers inside. But the massive shelling was indiscriminate, and civilians, too, were at risk.

The fate of the city's residents was in the hands of General Scott and General Morales. On March 22, before the U.S. mortars began firing on Veracruz, General Morales had refused a surrender demand from Scott that

Within the walls of Veracruz, "eighty soldiers had been killed or wounded, and of the civilians a hundred had been killed, and an unknown number wounded," notes Alfred Hoyt Bill. "The whole southwest quarter of the city had been destroyed."

included an offer of safe conduct for civilians. After several days and nights of constant bombardment, the Mexicans pleaded for a cease-fire and the evacuation of women and children from the city. The cease-fire was granted but not the humanitarian evacuation. When the cease-fire ended, the U.S. command resumed the heavy shelling until Veracruz surrendered.

Mexican commentators bitterly criticized Scott's decision to attack the civilian population but commended his conciliatory policy, once Veracruz was taken. Then he distributed food and issued proclamations promising security to the inhabitants. He also promised to prosecute soldiers for any attacks on civilians.

Each three-ton cannon was hauled up from the beach, across three miles of loose sand, by more than 200 men. From a hillside less than half a mile from the city walls, the cannons began their assault, fired by relays of sailors. Navy Lieutenant Raphael Semmes called these weapons "the heaviest battery . . . that had ever been mounted in a [U.S.] siege."

Surrender of the City

By March 25, the barrage of thirty-two-pound shells from the U.S. naval cannons had opened a fifty-foot-wide hole in the walls defending Veracruz and had demoralized its inhabitants. After a brief cease-fire, U.S. guns—and another vicious winter storm—pounded the city for one more night. The city's foreign consuls went to General Morales and pressured him to yield. Instead, Morales resigned his commission. On the morning of March 26, Brigadier General José Juan Landero called a truce and then surrendered both the city and the Castillo de San Juan. The U.S. army entered Veracruz. The Mexican army gave up its flags and weapons, including 300 to 400 muskets and sixteen British artillery pieces. Although the U.S. troops did not use all these weapons, they made a significant addition to the U.S. supply.

The siege and bombardment at Veracruz took the lives of only fifteen U.S. soldiers and wounded fifty-five others. It had been a "textbook" siege: Scott's careful planning had kept his men, supplies, and equipment strong. But with fever season approaching, the U.S. troops could not delay long before beginning the march to Mexico City.

COMBAT EXPERIENCE

At the time of the war with Mexico, Robert E. Lee had twenty years' army experience, but he got his first combat experience with Scott in Mexico, where his engineering skill was needed for such tasks as planning the emplacement of the three-ton cannons on the beach outside Veracruz and calculating the trajectory of the cannon fire. The bravery of this captain of engineers in surveying battle sites—swamps, lava fields, hostile territory—was invaluable to Scott in planning the strategies that carried the U.S. campaign.

U.S. Reactions to the Victories

News of the battles at Buena Vista and Veracruz arrived in the United States at about the same time. Taylor's Battle of Buena Vista captured the public imagination. Scott's Battle of Veracruz did not.

John S. D. Eisenhower has called the landing of Scott's army one of the great feats in world military history. But "the people were not ready to grasp the significance of the landing of the troops at Veracruz and the capture of that city."

Throughout the winter of 1846–47, the street boys in Philadelphia were singing:
 Old Zac's at Monterrey,
 Bring out your Santa Anner;
 For every time we raise a gun,
 Down goes a Mexicaner.
But after the war, Taylor was reminded of the toll on U.S. lives.

After the Battle of Buena Vista, General Taylor saw his reputation soar. With its hand-to-hand combat and ghastly casualties, Buena Vista fit the romantic image of battlefield glory. Historian Robert W. Johannsen described the story's appeal: "To an admiring nation, a 'handful' of raw, inexperienced citizen-soldiers, fighting in a foreign land thousands of miles from their homes, challenged and defeated a 'host' of professional combat-hardened veterans five times their number." The story was retold in music, in books, and on the stage.

General Scott had foreseen the U.S. response when he devised his strategy to capture Veracruz. Going against his officers' recommendation for an assault, he commented: "Although I know our countrymen will hardly acknowledge a victory unaccompanied by a long butcher's bill, I am strongly inclined to take the city with the least possible loss of life" of U.S. soldiers.

Scott's anticipation of public reaction did not alter his strategy—or make him any more beloved by the U.S. citizenry. The populace found Taylor "a much more attractive personality"—a populist, says Robert W. Johannsen. Scott was viewed as an aristocrat.

In the presidential campaign that followed the war, however, some commentators revived wartime criticism of Taylor's tactics, which had been careless of life on more than one occasion.

Mexican Reactions: Civil War

When U.S. Navy Lieutenant Raphael Semmes boasted, on the eve of the assault on Veracruz, that U.S. forces would "sweep away the moldering institutions" of Mexico, he was inspired, at least in part, by anti-Catholicism, a Yankee mistrust of the role of the church in Mexican society. It is ironic, then, that the church played a part in the U.S. victory in Veracruz.

THE POLKOS REVOLT
The Mexican church was wealthy, powerful, and fervently opposed to the efforts of Santa Anna's vice-president, Valentín Gómez Farías, to finance the war by auctioning church property. Opposition to Gómez Farías's scheme—in Mexico City and other parts of the country—united the church and the upper class.

Fearing this opposition, Gómez Farías sought to limit the power of Mexico City's civilian militia, the National Guard. He ordered one of the best units of this volunteer army to go to Veracruz to help defend the port city. Instead the wealthy upper-class soldiers took up arms against Gómez Farías.

Critics of the rebels called them "Polkos," says Guillermo Prieto. They sought to "hold them up to ridicule, by naming them for the dance that was in style" at the time. Battles between militia factions broke out in the streets of the capital, and Gómez Farías's government was threatened. The civil war, known as the Polkos Revolt, cost the church 300,000 pesos. Most of the leaders of the revolt were not the nation's conservatives but instead liberals and moderates. They felt that Gómez Farías's attack on the state religion went too far. This irony, says Miguel Soto, "adds one more tragic element to their rebellion."

José Fernando Ramírez was a government minister when the law that provoked the Polkos Revolt was passed. During the war, Ramírez (who was Mexico's minister of foreign affairs for a few weeks) spoke bitterly of the role the church played in the uprising:

> Members of the clergy, who had been spying about, dealing in hatreds and fears, seized the opportune moment . . . to open their money chests and start a civil war at the very time the foreign enemy was casting anchor in Veracruz harbor. Their treasury, which they had declared exhausted when it was a matter of defending the nation and the faith that these clergymen represent, was found to be full to overflowing when it came to killing Mexicans. The revolution broke out, and there were plenty of funds to finance uprisings, while the government and the few troops that were supposed to have made the bloody catastrophe at Veracruz an impossibility were eating their meager little loaves.

Ramírez's criticisms were contained in letters to his friend the governor of Durango, an epistolary record that combined personal memoir, political and philosophical speculation, and a history of the events of the war.

"You have probably noticed that history records innumerable cases substantiating the oft-repeated saying that 'a war with a foreign foe preserves a feeling of nationality and strengthens institutions,'" Ramírez observed. "In our privileged country quite the contrary has happened on the only two occasions to prove the truth of the maxim: namely, the Spanish conquest under Cortés, and the Yankee conquest under Scott. And to make the terrible comparison complete, both set foot upon the shores of Veracruz during Holy Week."

"What madness had seized the Mexicans, to provoke a civil war while a foreign enemy was lording over our cities and occupying our territory?"

—*Apuntes para la historia de la guerra*

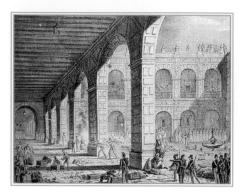

Rioting in Mexico City.

In another letter, Ramírez laments that the battle of "the ancient Mexicans" against the "intrepid conquistadors" is enough to make him "ashamed" of his age's war with the United States, a losing battle "against a gang of adventurers"—as he called the undisciplined volunteers who occupied his country.

END OF THE REVOLT

José Fernando Ramírez, who otherwise had very little good to say about Santa Anna, credited him with ending the revolt in the capital. After the Battle of Buena Vista, Santa Anna left most of his troops in San Luis Potosí and hurried to Mexico City with a small group of cavalry. Some 6,000 soldiers followed more slowly.

Santa Anna had to secure his government before he could pursue the war with the United States. As he approached Mexico City, riders came out to bring him appeals from both sides of the dispute that was fueling the Polkos Revolt. Sworn in as president before he entered the capital, he refused to enter the city until order had been restored. He negotiated an agreement with the clergy whereby Gómez Farías's measures to auction church property would be rescinded in exchange for the church's contribution of $2 million toward the war effort.

Santa Anna's alliance with Gómez Farías was over. When Gómez Farías refused to resign, Congress abolished the position of vice-president. Congress then named an acting president, Pedro María Anaya, to conduct business while Santa Anna was out of the capital preparing to stop the U.S. advance along the National Highway. The perilousness of the Mexican situation was apparent. Even Santa Anna, Ramírez reported, "expressed sad presentiments."

CHAPTER 13

THE DEFENSE OF CERRO GORDO

THE BATTLE OF CERRO GORDO.

Rather than see the U.S. army in the capital, Santa Anna swore, he would die fighting. But his ability to stop Scott's troops depended on his ability to muster his shattered army for another battle. The defense of Mexico had become a desperate effort to prevent the U.S. invaders from penetrating its heartland and reaching the capital.

ANTA ANNA was on home ground when he planned his stand against Scott. His hacienda, El Encero, was near Jalapa, and he prepared to confront U.S. troops at Cerro Gordo, about twenty miles east of Jalapa. The site, says John S. D. Eisenhower, was "the ideal defensive position between Veracruz and Mexico City." He calls Santa Anna's choice of battleground "close to masterful."

An Ideal Site

About fifty miles along the National Highway from Veracruz, Cerro Gordo (the name of a hill and a pass protecting a small village) was in the first foothills above the coastal plain, on the edge of the mountain range enclosing the central plateau. Cerro Gordo was the highest of the hills. A lower one, La Atalaya, was not quite half a mile away, and a series of smaller chaparral-covered hills ran down to the Rio del Plan. The road to Jalapa crossed a narrow bridge over the river and zigzagged up the hills, before running through a narrow pass at Cerro Gordo. Here the road veered toward the river as it cut through a deep, narrow canyon. The terrain would constrain Scott's army between the river and the rough high ground, Santa Anna felt, and he deployed his army and artillery accordingly.

The chapel at El Encero, Santa Anna's estate near Jalapa.

Gathering the Defense Forces

Santa Anna assembled 12,000 troops for the defense of Cerro Gordo. Many of his soldiers were new recruits from Mexico City, Puebla, and neighboring areas. About 6,000 who had marched to Jalapa from San Luis Potosí were exhausted veterans of the Battle at Buena Vista. In ten weeks, they had marched more than 1,000 miles. One observer called them ranks of dead men. *Apuntes para la historia de la guerra* describes their pitiful state: "They had suffered from hunger and heat, thirst and cold, storms and sickness, pestilence and snows. They had twice traversed the desert; for two and a half months they had had no rest."

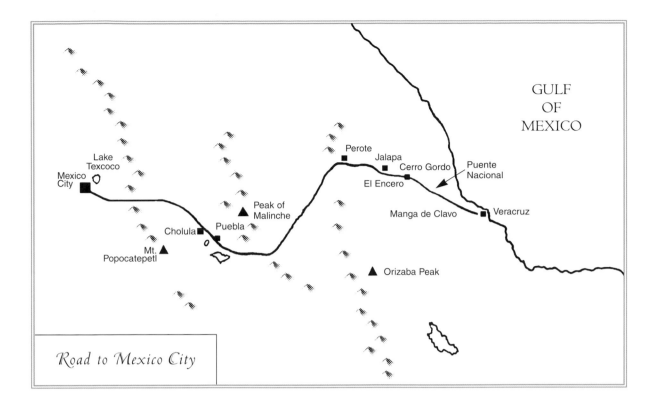

Road to Mexico City

The Mexican army spent a week fortifying its position. On the three rugged hills that extended like fingers between the river and the National Highway to Jalapa were seventeen guns and almost 2,000 troops. A battery of guns was mounted on the road at the pass, reinforced with trenches in which 1,300 infantry lay waiting. Cerro Gordo, which dominated the area, was topped with yet another battery of guns and protected by trenches, barricades, and more infantry. The main body of Mexican troops formed a line more than a mile long, which snaked around the curve of the road. Perhaps profiting from the lesson of Buena Vista, Santa Anna had arranged for forage for the animals, provisions for the troops, and a pipeline to carry water from his estate, El Encero, seven miles upriver, since the paths to the river were too steep to allow the troops easy access.

Santa Anna knew that he had a strong position, admirably fortified. The U.S. troops would be in for a bloodbath.

U.S. Troops Begin to March

Only a week after the surrender of Veracruz, Scott ordered the first U.S. troops to begin their advance to the capital. Additional groups would join them in the next few days. Scott and a small security force remained in Veracruz, along with a group of cavalry awaiting horses from the United States.

Rumors abounded of the reception they would receive along the road to Mexico City. Speculation about where and when the Mexican forces would choose to meet them soon ended. Lieutenant Napoleon

General Scott and his army followed the route of Cortés and the Spanish conquistadores from coastal Veracruz to Mexico City. In Veracruz the U.S. troops were within 260 miles of the capital.

Dana reported, after a long day's march up the "excellent . . . grand National Road to the City of Mexico," that the U.S. troops were passed by a wagon train from the army camp twenty-five miles away. Santa Anna is reported to have chosen a position in "a strong mountain pass . . . and has fortified himself there upon the hills." Still, Dana predicted that Scott would "put Santa Anna in a mighty bad fix . . . [and] give him such a whipping that the war will be finished at a blow."

Scott joined his troops on April 14. His subordinates had been considering a frontal assault, despite the obvious strength of the Mexican forces. Scott decided that such a strategy would be too deadly, and he ordered a detailed reconnaissance of the Mexican position.

The Advice of Engineers

At dawn the next day, Captain Robert E. Lee and Lieutenant Pierre G. T. Beauregard went behind enemy lines to scout the area. Surprised by a Mexican patrol, Lee dropped behind a fallen log in a spring-fed clearing. It was a popular watering hole. Unable to make his escape undetected, Lee lay beneath the log for hours, hardly breathing, bitten by insects he couldn't see. The information he brought back from this and subsequent scouting missions changed the course of the battle. His sketches of the area convinced Scott that it would be possible to clear a path through a ravine around the Mexicans' left flank, allowing the U.S. troops and their artillery to circle the Mexican troops, control the road, and turn their line.

Santa Anna's officers warned him that his flank was exposed, but he did not listen. Two of the men who tried to warn him were experienced engineers. Lieutenant Colonel Manuel Robles had just come from the fighting at Veracruz. Lieutenant Colonel Juan Cano had studied in the United States and Europe. Both officers recommended fortifying La Atalaya to protect the exposed flank, but Santa Anna maintained that it would be impossible for troops or cannons to get through the rough terrain around the hill.

Preparing the Attack

On April 17, Scott sent his troops into action to prepare the flank attack. They followed Lee and Beauregard, using the scouts' map. Ulysses S. Grant later described the route in his *Memoirs:* "the walls were so steep

BATTLE PORTRAITS

Depiction of the Battle of Cerro Gordo by an unknown artist.

GENERAL SCOTT'S CAMPAIGN was well documented by lithographers who traveled with the U.S. forces. George Kendall, editor and reporter of the New Orleans *Picayune,* accompanied Scott on his march to Mexico City; his stories inspired even artists not present in Mexico to draw war scenes, some of which displayed fanciful notions of Mexican geography. To produce more accurate images, Kendall hired Carl Nebel, a German artist who had spent some years in Mexico.

Nebel's lithographs, based on battlefield sketches, are among the most accurate depictions of U.S. combat positions. However, they glamorize U.S. combatants and often fail entirely to depict Mexican ones. They also contain numerous errors in the representation of Mexican topography. Anyone looking at Nebel's treeless lithograph of Chapultepec, for example, would have a hard time reconciling it with Guillermo Prieto's description of the forests around it.

This image of the Battle of Cerro Gordo, by H. Méndez, is one of the relatively few Mexican prints of the war. It shows the U.S. position at La Atalaya on April 18, 1847.

that men could barely climb them. . . . Animals could not." The artillery troops moved their cannons, Grant says, by tying rope around their axles and playing the rope out, up or down the slopes, with men at the opposite end giving directions.

The Mexican forces discovered the division moving along Lee's trail to La Atalaya and fired upon it. In their eagerness to engage the enemy, some of the U.S. soldiers went running forward, "shouting and hurrahing as if we were going to some delightful entertainment," said an account by one U.S. soldier. They ran straight into the line of fire of 3,000 Mexicans protecting Cerro Gordo. Cut off by the hills and without support from other U.S. troops, they faced withering fire until darkness fell. This first loss was "a shocking sight," said a U.S. soldier: 100 wounded U.S. troops, "lying on the ground with legs shot off, arms gone, and cut in every part."

That night Robert E. Lee supervised the placement of three heavy cannons—one of the gun barrels weighed almost three tons—on La Atalaya. Working in a steady rain, a team of 500 U.S. soldiers hauled the cannons up the hill piece by piece. When the first men were exhausted, 500 more took their place. "The night . . . was the most distressing one I have ever passed," said a U.S. artillery officer. "Many of our strongest men gave out. By the time the last gun was dragged up—I should judge about three in the morning—the track over which they had passed was strewn with tired, exhausted, and sleeping men from the top to the base of the mountain."

As dawn broke on April 18, the weary soldiers on La Atalaya could see the entire Mexican camp arrayed before them. Said one soldier, "I was awakened by a sweet, plaintive, melancholy strain of music. It was the Mexican reveille. . . . The Mexican army was turning out. The lancers—the chivalry of Mexico—were there, and far down the slope, by hundreds and thousands, the Mexican infantry. It was a beautiful morning." General Scott predicted that the fighting would end with a U.S. victory before ten in the morning. He was almost exactly right.

Surprise Shelling

At 7 A.M. on April 18, the U.S. battery opened fire from La Atalaya, the hill that Santa Anna had considered too steep to require fortifying. When the Mexican battery on Cerro Gordo returned the fire, a column of U.S. troops launched an attack on the most heavily defended route, the hills along the river, the action that Santa Anna had expected. These diver-

> *"Our whole force with a loud shout leaped the breastwork and met [the Mexicans] at the point of the bayonet. Here for just one short minute ensued a kind of fighting I hope never to see again. It seemed like murder to see men running bayonets into each other's breasts."*
> —A MASSACHUSETTS VOLUNTEER IN THE FIRST ASSAULT FROM LA ATALAYA ON CERRO GORDO

THE GULF SQUADRON

Ascending the Tabasco River *by Henry Walke.*

*A naval expedition under Commodore Perry makes its way past Devil's Bend
en route to its second assault on Tabasco in June 1847.*

The Road to Mexico City

The Battle of Veracruz *by Henry Walke.*

*The Naval Battery (large naval guns) joined General Scott's attack on the Gulf Coast
city of Veracruz and the Castillo de San Juan de Ulúa, which protected it.*

The Battle of Cerro Gordo *by Carl Nebel.*

*The U.S. assault on the Mexican army in the pass at Cerro Gordo. The large hill
in the background is protected by a Mexican battery. The smaller hill on the left
is held by a U.S. battery.*

IN THE VALLEY OF MEXICO

The Battle of Contreras *by James Walker.*

Mexican General Valencia and his ill-fated troops are in the center background.

The Battle of Churubusco *by Carl Nebel.*

The convent known as the Church of Churubusco (center) was the main focus of the fighting on August 20, 1847. Here it is seen in the distance, past a muddy battleground where U.S. troops were launching an attack that had little effect on the battle's outcome.

THE FIGHT FOR THE CAPITAL

The Battle of Churubusco *by James Walker.*

*The capture of the San Mateo Convent at Churubusco took the advancing U.S. troops
another step closer to Mexico City.*

The Battle of Chapultepec *by Carl Nebel.*

The U.S. troops made a two-pronged attack on the Mexican military academy, the hilltop citadel defending the capital.

Heroic Defense of the Garita de Belén *by an unknown artist.*

Mexican artillerymen fire at U.S. troops closing in on the Bethlehem Gate, as a
wagonload of wounded Mexican soldiers tries to pull away. Mexico City's last defenses,
the Belén and San Cosme garitas, *fell on the afternoon of September 13, 1847.*

sionary forces were led by General Gideon Pillow—an ally of President Polk's who had been promoted through political patronage. General Pillow took a somewhat different route from the one Scott had selected and conducted the feint so recklessly that his troops sustained heavy casualties.

With Pillow engaging the Mexican front line, Scott's main attack proceeded exactly as planned. U.S. troops charged furiously from La Atalaya toward Cerro Gordo, rushing the fortifications that protected the hilltop artillery. They pushed past one barrier after another, driving the Mexican troops before them. As the hilltop was abandoned, the U.S. forces turned the Cerro Gordo guns on the fleeing Mexican troops, who were thrown into confusion. Thousands ran in a blind panic. "Every chain of command and obedience now broken among our troops," says *Apuntes para la historia de la guerra,* "they rushed desperately to the narrow pass . . . that descends to the Rio del Plan . . . leaving a trail of blood on the road."

Other U.S. troops succeeded in moving around the Mexican position to attack it from the rear. This onslaught, combined with fire from the position taken atop Cerro Gordo, put more Mexican dragoons and infantry to flight. The U.S. troops soon controlled the road to Jalapa, surrounding the Mexican troops that had not fled, and forcing them to surrender. U.S. cavalry pursued fleeing Mexican troops as far as ten miles up the road to Jalapa to ensure that they would disperse rather than regroup.

Some 3,000 Mexican soldiers and 200 officers were taken prisoner. Five of Santa Anna's top generals were captured. Santa Anna himself barely escaped. Like many of his soldiers, he fled down to the river and then to El Encero—on a mule and pursued by U.S. cavalry, according to popular U.S. stories and cartoons. He didn't stop until he could rest in the shelter of Orizaba Peak, thirty miles from the battlefield.

SANTA ANNA'S FLIGHT

CERRO GORDO was a devastating loss, both for the army and for its leader. The *Apuntes* records sorrowfully: "Santa Anna . . . the first chief of our nation and our army . . . a few hours before . . . erect and proud, . . . [was] now humbled and confused, seeking among the wretched a refuge to flee to . . . a vivid picture of the fall of our country, of the debasement of our name, of the anathema pronounced against our race."

Spoils of War

The next day Scott and a small party rode into Santa Anna's estate, El Encero—"a princely place" in elevated country, "with mountains in the distance," in one soldier's account. Scott put the property under guard.

All of the Mexican artillery and ammunition had been left at Cerro Gordo for the U.S. victors. "Forty-three cannon and some four thousand small arms were taken and destroyed," says Alfred Hoyt Bill, "since Scott lacked the means to move the former, and the latter were too old to be worth keeping. Large stores of ammunition were found in caverns near the batteries. Quantities of clothing and provisions were captured and the Mexican military chest, containing eleven thousand dollars in specie, of which one broken bag supplied some vigilant volunteers with the first money they had seen since they had been paid at Tampico." This was money that Santa Anna had raised to pay the Mexican troops now fleeing through the countryside.

To General Scott, the U.S. victory seemed complete. He sent a message to President Polk: "Mexico . . . no longer has an army." But once again Santa Anna refused to accept defeat. Even as Scott's victory message was making its way to Washington, Santa Anna was organizing an army of almost 4,000 soldiers. Falling back to a small town near Puebla, his cavalry skirmished with U.S. artillery. Not finding the support he needed in Puebla, he decided not to defend it or any other town on the National Highway. Instead, he hurried on to the capital. By the end of May, Mexico's president and commander-in-chief was preparing for the defense of the capital, enlisting every willing soldier to join him.

"The North Americans, who believed that Santa Anna was destroyed forever," said the *Apuntes,* "did not imagine we would . . . collect a respectable force. . . . They were surprised to learn that . . . with regard to perseverance and obstinacy, we were like our predecessors, the Spanish."

The General's Leg

"Santa Anna lost his campaign carriage, which contained his official and private papers, and three of its team of fine black mules," according to Alfred Hoyt Bill. "He was said to have fled on the fourth, and a wooden leg that was advertised as his became an attraction at Barnum's Museum in New York the following winter."

El Republicano *newspaper, April 24, 1847, containing a letter from Santa Anna to Anaya describing the "esfuerzo estraordinario" (extraordinary strength) of the enemy at Cerro Gordo.*

CHAPTER 14

GATHERING FORCES

U.S. TROOPS ENTERING PUEBLA.

After burying the dead at Cerro Gordo, Scott's army continued its march up the National Highway. Santa Anna had chosen not to defend the towns along the way, and the towns themselves did not oppose the U.S. forces. Jalapa surrendered first, then tiny Perote. By the end of May, U.S. soldiers had entered Puebla, within 100 miles of Mexico City.

"At 12 o'clock precisely, the vanguard of the invading army entered the south gate and marched to the Grand Plaza fronting the Cathedral. They stacked their arms, and supplied themselves with water from a fountain."

—A SOLDIER IN
GENERAL SCOTT'S ARMY

*P*UEBLA, A LOVELY colonial city set in a high valley surrounded by volcanoes, was Mexico's second largest city, with 60,000 residents. It surrendered without resistance, and the entering U.S. troops were met by the inhabitants. "The streets . . . were swarming with the multitude as far as the eye could reach," said one soldier. "Our little army of 4,000 was completely lost in the crowds that pressed around us, examining us pretty much as they would the animals in a menagerie."

Puebla residents felt hostility and resentment. Wrote one: "I gave in to curiosity, and went out to meet our future masters. . . . The many stories about their Herculean size and elegant athletic forms were exaggerations. . . . I saw a hundred harrowed-looking men whose uniforms were poor and inelegant . . . feeble, skinny, and even crippled men . . . everything that bad taste and stinginess can produce of the ridiculous, sordid, and gross."

During the three-month occupation of Puebla, the U.S. and Mexican governments struggled with private negotiations they hoped would end the war. Many of the Mexican soldiers who had dispersed from Cerro Gordo were still in the area, harassing the countryside with guerrilla attacks, destroying bridges, and attacking U.S. troops and wagons as they traveled along the National Highway.

Scott prepared to move against the capital—a daunting prospect. His army, perilously small, was surrounded by a hostile and much larger civilian population. Some military observers thought he was doomed. The Duke of Wellington, whose credentials included defeating Napoleon at Waterloo, commented that Scott would have to ask the Mexicans for permission to leave.

Organizing U.S. Forces

To attack Mexico City, Scott needed to assemble soldiers and supplies. Like Taylor, he complained that the War Department undermined his campaign by failing to provide them. But the task of sending an army thousands of miles to Mexico—through Veracruz and the pestilent coastal lowlands, in Scott's case—was clearly greater than anyone in the War Department had anticipated.

Wagonloads of supplies were sent from the United States. After the Battle of Cerro Gordo, the chief quartermaster in Washington received Scott's request for essential goods: "medicines and hospital stores, clothing for troops, salt, ammunition, shoes for animals, and coffee; articles only a little inferior in importance are knapsacks, blankets [the highlands of Mexico were proving uncomfortably cool], hard bread, bacon and camp kettles." For the officers, cigars and brandy were also considered essential. The quartermaster calculated that, by the time the soldiers reached Mexico City, the army would require almost 3,000,000 pounds of supplies carried by more than 9,000 wagons and 17,000 mules. Scott's subordinate General William Worth hired Manuel Domínguez and 200 Mexicans to act as messengers and to protect U.S. wagon trains from attack by bandits and guerrillas.

As an experienced commander, Scott knew that his army had to obtain some supplies locally. He had written to the quartermaster that certain "indispensable articles . . . sugar, flour, rice, fresh meat, beans and forage, we hope to find in the country." The land around Puebla was very rich. "Winfield Scott's army on its way to Mexico City was always followed by a great crowd of Mexican vendors trying to sell all kinds of things to the soldiers, including food," says Robert W. Johannsen. "And, of course, the food was something that the soldiers had trouble getting used to." Fresh tropical fruits and hot peppers, it was said, were among Mexico's best weapons against the occupying forces.

In fact, disease took a greater toll on Scott's men than death in battle. Besides diarrhea, fevers disabled many men. Illness greatly reduced the effectiveness of Scott's force, said a U.S. officer after the war: at least a quarter of the regular troops and half of the volunteers were usually too sick to fight. Many had to be sent home. Seven regiments of twelve-month volunteers went back to the United States after the battle of Cerro Gordo, thus avoiding the worst of the yellow fever season.

The Volunteers Go Home

Half of Scott's troops were volunteers who had signed up for one year of service. For most of the men, the year was up, and they could now go home if they wanted. The vast majority, about 3,700, chose to leave "Camp Misery" and return to their families.

Twelve-month volunteer leaving Mexico.

In July Scott reported to the War Department that he had about 8,000 reasonably healthy troops and another 2,000 who were sick, spread over almost 200 miles between Puebla and Veracruz. Scott's manpower shortage along the National Highway was similar to Taylor's along the Saltillo line. Like Taylor, Scott found himself establishing small garrisons in some towns, no garrisons in others. And he refused to consider any further offensive action until he got reinforcements.

Courting the Mexican Populace

The United States had fewer than 20,000 soldiers in central and northeastern Mexico, divided between two distant fronts. Taylor and Scott were attempting to control a large, widely scattered populace. They hoped to convince the occupied populations to see the U.S. troops (as they saw themselves) as liberators. Considering the Mexican government "anything but democratic," says Robert W. Johannsen, many U.S. soldiers wondered "why there wasn't a popular revolution to try to restore republican government."

The attitude was widespread in the United States. Polk's advisers suggested that Mexicans might well be tired of the war, of the endless requests for money and men. They might be dissatisfied with their ever-shifting government, less loyal to their state than to their church. So, Polk established an occupation policy intended to reassure Mexicans that their church would be respected, that the United States guaranteed freedom of religion. In Puebla, Polk's policy could be tested.

Para mujeres y campanas, las Poblanas, goes the Mexican saying: *Puebla is the city of bells and belles.* The city had fifty or more churches. Months before the U.S. army invaded, the newspaper *Diario* described the force as "made up of adventurers who have no . . . religious creed, no moral principles or sentiments; for whom there are no priests or magistrates, and for whom the house of God, the Senate, a drawing-room, a theatre, and a circus are all the same." The editorial went on to suggest that the church contribute to the defense of the Mexican religion against this advancing horde of heathens.

CHURCH AND STATE

RELIGIOUS DIFFERENCES lay beneath much of the intolerance expressed during the war. Broadsides warned Mexican residents of the dangers of impious heretics from the United States. Priests in Puebla, fearing verbal if not physical abuse, conducted Corpus Christi ceremonies in the churches rather than the streets.

There was significant anti-Catholic sentiment in the United States and among the U.S. troops. This lithograph depicts the clergy fleeing Matamoros.

While in Puebla, General Scott issued a proclamation. He accused Mexico's generals of both "idleness" and an excess of ambition—the reasons they levied such outrageous taxes. He insisted that U.S. troops were "friends of the peaceful inhabitants of the country we occupy . . . friends of your holy religion and its priesthood. The same church is found in all parts of our country, crowded with devout Catholics, and respected by our government, laws and people."

Scott courted the church, especially after clergy in Puebla encouraged him in the belief that a religious revolt would soon sweep Mexico City. He instructed his soldiers to salute priests they met on the streets. In full dress uniform he and his staff attended Catholic mass (which cost him support in the mainly Protestant United States). Many Protestant soldiers from New England, the Midwest, and the frontier also visited Mexican churches. These beautiful buildings epitomized the richness of what was once Europe's most valued possession in the New World. The opulence dazzled the U.S. troops. But the soldiers also admired the "equality of all ranks before the altar." As one said: "The distinction of races, of color, of wealth were disregarded, and they all seemed to regard each other, at least in the sanctuary, as equal before God."

Most U.S. soldiers, however, were seen in the streets of Puebla more often than in its churches. U.S. regimental bands played dance music in the plaza every afternoon during the three-month occupation. Yet, as one soldier described the occupation, "Our duty has been extremely severe, especially guard duty, for we have been threatened with insurrections and all sorts of diabolical attempts to destroy the Yankees. A family that showed us some civility has been placarded and forced to leave the city, from fear of being burned down."

SAINTS OR SOLDIERS?

WHEN SANTA ANNA read Scott's proclamation currying favor with Mexican Catholics, he was furious. Soon Mexico City newspapers were publishing warnings: "Mexicans, beware! These Yankees, when in Jalapa, where there were plenty of pretty women, and where gallantry was the order of the day, were obsequious and attentive beaux; but now they have arrived in Puebla de los Angeles, where religion is in vogue, they have suddenly become saints."

The U.S. soldiers were not saints, however seductive the Mexican devotions: "Mexico is full of poetry . . . especially that . . . called the 'poetry of the steeples,'" said Lieutenant John James Peck. "Bell-ringing is an occupation. Day and night are consecrated by bells pealing forth strains of praise. To me, a heretic, many a pleasant dream has been dissipated by such poetry."

The Price of War in the United States

It had been little more than a year since the United States had declared war on Mexico. In the past two months U.S. troops had landed at Veracruz and fought their way to within 100 miles of Mexico City. But President Polk was frustrated with what he regarded as Scott's too-deliberate progress. Polk, who had often criticized Taylor's too-irregular style of command, now complained about Scott in his *Diary,* "If I had a proper commander of the army who would lay aside the technical rules of war to be found in books . . . I have no doubt Santa Anna & his whole army could be destroyed or captured in a short time." Chafing at the delay, the president longed for troops that would "go light & move rapidly" and bring the war to an end.

Polk had never liked Scott, of course, but his criticism also reflected a new U.S. impatience with what was seen as a protracted and painful war. As the twelve-month volunteers began returning home—and as death notices from Buena Vista and casualties from Veracruz and Cerro Gordo reached the United States—public awareness of the price of the war had grown.

Congress Debates Again

There was renewed debate about the justice and purpose of the war in the spring of 1847. President Polk precipitated the argument himself when he addressed the December 1846 Congress with a speech that attempted to justify the war. Again he requested an appropriation to pay Mexico for land, should a treaty be signed. Again the Wilmot Proviso forbidding slavery in any land acquired in the war became an issue. Congress debated restricting the appropriation with such a clause. Polk believed that this was a "domestic question" that should play no part in a "Treaty with a Foreign Power."

Daniel Webster and many Whigs supported an amendment that the war should not lead to U.S. "acquisition by conquest of any portion of [Mexico's] territory." But more asked the question, if the United States nonetheless did acquire any lands through war—and there was general agreement that California would be an attractive acquisition—then should slavery be allowed in them? That would undo the balance of slave and free states in the Union.

In February and March 1847, Congress did authorize the sale of war bonds and the enlistment of regiments, but Polk still complained of the slavery debate, which he thought was "a mischievous and troublesome interjection into a war," says David Pletcher. The land to be acquired, Polk asserted, was not even suitable for slave agriculture. He wrote in his

RETURNING HEROES

As the sick and wounded from Taylor's and Scott's campaigns made their way back from Mexico to the United States, their condition shocked the folks at home. Husbands, sons, and brothers returned in broken health, some with missing limbs. It was enough to stop at least some of the nationalistic fervor. Their condition excited both sympathy and a certain amount of anti-war protest.

GOING TO AND RETURNING FROM MEXICO.

CITIZENS' DIALOGUE

FTER HIS SON was killed at Buena Vista, U.S. Senator Henry Clay said that he "would like to kill a Mexican." But in November 1847 he made his first public statement about the war: "This is no war of defense, but one of unnecessary and of offensive aggression. It is Mexico that is defending her firesides, her castles and her altars."

Quakers, abolitionists, and a few New England writers agreed with that accusation. New England was the home of literary protest. James Russell Lowell wrote satirical verse equating war and murder. Ralph Waldo Emerson, who had opposed the annexation of Texas, also opposed the war with Mexico. "We have a bad war," he said, "many victories—each of which converts the country into an immense chanticleer—and a very insincere political opposition."

CIVIL DISOBEDIENCE

Henry David Thoreau had built a small cabin near Walden Pond, not far from Ralph Waldo Emerson's house. The two spent long evenings discussing the war with Mexico.

In an essay later titled "On Civil Disobedience," Thoreau spoke out against both slavery and the war (Gandhi cited this work as an influence a century later): "When a sixth of the population of a nation which has undertaken to be a refuge of liberty are slaves, and a whole country is overrun and conquered by our foreign army and subjected to military law, I think it is not too soon for honest men to rebel and revolutionize.

"What makes this duty the more urgent is the fact that the country so overrun is not our own, but ours is the invading army. . . . This nation must cease to hold slaves, and to make war on Mexico, though it cost them their existence as a people."

Mrs. Philip N. Barbour received the following letter after her husband was killed in Monterrey: "My Dear Friend, . . . the loss you have sustained . . . is alike irreparable to the regiment and country. May God grant you support and consolation under the weighty affliction which has befallen you. . . . May God bless and protect you, and make you happy . . . are the sincere prayers of your friend, H. Bainbridge"

Thoreau criticized New Englanders who professed to be against slavery and war but stood by and did nothing. Nor did he spare Whig politicians who denounced the war but praised the warriors and voted them supplies.

When a poll tax was approved to help finance the war, Thoreau refused to pay it, and he was put in the Concord jail. The story goes that Emerson, visiting him there, asked, "Henry, what are you doing in there?"

To which Thoreau replied, "What are you doing out there?"

EXPANSIONIST EDITORIALS

Most U.S. citizens supported the war, however. Expansionist newspapers such as the New York *Herald* thundered lofty sentiments: "The universal Yankee nation can regenerate and disenthrall the people of Mexico in a few years; and we believe it is part of our destiny to civilize that beautiful country, and enable its inhabitants to appreciate many of the advantages and blessings they enjoy."

In the last months of the war, editorials like these inspired a new flood of volunteers, many of them from the New England states. As Thoreau sat in his jail cell in Concord, Massachusetts, other eager young men were rushing to join the "invading army." Drilled and trained, they would seek their own brand of honor on the battlefields of Mexico.

Diary that he was "perfectly disgusted with the want of patriotism which seems to control the votes and course of a portion of the Democratic members"—and, of course, the Whig members—of Congress.

Mounting Pressure on Mexico

After the Mexican defeat at Cerro Gordo, Santa Anna had returned to Mexico City to find that Congress no longer had confidence in him as a general or as a president.

Anticipating the fall of Santa Anna's government—and perhaps the end of Mexican independence, as well—various factions were vying for power. Their desire to advance their own political interests struggled against their desire to preserve the nation. Observer José Fernando Ramírez lamented, "Everything is done for persons and nothing for principles." While Scott's troops were preparing to advance on Mexico City, factional fighting in Congress "was so shameful and humiliating," Ramírez reported, that it reduced him to despair. Unable to "conceive how the representative system can survive," he felt that he was "witnessing a nation breathing its last breaths."

President Polk agreed. The United States was in an excellent position to obtain the treaty he wanted. How could Mexico refuse to discuss the sale of New Mexico and California now that U.S. troops occupied them? Taylor's and Scott's troops already had a solid hold on northeastern and central Mexico. When Scott's forces advanced toward the capital, there would be even more pressure on the weakened Mexican government to discuss a settlement.

Polk wanted a diplomat to travel with General Scott—someone qualified to conduct negotiations with Mexico, someone who could present the U.S. terms to Santa Anna. The president chose Nicholas Trist, a good Democrat though not a prominent politician. Trist went to Mexico with Polk's proposal. Its terms were strict: the United States would end its attack if Mexico would agree to sell Alta and Baja California, New Mexico, and Texas to the Rio Grande. Trist was authorized to offer up to $30 million in compensation.

A Mexican Peace Overture

Early in 1847, Mexico sent an envoy to Washington to discuss a peace proposal. The ambassador was Colonel Alexander Atocha, who had persuaded Polk the year before to allow Santa Anna through the U.S. Gulf blockade. Now, with letters from Santa Anna as credentials, he promised that Mexico would negotiate if the blockade of the Gulf were lifted.

This time Polk refused Atocha, suspecting that Mexico would merely use the opportunity to obtain arms and munitions. That would, in his words, "subject the administration to the ridicule of the whole world for its credulity and weakness."

A Poor Start to Peace

Nicholas Trist arrived in Veracruz on May 6, 1847, with a sealed proposal from President Polk. Scott was at his headquarters in Jalapa. Trist's first contact with Scott did not demonstrate his skill as a diplomat. The presidential envoy should have waited to meet personally with Scott. Instead he sent the president's sealed proposal to the general with instructions to pass it on to Mexican officials.

Both Trist and Scott were thin-skinned and touchy on points of honor. Scott refused to deliver a proposal he knew nothing about. He resented the challenge to his authority and wasted no time informing Trist: "The Secretary of War proposes to degrade me by requiring that I, the commander of this army, shall defer to you, the chief clerk of the Department of State, the question of discontinuing hostilities. . . .

"Here in the heart of a hostile country," Scott wrote, any question of an armistice was "a military question," which could be decided by "the commander of the invading forces," and no one else. "The safety of this army . . . demands no less."

Besides protecting his troops, Scott may have been protecting his pride. He already felt that he had not been sufficiently appreciated for his successes at Veracruz and Cerro Gordo. Now Polk had sent a negotiator over his head. Was the intention to deprive Scott of a final victory over Mexico? So went the talk among his men.

Trist replied to Scott's huffy declaration in a long and sarcastic letter: "The course determined upon by our government is what any man of plain common sense would take for granted that it must be, and it is not what your exuberant fancy and overcultivated imagination would make."

Scott replied, "If you dare to use this style of address again, or indulge yourself in a single discourteous phrase, I shall throw back the orders and instructions with the contempt and scorn which you merit at my hands."

When Trist finally caught up with Scott's troops in Jalapa on May 14, Scott refused to see him. Scott moved to Puebla, and Trist followed.

A Spirited Diplomat

For the critical mission of negotiating an end to the war, Polk decided "not to send a major politician, with many friends and enemies in American politics," says David Pletcher. "It would be safer to choose an obscure man." The president appointed Nicholas Trist, who held the then-prestigious title of chief clerk at the State Department. Trist was fluent in Spanish, having served for eight years as U.S. consul in Cuba. Although not well known, he was well connected. He was married to Thomas Jefferson's granddaughter and had worked closely with Presidents Andrew Jackson and James Madison. But, Pletcher notes, he had "a rather hot temper" and was "a compulsive writer who wrote long dispatches and letters in which he said many things that he should not have said."

But for six weeks the two would not speak to one another, and Polk's proposal was not delivered. Finally, Trist asked for help from an old acquaintance, the British foreign minister to Mexico. He made arrangements to have Polk's proposal forwarded to Santa Anna in Mexico City.

In late June, Trist sent Scott a conciliatory letter and then collapsed with dysentery. The letter included a copy of Trist's commission, which finally satisfied Scott. The general responded with a gift, a jar of guava marmalade supposed to soothe an upset digestive system. When Trist recovered, the two men met for the first time. It was the beginning of a friendship that soon became as intense as their previous feud.

In negotiating with the enemy, Santa Anna was risking a charge of treason. But in public he gave no indication that he was looking for ways to make peace. "My duty," he declared, "is to sacrifice myself, and I will know how to do it! The North American armies may parade in the ancient capital of Azteca, but I will not witness the shame, for I am determined to die fighting first."

Buying Peace

Santa Anna was prepared to talk to Trist, but he no longer had the authority to negotiate. After the defeat at Cerro Gordo, Congress had passed a law making it illegal to deal directly with the United States—in fact, making it high treason even to receive a proposal from Polk. The law was intended to limit Santa Anna's power—Congress did not trust him.

Santa Anna asked Congress for authorization to start negotiations. Congress responded that he could, says Miguel Soto, but that "they would determine if the negotiation was valid or not." As they all knew, talk about selling Mexican land would bring down Santa Anna's government. To discuss a treaty with the United States, says Soto, Santa Anna would have had "to sacrifice himself politically."

Santa Anna wanted Congress to take responsibility for any discussions. In early July, he sent Scott and Trist a reply to Polk's proposal. It hinted that a certain amount of cash might help him influence key Mexican leaders. Scott discussed the matter with Trist and his generals and advanced Santa Anna $10,000 with the promise of $1 million more on the signing of a treaty. Scott had some misgivings. He and his advisers considered the money a bribe (it was concealed from the public, and there is still no agreement about what Santa Anna did with it). But Trist reported that he and Scott were "both convinced" that it was "the only way in which the indefinite protraction of this war can possibly be prevented." They were mistaken: the money failed to produce any movement toward peace. Santa Anna sent Trist's proposal to the Mexican Congress, but Congress voted against beginning negotiations.

Santa Anna's "position after Congress scattered in mid-July," according to K. Jack Bauer, was apparently "that he should negotiate a peace

SITES OF ANCIENT CONQUESTS

SCOTT ARRANGED FOR U.S. troops in Puebla to make excursions to nearby Cholula. The town was a vast complex of plazas, altars, and pyramids, among them Tepanapa, considered the largest, though not highest, pyramid in the world. More than 1,000 years old, Tepanapa was built by Toltec peoples to honor their god Quetzalcoatl. The Spanish built a church over its base—as they did over more than forty other temples—after massacring at least 3,000 Indians there. The Spanish church is seen by Mexican author Octavio Paz as a metaphor for the conquerors' adoption of the natives' structures of power.

U.S. soldiers, too, saw special meaning in the site. They speculated—as the Spanish conquistadores had centuries before—that the pyramid might be the ruins of the Tower of Babel. And they were inspired in that speculation by an 1843 book, *The History of the Conquest of Mexico,* by historian William Prescott, who described how the Spanish had seen "analogies between the Aztec and Scripture histories."

The U.S.–Mexican War had made Prescott's book enormously popular, with publishers bringing out new editions to meet the demand. "Many soldiers carried copies of the book with them into Mexico," says Robert W. Johannsen, "especially those in Scott's army who marched from Veracruz to Mexico City. They used it as a kind of guidebook. They wanted to visit all of the sights that Cortés had, and they identified with what they had read about in Prescott's book."

Prescott comments dryly on the eagerness of a conquering people to find "points of resemblance" with the conquered people, so that they are "perpetually cheated by the illusions of their own imaginations." Bearing him out, enthusiastic U.S. army officers were inspired to see themselves playing a role in a grand historical drama. They had picnics on top of the pyramids at Cholula, regimental bands played patriotic tunes, and the soldiers dreamed of glory: "To conquer the descendants of the Spanish conquerors," wrote an Ohio volunteer, "and to plant the flag of our young republic upon the capitol reared centuries ago above the ruins of Montezuma's palaces! What prospect more captivating to the youthful imagination!"

The churches and pyramids of Cholula.

and use the money it produced to smooth any ruffled feelings. [But] he evidently believed that he could not make such a peace without at least appearing to defend the nation's capital. Trist forwarded to Washington on July 23 the comments of one of his sources within Mexico City . . . [that] 'S. A. now says secretly, that he shall allow your army to approach this city, even as far as the Peñon, and then endeavour to make peace.'" Trist predicted that "the Army would not have to enter Mexico City in order to secure a peace"—that Santa Anna would put up a show but not a fight.

Advance to the Valley of Mexico

In August, more than 2,000 new troops landed in Veracruz, which was at that season "the very habitation of pestilence" according to General Franklin Pierce. Scott assembled as many of these troops as possible in Puebla, moving them from the garrisons stretching to the coast. Scott's army was now "isolated and abandoned," he wrote to the War Department, without the possibility of retreat or reinforcement. He had cut his supply line and "resolved no longer to depend on Veracruz, but to render my little army a self-sustaining machine . . . to throw away the scabbard, and to advance with the naked blade in hand."

On August 7, the U.S. troops began their advance on the capital. Some had doubts about their chances of success. Lieutenant John James Peck wrote: "General Scott . . . has been inveigled into an advance by his wily enemy. Our force is small, not quite 10,000, with an inadequate siege train and small supply of ammunition. . . . We must oppose great odds and decide by the bayonet." But their advance was not opposed.

The "long train of wagons and camp-followers" that moved out of Puebla toward the Valley of Mexico was trailed by a "rabble rout inconceivable according to modern ideas of war," a line of "sutlers, printers with their presses, editors and reporters, actors and circus riders, gamblers, jobbers, 'certain frail but daring fair ones,' *damas cortesanas,* sailors turned teamsters, and discharged soldiers," enumerates Alfred Hoyt Bill. They moved unopposed, even at passes that Scott considered dangerous.

Three days later, Scott's army reached the base of the volcano Popocatepetl, a mountain pass two miles high. More than 3,000 feet below, the brilliant Valley of Mexico was spread out before them. William Prescott's *History of the Conquest of Mexico* had described it as a "gay and gorgeous

"We hear from all quarters that the Mexicans, more than 20,000 strong, are prepared to oppose our march to the capital. We must have at least one tremendous battle. Welcome the danger, welcome the toil, welcome the fierce conflict and the bloody field, if it will but close the war. . . . Mexico must fall or we must all find a grave."

—CAPTAIN KIRBY SMITH
OF THE U.S. REGULAR ARMY

panorama." Remnants of ancient lakes glittered in the golden sunlight. In their center, Mexico City arose like an enchanted island.

For Prescott, this "fair city of Mexico" was "like some Indian empress with her coronet of pearls." For Scott, it was "the object of all our dreams and hopes, toils and dangers; once the gorgeous seat of the Montezumas. . . . Probably not a man in the column failed to say to his neighbor or to himself: That splendid city shall soon be ours."

Not all of the troops were so confident. Captain Kirby Smith wrote simply, "Mexico must fall or we must all find a grave."

CHAPTER 15

THE SPLENDID CITY

U.S. TROOPS IN THE VALLEY OF MEXICO.

*The Valley of Mexico was a basin about 120 miles
around. Three large lakes edged by soggy marshland
surrounded Mexico City, forming a natural defense.
Over this moat only a few heavily defended roads
and causeways led to the capital.*

*H*OPING TO AVOID a bombardment of the city, Santa Anna chose to defend the areas around it. He had assembled professional soldiers and volunteers. Thousands of men had joined the four National Guard battalions: the Victoria and Hidalgo Brigades, composed of the city's upper classes, and the Bravo and Independencia Brigades, composed of laborers and artisans.

Two days before Scott's arrival, a signal sounded notifying all men between fifteen and sixty to report to key points around the capital. Santa Anna paraded the troops through the city streets. *Apuntes para la historia de la guerra* recalls: "The spirit of the inhabitants of the capital . . . began to recover confidence. . . . The music of the Eleventh Infantry filled the air, a thousand *'Viva'*s answered it, and the National Guard marched, bearing with them the good wishes of all."

The men paraded out the city gates to El Peñón, seven miles away. This large hill commanded the main road, which entered the capital from the east. Here 7,000 troops camped for several days, waiting to attack the U.S. forces as they approached the city.

Scott's Approach

Scott had reconnoitered the roads to Mexico City while he was still at Puebla. But questions remained: Could the road that passed between Lake Chalco and Lake Xochimilco support artillery? A second surveying team, sent out after the U.S. troops entered the Valley of Mexico, recommended passing along a narrow muddy track between those lakes and the mountains enclosing the valley.

Rather than risk a battle at El Peñón, which would have cost many lives, Scott and more than 10,000 U.S. troops made a "sudden inversion" (as Scott wrote in his autobiography) to approach Mexico City by the road beyond Lake Chalco, which Santa Anna had decided was impassable. The U.S. army moved within a few miles of the capital without a battle.

When Mexico City residents learned that Scott had bypassed the well-defended El Peñón to approach the city from the south, their hope

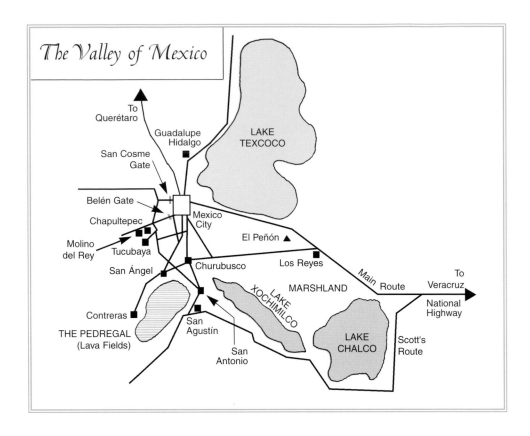

The Valley of Mexico

turned to fear. Many families left the city, says the *Apuntes:* "the doors and balconies were closed and the echo of the tramp of the soldiers could be heard in the distance."

U.S. troops had advanced to San Agustín, but there were two well-fortified areas guarding the capital from attack: San Antonio, a hacienda a mile to the north, and Churubusco, a fortified bridge and convent two miles farther. Santa Anna ordered most of his troops to protect these two strongholds. Soon 20,000 Mexican soldiers had formed a defensive line along the Churubusco River, stretching beyond the town of San Antonio to San Ángel. The line blocked the two main roads entering Mexico City from the south.

The Pedregal

Scott's army was concentrated in San Agustín, just south of San Antonio. He knew the strength of the Mexican position. Again, he looked for a way around the Mexican troops. But the way around was blocked by the Pedregal, a roughly circular, five-mile-wide barrier of hardened lava. Its surface was so sharp it could tear a horse's hooves to shreds. The area was cut with deep gullies and choked with thick brush and scrub. One U.S. volunteer called it "hell with the fires out." There seemed to be no way an army could cross the Pedregal.

Scott turned to one of his trusted engineers—Robert E. Lee. When Lee's scouting party got to the Pedregal's western edge, they met some

"The mere sight of the deserted city inspired sorrow and fear. It resembled beauty without life, the naked bones of a skull where lovely eyes had sparkled."

—Apuntes para la historia de la guerra

Mexican horsemen and foot soldiers. After a brief skirmish, the Mexicans retreated, leading Lee to a path through the lava fields.

The next morning, August 19, Lee set out with about 500 soldiers to improve the path he had scouted. Suddenly his men were fired on by General Gabriel Valencia's troops, part of the Army of the North. Santa Anna had ordered Valencia to stay in San Ángel. But the two were rivals. Valencia distrusted Santa Anna and disobeyed his orders. He advanced his 7,000 troops south to a position near the town of Contreras, thinking it would be a good defensive position. In fact, it was outside the Mexican defensive line.

The Battle of Contreras

Neither Scott nor Santa Anna had intended to fight at Contreras that day. But the skirmish between Valencia's troops and the U.S. advance party soon turned into a battle. When U.S. reinforcements arrived, the fighting intensified. Captain Kirby Smith described the afternoon: "The firing soon became tremendous. . . . The crash of small arms mingled with the incessant roar of artillery, the firing continuing for hours without our being able to perceive that our forces gained an inch."

Late in the day, a Mexican force led by Santa Anna arrived from the north. The U.S. troops were caught between two large Mexican armies. But it was getting dark, a storm was coming, and Santa Anna decided not to attack.

As night fell, Valencia began to celebrate what he thought would be certain victory the following morning. But his satisfaction turned to rage when a messenger brought the news that Santa Anna would not support him. Instead, Valencia was ordered to retreat. Santa Anna did not want to bail out his rival. "Valencia is an ambitious, insubordinate sot," Santa Anna was reported to have said. "He deserves to have his brains blown out, and I will not expose my men to the storm for him. Let him spike his guns, make the ammunition useless, and retreat."

Valencia stormed through the camp, cursing Santa Anna as a traitor. Again he refused to obey. He would not retreat. His soldiers were hungry, exhausted, and soaked with rain. The news made their hearts sink. "The impression . . . was frightful," the *Apuntes* reported. "Discontent spread

A RIVAL GENERAL

General Gabriel Valencia was considered the major threat to Santa Anna's leadership in Mexico. The two generals had long been hostile to each other. The British envoy who had carried Trist's proposal to Santa Anna considered Valencia one of several military leaders who were looking to rise through Mexico's fall. The envoy thought Valencia was foremost among Santa Anna's "many enemies who are raising a war cry merely for the purpose of bringing on his overthrow."

The Battle of Contreras.

rapidly. . . . This new message brought shudders to those who were already suffering so much. . . . All turned their eyes anxiously to the road at San Ángel, and, when convinced that no support would arrive, some soldiers abandoned the camp. From that time all were deeply disheartened."

For the outnumbered U.S. troops, the night seemed just as desperate. But Brigadier General Persifor Smith had a plan. U.S. scouts had found a ravine that led to a position behind Valencia's troops. He would launch his main attack from the rear, a surprise attack over a route that was considered impassable. But Smith needed reinforcements to conduct a diversion against Valencia's front.

By now, the rain was coming down in sheets. Jagged bolts of lightning lit the sky. Captain Robert E. Lee picked his way across the Pedregal, found Scott at San Agustín, and then led reinforcements back across the lava field. Scott later called this the greatest feat of physical and moral courage performed by anyone during the entire campaign.

During the night the U.S. troops moved to a position surrounding Valencia's forces. At daybreak on August 20, the U.S. soldiers launched an attack that seemed to come from everywhere at once. In seventeen brutal minutes, 700 Mexican soldiers were killed and 813 were taken prisoner, among them four generals.

"When it was over," a Mexican writer would say, "ambition and envy smiled with satisfaction." Valencia's elite Army of the North was no more. Valencia started toward San Ángel but changed his route when told that Santa Anna had ordered him shot. Most of his troops fled up the road to San Ángel and nearby Churubusco.

"The Americans turned our position around with the speed of lightning, aiming their artillery and our own at the scattering forces fleeing down the hills," the *Apuntes* noted. "That avalanche rolled, frightened and maddened, in the direction of Churubusco."

Defense at Churubusco

The bridge at the Churubusco River was a crucial defensive position, and Santa Anna had ordered his troops to hold it at all costs. Both the bridge and a nearby convent were heavily fortified.

U.S. troops paid dearly in attacking these positions. Lieutenant John James Peck wrote: "Here we fought . . . against hope. The thundering of the artillery was deafening, and the roaring of the musketry was awful, making the ground tremble. . . . Heads of columns were swept away like

"What has occurred is the result of . . . the stupidity committed by the disobedient Valencia . . . and the inconceivable conduct of Santa Anna when he stood by as a motionless spectator watching the ruination of his rival. It is not the first time, nor will it be the last, that the criminal desire of generals to surpass one another results in the loss of nations."
—Manuel Gómez Pedraza

chaff, and companies cut in pieces. . . . Lieutenant Halloway was cut down while talking with me, and I thought of the passage, 'one shall be taken and another left.' "

Using abandoned wagons as cover, U.S. troops spread out to attack the convent. A week before, most of the men inside had been stonecutters, shopkeepers, lawyers. Now they found themselves fighting a desperate, close-range battle. They defended their position "with great valor and patriotism," says military historian General Martinez Caraza, "though they were not regular soldiers." Even after their ammunition began to run out, they fought on. Lieutenant Colonel Juan Cano, the engineer who had been with Santa Anna at Cerro Gordo, was among the bloodied defenders of the convent. "After a fatal delay, Santa Anna sent munitions. They rushed to it. The bullets were for weapons of a larger caliber! They say those desperate men tried to load their rifles with stones."

Among the Mexican troops at the convent, none fought with more desperation than the two companies of soldiers from the San Patricio Battalion. They had fought well in other battles. John S. D. Eisenhower says, "The San Patricio Battalion of American deserters, who knew that they would be hanged if they were captured, really stiffened the backbone of the Mexican resistance . . . and brought about a more serious battle than Scott had any reason to expect. It was expensive. Scott couldn't spare a man in this campaign. He was now down to about 8,000 effective troops, alone, in a foreign country."

Finally, after nearly three hours of savage fighting, the U.S. forces overwhelmed the convent. Seventy-two San Patricios, including Captain John Riley, were taken prisoner.

From the dawn attack on Valencia's troops at Contreras to the bloody fighting at Churubusco, August 20 had been a long and costly day for both armies. The two unexpected battles had cost Scott 1,000 dead and wounded, twice the number he had lost at Cerro Gordo. Santa Anna had lost almost a third of his 10,000 men. Some 3,000 Mexican troops had been taken prisoner, including eight generals, one a former president of Mexico.

The Mexican army was broken and in retreat, but Scott decided to halt his troops at the threshold of victory. He gave up "the greatest advantage," says John S. D. Eisenhower. "When the enemy is running and disorganized, the pursuer does the most killing and makes the greatest advances. But, oddly enough, the ability of a commander to pursue is the rarest thing you'll find."

"It was with much difficulty that the American soldiers could be prevented from bayoneting these miscreants [captured U.S. deserters of the San Patricio Battalion] on the spot, so deep was their indignation against them."
—GEORGE KENDALL, EDITOR OF THE NEW ORLEANS *Picayune*

Deserters or Defenders?

Less than a month after the Battle of Churubusco, thirty of the captured U.S. deserters from the San Patricio Battalion watched the U.S. storming of the Castle of Chapultepec with ropes around their necks. It was the last image they would see. General Luis Garfias provides a Mexican perspective: "The North American army acted correctly from the point of view of military law. From the Mexican point of view we use another criterion. We see a group who, for religious and political ideas, join the Mexicans and are hung. . . . We understand that the decision of the North American army is correct. But Mexico remembers [the San Patricios] with respect because they were men who gave their lives for Mexico."

The hanging of the captives from the San Patricio Battalion.

Again Scott was conciliatory. He explained that he and Trist "had been admonished by the friends of peace . . . against precipitation—lest by wantonly driving away the government and others . . . we might scatter the elements of peace, excite a spirit of national desperation, and thus indefinitely postpone the hope of an accommodation. Willing to leave something to this Republic—of no immediate value to us—on which to rest her pride . . . I halted our victorious corps at the gates of the city."

A Temporary Peace

Scott had given Santa Anna and the Mexican government another chance to make peace. But few in the capital had any faith in their leaders. Lawyer and legislator José Fernando Ramírez wrote, "Everything, everything has been lost, except our honor. That was lost a long time ago. . . . Preparations to resist the enemy still continue. . . . But all this seems to me like so much sound and fury. . . . From my point of view it is all over. . . . What frightens me is the future. I cannot even guess what will become of us."

Santa Anna's situation seemed hopeless. The U.S. army was at the gates of Mexico City. Some of his own generals were plotting against him. General Valencia, who still had 1,400 troops, had announced that he would have Santa Anna beheaded. At a meeting of generals still loyal to him, Santa Anna offered his place to anyone who would take it. No one stepped forward.

U.S. troops hoped that Santa Anna's weakness would favor the peace efforts. Captain Kirby Smith observed that "Santa Anna may be compelled to make a peace to save himself from his own countrymen who will certainly kill him if deserted by his troops, as he surely will be if we fight again."

However desperate his situation, Santa Anna maintained the illusion of absolute control. On the day after the fall of Churubusco, he sent a message to Scott: "The Chief of the United Mexican States has resolved to listen to the proposals that Mr. Nicholas Trist . . . may have to make, provided they . . . safeguard the honor of the Mexican Republic." Scott agreed to an armistice. Santa Anna used the time to fortify the city, in violation of the armistice terms.

SCOTT'S GRUMBLING SUBORDINATES

WITH THE U.S. army at the gates of Mexico's capital, General Scott's junior officers were all in favor of going on. He was bitterly criticized by some of his subordinates for allowing an armistice.

"We . . . learned that a flag of truce had been received from Santa Anna preparatory to negotiations for peace," wrote Captain Kirby Smith, "and that we were not to enter the city. There was much muttering and grumbling throughout the army when it was known that these were to be the fruits of all our fatigue and fighting."

On August 27, Nicholas Trist met with former President José Joaquín de Herrera and three other Mexican commissioners to discuss terms of peace. For Herrera, it was an ironic assignment. He had favored peaceful negotiations at the beginning of the war. For that, he had been overthrown.

The negotiations began cordially but soon became deadlocked over the disputed territory between the Rio Grande and Nueces Rivers. Santa Anna would offer only minor concessions. David Pletcher notes the difficulty of trying to negotiate with Santa Anna, who was concerned about exposing himself to accusations of treason from his subordinate generals. "He was willing to negotiate but he was not willing to offer terms that the Americans could even consider."

Trist expressed disappointment that Santa Anna "could not bring himself to take the plunge into his Rubicon [that is, negotiate a peace treaty] . . . and allowed himself to be carried along by a flood of circumstance . . . staking all upon a battle everyone felt sure he would lose." Trist was forced to terminate the negotiations, and the temporary peace ended.

On September 6, Scott demanded that Santa Anna surrender by noon the next day. Santa Anna declined, writing back: "Yours will be the responsibility before the world, which readily will perceive whose is the part of moderation and justice." He issued a public proclamation: "Countrymen. The enemy . . . expected that I should subscribe to a treaty by which the territory of the republic would have been considerably reduced and the republic covered with shame. . . . The enemy lifts the sword to strike your front ranks; we too will raise it to punish the rancorous pride of the invader."

Once more, soldiers on both sides prepared for battle.

Slaughter at Molino del Rey

Scott had received reports that a foundry just outside Mexico City was turning church bells into cannons. The foundry was in the mill at a compound called Molino del Rey—a group of stone buildings less than

"Our troops fought like heroes and were mowed like grass."
—LIEUTENANT JOHN JAMES PECK

1,000 yards from the Castle of Chapultepec, two miles southwest of the city. Scott ordered its capture. On the morning of September 8, General William J. Worth's artillery began to fire, and the U.S. infantry moved in. Mexican soldiers opened fire from behind the stone walls, stunning U.S. soldiers by the intensity of the barrage from hidden artillery.

The battle raged for two hours. Half of Scott's army threw themselves against a much larger Mexican force. The defenders included the brigades of Generals Antonio Léon, Joaquín Rangel, Francisco Pérez, and Simeón Ramírez—a force estimated at 12,000 to 15,000 men by contemporary accounts but in fact probably under 10,000. Overwhelmed by the near-suicidal assault, the Mexican defenders were finally driven from their positions. But the U.S. victory had come at a terrible price, as K. Jack Bauer observes:

U.S. troops storming Molino del Rey.

> After two hours of fighting and the loss of 116 men killed, 665 wounded, and eighteen missing—one quarter of his command—Worth held the mill. Clarke's brigade, which took the heaviest casualties, lost half its officers and nearly a third of its men. The irony of the attack became clear when a search of the building produced only a few gun molds but no pieces. Scott ordered the buildings destroyed and abandoned. . . . By one o'clock in the afternoon the American troops were back in their old positions. All that Scott had to show for the casualties was 685 prisoners, fifty-three of them officers, and three additional trophy guns for the artillery park. Perhaps 2,000 Mexican soldiers had been killed or wounded. Colonel Hitchcock spoke the truth when he called it a pyrrhic victory.

The decision to fight had been based on faulty intelligence. Scott had lost a substantial portion of his army in a battle that may have been unnecessary. There had been heavy Mexican losses, but the U.S. troops now faced the capital city.

Attack on Chapultepec

Inside the gates of Mexico City, the residents suffered the agony of waiting, wondering when and where the final attack would come. "The church bells, which have been silent for many days, ring only to spread the alarm," said José Fernando Ramírez, "and this sound of alarm bells, which produces feverish excitement in the streets and public

General William J. Worth had been instrumental in the U.S. victory at Monterrey and had fought with distinction all along the march from Veracruz to Mexico City. But he was not optimistic about the assault on Chapultepec. Before the battle he was heard to predict, "We shall be defeated."

A Mexican soldier and a civilian.

squares, is followed by the silence of desolation, because half the inhabitants crowd the rooftops to see what their fate may be, while the other half lock themselves indoors or rush to prepare to defend themselves to the last."

The western approach to the capital was dominated by the imposing Castle of Chapultepec, which stood at the top of a rocky hill towering 200 feet above the surrounding plain. For the U.S. soldiers, these were the fabled "Halls of the Montezumas," ancient home to Aztec kings and Spanish conquistadores. In fact, the building had been a summer palace for the Spanish viceroys. Now it housed the Mexican military institute.

Scott could have sent his troops around the castle, but he did not want to leave such an important Mexican stronghold to his rear. On the night of September 11, he called a meeting of his top staff. All of the officers and engineers were in favor of bypassing Chapultepec except Lieutenant P. T. Beauregard and later Franklin Pierce, who switched his vote. Nonetheless, Scott decided to make an all-out attack on the castle. It was a risky strategy. Even Scott admitted, "I have my misgivings."

At sunrise on September 12, U.S. artillery began blasting at Chapultepec's walls and rooftops. The shelling lasted fourteen hours, but the Mexican troops held firm. The commanding officer, General Nicolás Bravo, led 832 defenders, including about eighty young cadets who were students at the military institute. Bravo sent an urgent request to Santa Anna for reinforcements but was refused.

General Luis Garfias can sympathize with Santa Anna's position: "What purpose would it serve to send additional troops? In the end, it would only result in a useless bloodshed. It wouldn't change the course of the operation. It wouldn't change the outcome of the war—the war [was] lost. At times I believe one has to make grave decisions . . . that will save the lives of some, but [send] others . . . to an almost certain death. That's the way it was here."

Inside the castle, the bombardment had taken its toll. The dead and wounded lay along the corridors. Without medicine or supplies, their fellow soldiers could do nothing for them.

A Brother's Life

Lieutenant Colonel Juan Cano had survived the battles at Cerro Gordo and Churubusco. Now he was at Chapultepec, fighting desperately to repair the battered fortifications. Cano knew that the next day would bring disaster. That night, he ordered his brother, Lorenzo, to slip out of the castle with a sealed message for their uncle. Cano told his brother that the message was a request for supplies.

When Lorenzo delivered it, he learned the truth.

Dear Uncle,
I am certain that tomorrow we will die, and because I don't want to give my elderly parents the unbearable bitterness of receiving news of the death of two sons at the same time, I beg you to keep my brother Lorenzo from returning to my side, as I am sure that he would die with me if he remained at Chapultepec.

Storming the Castle

On the morning of September 13, the U.S. infantry attacked. The lead storming party was called the Forlorn Hope, 500 soldiers who had volunteered to scale the walls of the castle carrying muskets and bayonets. First they had to fight their way through the woods at the base of the castle, carrying ladders, while the Mexican soldiers defended the approach with artillery and musket fire.

U.S. troops launched a diversionary attack on one of the causeways leading to the castle, while two divisions struggled toward the ditch and retaining wall at the base of the castle's walls. The defenders rained death on those below. But the men of the Forlorn Hope and the divisions that had joined them scrambled up their ladders and swept over the top of the parapets.

The fight for Chapultepec ended in bloody, hand-to-hand combat. A force of 400 Mexican sharpshooters, the San Blas Battalion, appeared as the battle was in progress. Courageously, they tried to fight their way to the top of the hill to join the defenders of the castle. Most were cut down in the attempt.

The U.S. troops prevailed and many of the Mexican soldiers fled. Among those who remained to fight were some student cadets. Most were teenagers, the youngest thirteen. According to legend, six chose to die rather than surrender: Agustín Melgar, Juan Escutia, Fernando Montes de Oca, Vicente Suárez, Francisco Márquez, and Juan de la Barrera. Juan Escutia is said to have wrapped himself in the flag of Mexico before leaping to his death from the castle wall. Known as the *Niños Héroes* (boy heroes), they are remembered every year in a national

Santa Anna's Last Comeback

AFTER LEAVING MEXICO CITY, Santa Anna continued to fight U.S. troops, leading an unsuccessful attempt to reconquer Puebla. Near there, at the town of Huamantla, Santa Anna and about 1,000 soldiers were met by 3,000 U.S. troops. The U.S. forces charged; Santa Anna counterattacked. Samuel Walker of the Texas Rangers was among those killed in this encounter, while the U.S. army was still trying to consolidate its control.

On October 11, Santa Anna received an order containing painful news. Acting President Peña y Peña ordered him court-martialed and stripped of his command. The bitter Santa Anna issued a farewell to his troops: "The president separates me from you and from the theater of war perhaps to sacrifice me to the vengeance of my enemies or to carry out a disgraceful peace, which I could never accept because my conscience finds it repulsive.

"Soldiers! Be true servants of your country: in spite of the misfortune we have faced, perhaps the

moment is not far off in which you will be led by another, more fortunate general and your luck will change."

Wanted by his own government, pursued by Texas Rangers, Santa Anna took refuge in southern Mexico before departing for Jamaica to live in exile.

Again, he found a way to return. In April 1853, Santa Anna became president of Mexico again, his last triumph in Mexican politics. His presidency was, ironically, strengthened by an infusion of money from the United States, when he sold the southern portions of New Mexico and Arizona for $10 million in the Gadsden Purchase of 1853.

In an autobiography written near the end of his life, Santa Anna asked his countrymen to honor his memory. "Mexicans!" he wrote. "I am a man, and I have defects, but I have never sinned against my country. . . . I have earnestly longed for everything great and glorious for Mexico, and to obtain it I have not spared my own blood. You know this and will do me justice."

Antonio López de Santa Anna in 1848.

patriotic ceremony. There is no historical evidence of how the cadets died, but the six remain a powerful symbol of honor and courage in defense of the nation.

By 9:30 A.M., the battle was over. The U.S. flag was raised over the castle. Now Scott's army battled its way up the heavily defended causeways toward the Gates of San Cosme and Belén. The Mexican soldiers fought a desperate battle, knowing that behind them were their homes and families. But the defenders could not hold their positions. The U.S. soldiers broke through, entering the city, and the fighting spread down its streets, from inside buildings to rooftops.

As night fell, the shooting stopped. Scott's forces had been further reduced. Only 6,000 of his hungry, exhausted men were still able to fight. Each side wondered how it would end.

Mexico Surrenders

The night of September 13, Santa Anna, his generals, and his staff met with political leaders in La Ciudadela, the city's military barracks. Most believed that the defense of Mexico City had become a lost cause. Santa Anna decided to renounce his presidency and withdraw from the city. After a period of confusion, Manuel de la Peña y Peña, a fifty-eight-year-old Supreme Court justice and former foreign minister, was named acting president.

At four o'clock in the morning on September 14, a delegation of city leaders went to Scott's headquarters and surrendered the capital. A few hours later, the U.S. flag waved over the National Palace. A military band played "Yankee Doodle." Winfield Scott, dressed in full uniform and accompanied by Nicholas Trist and an honor guard, rode into the main plaza of Mexico City. The Duke of Wellington commented: "His campaign is unsurpassed in military annals. He is the greatest living soldier."

Manuel de la Peña y Peña.

Winfield Scott.

CABALLEROS AT A PLAZA FIESTA, 1901.

Epilogue

LEGACY

"Los Estados-Unidos mexicanos y los Estados-Unidos de América, animados de un sincero deseo de poner término a las calamidades de la guerra que desgraciadamente existe entre ambas Repúblicas y de establecer sobre bases sólidas relaciónes de paz y buena amistad . . . [han] firmado el siguiente Tratado de Paz, Amistad, Límites y Arreglo."

"The United States of America and the United Mexican States, animated by a sincere desire to put an end to the calamities of the war which unhappily exists between the two Republics, and to establish upon a solid basis relations of peace and friendship . . . [have] signed the following Treaty of Peace, Friendship, Limits, and Settlement."
—*Treaty of Guadalupe Hidalgo, 1848*

GENERAL SCOTT REVELLING IN THE HALLS OF THE MONTEZUMAS.

Despite his military success, Winfield Scott was caricatured in U.S. anti-war broadsides as "revelling in the halls of the Montezumas." President Polk, too, denounced Scott's "vanity and tyrannical temper" and informed Scott that a military court of inquiry would be held to consider charges that Scott had bribed Santa Anna during the Puebla negotiations.

W HILE THE U.S. ARMY occupied Mexico City, the Mexican government moved to the town of Querétaro, 170 miles northwest of the capital. There, Acting President Manuel de la Peña y Peña attempted to form a coalition that could hold the war-torn country together.

Nicholas Trist hoped that the moderate Peña y Peña would be able to persuade the Mexican Congress to accept a treaty to end the war. But before negotiations could begin, Trist received stunning news. In a letter dated October 6, Polk's secretary of state, James Buchanan, wrote: "The President, believing that your continued presence with the army can be productive of no good, but may do much harm by encouraging the delusive hopes and false impressions of the Mexicans, has directed me to recall you from your mission. . . . He has determined not to make another offer to treat with the Mexican government. . . . They must now sue for peace."

Polk's Instructions

Six weeks before Trist's dismissal, reports had reached President Polk of the peace negotiations that had taken place after the Battle of Churubusco, during the brief armistice before U.S. troops made their final assault on Mexico City.

Polk had sent Trist to Mexico to present and enforce an ultimatum. He was furious when he learned that Trist had discussed setting the Texas border at the Nueces River (even though Trist had quickly realized his error and withdrawn the offer). There must be no talk of any but a Rio Grande border to legitimize Polk's claim that U.S. blood had been spilled on U.S. soil.

Polk's decision to recall Trist and insist that the Mexicans send an emissary of their own was "a very dangerous sort of maneuver," says David Pletcher. It put the occupying army in a difficult position. Without a negotiated peace, General Scott had two alternatives: He could keep his troops where they were, risking continued raids by the Mexicans on the

U.S. supply line, or he could try to expand the occupied area, risking defeat at the hands of the Mexicans.

In October the U.S. secretary of war sent Scott instructions to expand his occupation. He was to "carry on further aggressive operations; to achieve new conquests; to disperse the remaining army of the enemy." Although Scott did not move U.S. forces far from the capital, he did announce his intention to occupy Zacatecas and San Luis Potosí as soon as more U.S. troops were sent.

Scott's warning put additional pressure on the Mexican peace commission. Because no armistice was in effect, the threat of further conquest by U.S. troops was significant. "It was necessary for the Mexicans to negotiate, because they were afraid of losing all of their territory or even more territory than the United States was occupying in the north," says Jesús Velasco-Márquez. In Mexico City, newspapers reprinted U.S. editorials calling for the acquisition of all of Mexico. A New York *Herald* article, for example, said, "A force must be poured into the country sufficiently powerful to overawe resistance. . . . It is a glorious prospect, this annexation of all Mexico."

Trist's Decision to Stay

Would the U.S. government now demand more Mexican territory than Trist's original offer (and Polk's original design) had included? Fearing that it would, Scott encouraged Trist to remain in Mexico and negotiate with the treaty commission. Peña y Peña and the appointees to the treaty commission also wanted Trist to stay. The Mexican president wrote to one treaty commissioner that, if Trist could not "conclude a treaty with us, assuming his powers have been revoked," then he should at least be able to "require his government to continue the negotiations begun in due season by its own agent."

A group of moderates led by Peña y Peña was willing to negotiate on the terms the United States had proposed a few months before. Both they and Trist were afraid that an overthrow of Peña y Peña's government would result in further disruption of Mexican society, and perhaps even a resumption of hostilities, since many factions opposed the treaty process.

Knowing that peace was hanging by the fragile thread of Peña y Peña's leadership, Trist chose to disobey his own president. Instead of returning to the United States, he wrote to Polk that if the present "opportunity be not seized at once, all chance of making a treaty at all will be

"Poor people! Unfortunate nation, which always loses and never wins!" Between 1846 and 1851, many newspapers in Mexico City printed satirical commentaries on the war and the peace that followed: images of a ravaged Mexico, poems, songs, "deathbed" confessions about Mexican military failures, laments of "the great depression" that followed the war, and descriptions of the "degradation" of the occupying army, with its drunken soldiers, the rowdy red-faced volunteers, turning the capital "into a camp of savages." The image is from Irene Vázquez Valle's Sátira de un año infausto *(Satire of an Ill-fated Year).*

THE MEXICAN GOVERNORS MEET

"FROM THE MEXICAN perspective," says Miguel Soto, "with the occupation of Mexico City, you have a lack of authority, a division at the highest level. Divisions within the government are deeper and more dangerous than before, and the nation's defense, the army, is dispersed."

The largest portion of the Mexican army was in Querétaro, where political leaders from the various Mexican states were attempting to put together a government. According to a November meeting of the Mexican governors, this main body of the army now consisted of no more than 3,000 men. The governors heard reports that the entire Mexican army numbered about 8,000 men, scattered around the nation; that the U.S. army had captured or destroyed virtually all the Mexican artillery and ammunition; and that the occupying forces numbered more than 40,000 men, with more than 30,000 under Scott's direct command. This news did not prompt the governors to support the foundering central government.

By occupying several major cities, the United States had gained control of a number of Mexican customhouses, a key source of Mexican revenue. The need for a treaty was clear.

lost . . . probably forever." He planned to conduct peace talks while the letter was on its way to Washington, gambling that Polk and the Congress would approve the treaty he negotiated.

"There are few examples in history of how a single person can so greatly affect the destinies of so many people, or of two countries," notes Miguel Soto. "The negotiating committees were there, but the war could have continued, and the consequences could have been very different" had Trist obeyed Polk's directive.

Negotiating the Treaty

By the third week of January, Trist and three Mexican peace commissioners had agreed on most of the terms of the treaty. Mexico paid dearly for this treaty, says Josefina Zoraida Vázquez. Trist proved a tough negotiator.

As a condition for opening talks, the Mexican commissioners had been forced to accept the loss of Texas, with its border drawn at the Rio Grande. During the negotiations, the Mexicans fought for and lost the right to keep New Mexico. They wanted to keep southern California, which had a large Mexican population, and San Diego Bay with its excellent harbor, but the new border was drawn south of the port. Trist ceded only one point: Baja California was left in Mexican possession, along with a land bridge connecting it to the rest of Mexico.

The treaty commissioners were more successful in their careful provisions for the Mexicans who were left on the other side of the redrawn border. They demanded assurances that the land ceded to the United

Cartoon showing Trist asking Mexico for peace.

States be organized into U.S. states or territories quickly and that existing religious property and land grants be respected.

To draw boundary lines for Mexico's northwestern frontier, which had never been precisely mapped, the treaty commission used the 1847 Disturnell map, supplemented by a general description of the territory's edge, which would follow the Rio Grande, Gila, and Colorado Rivers before extending due west to the Pacific Ocean.

In exchange for the ceded territories, the long-standing claims for damages that the United States had pressed against Mexico were to be paid by the United States. The Mexican negotiators also wanted the United States to pay $30 million, but they finally agreed to accept $15 million "in consideration of the extension acquired by the boundaries of the United States." They asked that the treaty state that the government was not selling the land, that California and New Mexico had been taken by conquest, and that the money was indemnification.

On February 2, 1848, Nicholas Trist and the Mexican commissioners met in the town of Guadalupe Hidalgo near the sacred Basilica of the Virgin of Guadalupe. There, they signed the document that became known as the Treaty of Guadalupe Hidalgo.

"It was in the war, and not in the treaty, that the territory that now remains in the possession of the enemy was lost."

—DON BERNARDO COUTO,
ONE OF MEXICO'S
TREATY COMMISSIONERS

Ratifying the Treaty

When the treaty arrived in Washington on February 19, President Polk was still angry with Nicholas Trist (who, he wrote, had "proved himself to be an impudent and unqualified scoundrel"). But the document offered an end to the war on terms Polk could accept. Polk could say that the United States had gotten what it wanted: Mexico had ceded the land he had tried to purchase at the beginning of the war. He decided to present Trist's treaty to Congress with no amendments.

Although the Democrats had a majority in the 1847 Senate, the treaty could not be approved without the cooperation of several factions. There was the usual slavery debate, but one voice was missing: John Quincy Adams, the Whig who had influenced so many congressional votes on Texas and the war, had suffered a stroke just before the treaty was to be introduced. While the first arguments were made, he lay in a coma; a few days later, he died.

The war had produced several extremist groups in the Senate. Some politicians felt that the United States ought to take more land from Mexico. Some U.S. citizens wanted to annex the entire country. Polk did not want the "burden of responsibility" for such an action, says David Pletcher, preferring to shift it to the Senate.

Other groups did not want to accept any land at all. Daniel Webster maintained that this was the moral point of view. The extreme anti-slavery faction spoke out against acquiring any territory that might "strengthen the . . . pro-slavery point of view."

Still other politicians were opposed to accepting Mexicans as free citizens of the United States. Senator John C. Calhoun from South Carolina spoke for many: "We have never dreamt of incorporating into our Union any but the Caucasian race—the free white race. . . . The greatest misfortunes of Spanish America are to be traced to the fatal error of placing these coloured races on an equality with the white race."

The debate was intense, with extremists combined against the treaty supporters. Although many questions were raised by the acquisition of so large a territory, much of the debate centered not on the effects but on the causes of the war and seemed aimed at the next year's presidential election. In the end, however, the vote was not close: on March 10, 1848, the Senate approved the treaty 38–14.

In Querétaro, President Peña y Peña also was pressured by extremist factions. The debate over the treaty in the Mexican Congress was

SHAME

MANY YEARS AFTER the treaty ending the war was signed, Nicholas Trist's wife, Virginia, wrote down what her husband had said happened that day: "Just as they were about to sign the treaty, one of the Mexicans, Don Bernardo Couto, remarked to him: 'This must be a proud moment for you—no less proud for you than it is humiliating for us.'

"To this Mr. Trist replied, 'We are making peace, let that be our only thought.' But—said he to us in relating it—'Could those Mexicans have seen into my heart at that moment, they would have known that my feeling of shame as an American was far stronger than theirs could be.'"

inflamed by rage and indignation. Many delegates urged the country to fight on, preferring heroic tragedy to dishonorable submission. There was "profound frustration among the Mexican people" at the consequences of the war, says Mexican General Luis Garfias. Every Mexican had been touched by the killing, and "after so much blood had been shed . . . all that was left to show [for it] was the loss of half of Mexico's territory."

At the beginning of the war, Manuel de la Peña y Peña had advocated a peaceful resolution of the issues between the United States and Mexico. Now he had to preside over the dismemberment of his nation. He called it his journey to the grave. Somberly, he urged his fellow Mexicans to accept the treaty:

> The people have an incontestable right not to have to suffer more. . . . It would be a great inhumanity to put them through all the horrors of a renewed and bloody battle, especially after the many years of civil war. . . . The territories have not been given up for the sum of $15 million but to recover our ports and invaded cities, to bring order to a people who have not ceased to suffer for thirty-seven years.
>
> Let us do the right thing, gentlemen. Let us strip off the veil that has prevented us from seeing the reality of things. Let us make a mighty effort, so that our children will not curse our memory.

On May 30, 1848, the Mexican Congress approved the treaty. The war was officially over. Says Josefina Zoraida Vázquez: "It was the end of a dream, the end finally of the greatness of New Spain. . . . Now all was history."

The countersigned Treaty of Guadalupe Hidalgo arrived back in Washington on the Fourth of July. War veterans led a grand victory parade, and the cornerstone was laid for the Washington Monument. After a long day of celebration, President Polk returned to the White House. In his *Diary,* he recorded, "I immediately saw the Secretary of State and caused a proclamation to be prepared announcing officially the definitive conclusion of peace with Mexico. At about 11 o'clock at night I signed the proclamation. I desired to sign it on the anniversary of Independence."

Polk's Gains and Losses

James K. Polk had finally fulfilled the goals he had set early in his presidency. He had settled the Oregon question, he had won California, and he had resolved the boundary dispute over Texas. And yet, says David

"The truth is that a fertile and beautiful part of our territory is being ceded. . . . I have no wish to obscure the truth, much less to deny the pain I feel at the separation from the Mexicans of California and New Mexico."
—MANUEL DE LA PEÑA Y PEÑA

Commodore Matthew Perry served in the Gulf and honed his diplomatic and naval skills during the U.S.–Mexican War. In 1853, he was sent to Japan on a mission to establish trade relations with that previously closed society. He took a copy of the history of the war with him. His success realized President Polk's vision of the United States as a Pacific Rim—and important world—power. The navy continued to grow in importance throughout the century and was instrumental in the acquisition of additional formerly Spanish territories, Cuba, the Philippines, and Puerto Rico.

Pletcher, "assessing Polk is difficult. . . . Over the years his reputation has risen and fallen. He's been called a very ordinary, mediocre president. He's been called a butcher. He's also been called one of the great presidents, perhaps the greatest—the most positive—president between Jackson and Lincoln." Josefina Zoraida Vázquez sees Polk as "an absolute expansionist. With him, there was no other possibility—war was inevitable. He was not a pleasant person, but he did convert the United States into a continental power." There is no doubt, says Pletcher, that Polk "was a winner of great prizes. He won great stakes. But he took great gambles to win." Polk's victory, says Pletcher, can be described as "the rewards of rashness."

After the treaty had already been approved by the U.S. Congress, Polk proposed to send new troops to Mexico to intervene in a civil war in Yucatán. Congress refused to support him.

Polk served only one term as president. Just as he had feared, the war brought a Whig to the presidency: Zachary Taylor, Old Rough and Ready, the victor of Monterrey and Buena Vista. James K. Polk's last official duty was a bitter one: attending the inauguration of his rival. Exhausted and in poor health, he retired to Tennessee. Within three months he was dead.

Aftermath of the War

The U.S.–Mexican War, and the transfer of territory that resulted from it, had a lasting impact. It caused shifts in power in both countries. In Mexico, Santa Anna was replaced by moderate figures who tried to forge a new government. In the United States, presidential power transferred from the Democrats to the Whigs, as war hero Zachary Taylor replaced departing President James Polk.

Internal conflicts increased in both nations in the next few decades. In Mexico, "criollo optimism" suffered a devastating collapse, and society was thrown into demoralization and turmoil. Several indigenous peasant uprisings occurred, as the nation's social system underwent a fundamental restructuring. Liberals and conservatives struggled for power before a new "republicanism" began to take shape. With new leaders, a slow path to regeneration and reform was begun, along with a reduction in the roles of the church and the military.

In the United States, regional north/south disputes, which the war had helped bring to the surface, continued to grow. The addition of new

TREATY OF GUADALUPE HIDALGO, 1848

ARTICLE V: The boundary line between the two Republics shall commence in the Gulf of Mexico, three leagues from the land, opposite the mouth of the Río Grande, otherwise called Río Bravo del Norte. . . . [The Treaty of December 30, 1853, redefined the border.]

Article VIII: Mexicans now established in territories previously belonging to Mexico, and which remain for the future within the limits of the United States, as defined by the present treaty, shall be free to continue where they now reside, or to remove at any time to the Mexican Republic. . . . Those who shall prefer to remain . . . may either retain the title and rights of Mexican citizens, or acquire those of citizens of the United States. . . . In the said territories, property of every kind, now belonging to

The treaty document.

Mexicans not established there, shall be inviolably respected. . . .

Article XI: Considering that a great part of the territories, which, by the present treaty, are to be comprehended for the future within the limits of the United States, is now occupied by savage tribes, who will hereafter be under the exclusive control of the Government of the United States, and whose incursions within the territory of Mexico would be prejudicial in the extreme, it is solemnly agreed that all such incursions shall be forcibly restrained by the Government of the United States . . . [and] when they cannot be prevented, they shall be punished. . . .

Article XII: . . . the Government of the United States engages to pay to that of the Mexican Republic the sum of fifteen millions of dollars. . . .

---

states brought fresh fuel to the slavery debate that eventually ignited the Civil War. And this was not the only racial conflict. Westward migration and resulting land disputes increased racial and ethnic conflicts with the Native American and Hispanic populations.

The political and social changes following the war were intensified by its economic effects. The conflict bankrupted Mexico while it created a boom in war industries in the United States. At the same time, Mexico lost and the United States gained Pacific Rim trade opportunities.

This increase in its international stature reinforced a U.S. self-image as the uplifter of "lesser" peoples and confirmed in the public mind the notion of Manifest Destiny. It helped to entrench racist and condescending attitudes toward Latin America and nonwhite peoples. For Latin Americans, the war established an image of the United States as "El Coloso del Norte"—the colossus of the north.

"There shall be firm and universal peace between the United States of America and the Mexican Republic. . . ."

—TREATY OF GUADALUPE HIDALGO, ARTICLE I

POLITICAL GAINS OF THE U.S. MILITARY

Lthough the Democratic Party's enthusiasm for expansion had built support for the war, it was the Whigs—especially the war's generals—who gained political advantage from it.

THE GENERALS

While camped in northern Mexico, General Zachary Taylor had begun to picture himself in the White House. In the first presidential election held after the war, this political unknown was easily nominated and elected. Taylor could be all things to all people: not only was he popular for his military successes, but he was also a Whig slaveholder, and thus likely to pick up votes among southerners. Unfortunately, the military skill that had led to the acquisition of so much new territory did not prepare him for the difficulties of administering the region. The admission of California and New Mexico to the Union provoked a series of debates (continuing the rancorous disputes of the war years). Taylor was ill-equipped to mediate the conflicts. He took sick on July 4, 1850, and died of cholera a few days later.

Fellow Whig General Winfield Scott had predicted Taylor's political success and his own failure to win popular support. Four years after losing his first bid for the presidential nomination to

President Taylor and his cabinet.

A campaign poster: Scott vs. Taylor.

Taylor, Scott was selected as the Whig candidate. But he lost to Franklin Pierce, who had served under him in the campaign to take Mexico City.

The war significantly promoted the rise of a professional military in the United States. The Mexican conflict had been a proving ground for West Point–style training, technology, and technique. It gave combat experience to the military leaders of the coming Civil War. After the U.S.–Mexican War, in which engineers and professional officers had served with distinction, there was little talk of an all-volunteer army. A professional military, with formal training in military strategy and technology suited the ambitious U.S. expansionist vision and became an established component of the nation's new role as a continental power.

THE NEXT U.S. CONFLICT

The U.S.–Mexican War was the defining experience for a generation whose young men were shaped by the decision to fight in Mexico. It was also a prelude to the great U.S. internal conflict, the Civil War, less than fifteen years later. Debates about slavery took on a new urgency with the U.S.–Mexican War, and the acquisition of new territory at the war's end complicated and intensified the arguments. By 1861, the officers who had fought side by side

The Mexican conflict had been a proving ground for West Point–style training, technology, and technique.

in Mexico were fighting against each other as generals on the bloody battlefields of the War between the States. Besides Grant, those who fought on the Union side included George McClellan, George Meade, and John Frémont; besides Lee, those who fought for the Confederacy included Thomas "Stonewall" Jackson, Gideon Pillow, and Albert Sidney Johnston.

During the U.S.–Mexican War, the techniques and technologies of warfare were changing. Fighting with lance, saber, and smoothbore musket was on its way out.

Ulysses S. Grant, who had gone to Texas as a young soldier with Zachary Taylor, served as President Lincoln's general-in-chief in the Civil War and then went on to become president.

With more artillery and the new long-range rifled musket, an army could cut down lines of men in massive numbers. The traditional battlefield charge had met its match, and the slaughter of young men in the U.S. Civil War reached staggering levels.

Seeing the bitter warfare that raged between nations and within the United States in the middle of the nineteenth century, some Native Americans believed that an evil spirit had enveloped the continent. They attributed it to frontier cruelty by all sides.

When sectional differences and the slavery issue tore the U.S. Union apart, it was U.S. homes, countryside, and cities that were destroyed.

Mexico's War of Reform

THE U.S.-MEXICAN WAR intensified internal conflicts that had divided Mexican society for years, but the civil war that followed, known as the War of Reform, made some crucial progress toward resolving opposing ideologies.

POSTWAR PRESIDENTS

Immediately after the war, Mexico was governed by many of the same leaders who had been prominent in the war years. José Joaquín de Herrera had been forced from the presidency in 1845 by Mariano Paredes just before hostilities erupted between Mexico and the United States. During the war, General Herrera had served in Santa Anna's army, commanding the troops at El Peñón. After ratification of the Treaty of Guadalupe Hidalgo, Herrera became Mexico's first elected president. He governed from a city outside the capital while Mexico waited for the occupying U.S. troops to leave. Herrera held office until 1851. Mariano Arista, the general of the Army of the North who had suffered the initial defeat by U.S. troops at Matamoros, was president from 1851 until January 1853. Both Herrera and Arista made valiant efforts to restore social and economic order to Mexican postwar society.

In April 1853 Antonio López de Santa Anna was given one more chance to govern the country. The next year, recounts Mexican writer Carlos Fuentes, "Santa Anna, who now called himself 'His Most Serene Highness,'... was overthrown by a reaction of disgust and national dignity, led by the Liberal Party." But Santa Anna's last presidency was also the last gasp of the era of *Santanismo,* an era of excess marked by frequent power shifts among generals and criollos.

José Joaquín de Herrera.

REEVALUATION

The devastation of the U.S.–Mexican War, the loss of so much life and land, the economic losses caused by destruction of property and by U.S. occupation of Mexican customhouses caused Mexican political thinkers to examine and analyze what had gone wrong. Along with hand-wringing about the failure of Mexican society to unite against a common enemy, they offered new insight into possible solutions. After winning independence from Spain, says Octavio Paz, Mexico had "changed its laws, not its social, economic, and cultural realities." After the cataclysm of seeing its capital occupied by a foreign power, Mexico slowly began to adjust those realities. By 1857, a new constitution greatly weakened the political power of the Catholic Church, and election of new leadership expanded the liberal influence of less-advantaged portions of society.

THE GREAT REFORMER

Benito Juárez oversaw many of these reforms. Essayist and novelist Carlos Fuentes describes this inspired reformer:

> An austere lawyer of Zapotec Indian stock, Juárez lived as a shepherd, illiterate and ignorant of the Spanish language, until he was twelve years old, when he joined his sister in the home of a parish priest in the city of Oaxaca. It was there that he learned to read and write Spanish. His mind was acute and his ambition great. . . .
>
> Juárez's first line of business, undertaken while he was minister of justice, was separating church and state. He confiscated the vast, unproductive wealth of the church and set it to circulate. He deprived the military and the aristocracy of their special courts of justice. He established civil laws and subjected all citizens to their rule. Known as the Reform Laws, these could not be countenanced by the

Santa Anna's last presidency was also the last gasp of the era of Santanismo, an era of excess marked by frequent power shifts among generals and criollos.

Conservative Party. Juárez and the Liberals had opted for a clear solution: subject the church and the army to the control of the national state, and then subject everyone, including the state, to the control of law. . . .

With Mexican conservatives in revolt against Juárez's reforms, Napoleon III of France attempted to establish an empire in Mexico. He was ultimately defeated by Juárez in 1867 and Mexican Emperor Maximilian was executed. It was the end of the Mexican flirtation with European powers. Juárez then discharged two-thirds of the army, decreasing military dominance. He formed a new civilian government, which launched a careful social program for national development. With the participation of Mexican intellectuals, new policies and a new national identity began to emerge.

Carlos Fuentes sees Benito Juárez as "the very embodiment of Indian fatality, Roman legality, and Spanish stoicism." Juárez possessed a personal integrity that inspired a new generation of Mexican presidents.

DICTATORSHIP

The pendulum swung back later in the century, when the more privileged criollo government returned, led by Porfirio Díaz, a military dictator who had served in the National Guard during the U.S.–Mexican War. In the 1960s Octavio Paz described the new form taken by the dictatorship:

Order was re-established, but at the expense of democracy. In the name of liberal ideology and the positivism of [Auguste] Comte and [Herbert] Spencer, a military dictatorship was imposed which lasted more than thirty years. It was a period of peace and appreciable material development—also of increasing penetration by foreign capital, especially from England and the United States. The Mexican Revolution of 1910 set itself to change direction. It succeeded only in part: Mexican democracy is not yet a reality, and the great advances achieved in certain quarters have been nullified or are in danger because of excessive political centralization, excessive population, and the actions of the economic monopolies, among them those from the United States.

A group of puros *(liberals) who opposed ending the war on unfavorable terms and later rose to political power. L to R back row: Miguel Lerdo de Tejada, Ignacio Ramírez, Guillermo Prieto, José María Lacunza, Vicente Riva Palacio, Manuel Romero Rubio; L to R front: Ignacio Mariscal, Benito Juárez, Matías Romero, and Carlos Pacheco.*

New U.S. Territories

The Gold Rush to California

Gold was discovered near Sutter's Fort in California on January 24, 1848. Within weeks of the signing of the Treaty of Guadalupe Hidalgo, news of the gold had reached the East. It precipitated furious development and a rush of gold seekers—including thousands of Mexicans, especially from Sonora and Chihuahua. They flocked to territory that had been largely unsettled only a few years before. By some estimates, the population of California increased from 15,000 to 260,000 in only four years.

The first California miners used methods that had been introduced by the Spanish in sixteenth-century Mexico. After 1852, however, Mexican miners were mainly excluded from northern California mines. The first state constitution established California as a bilingual state, but by 1878 that was no longer in effect. The gold rush shifted the wealth and power of the state to a new population of Anglos in northern California.

The "forty-niners" were the advance guard of U.S. migration across the continent to California. As ever greater numbers moved into the West, the development of agricultural and industrial wealth confirmed U.S. belief in its Manifest Destiny to occupy the continent from Atlantic to Pacific. As President Polk had hoped, the threat of French and British empire building in the North American continent faded.

Mapping the Land

After the war, teams of surveyors quickly set out to explore the lands acquired by the United States. John Charles Frémont returned to his role as "Pathfinder." He set out in the fall of 1848, this time to survey a transcontinental railroad route. Frémont made a foolhardy winter trip through the southern Rocky and San Juan Mountains. Some of his party, lost in the snow, were said to have resorted to cannibalism for survival.

The Wheeler survey party used flat-bottomed boats to carry heavy photographic equipment up the Colorado River to the Grand Canyon, bringing back the first photos of the area (Black Canyon is pictured here).

*The first state constitution established California as a bilingual state,
but by 1878 that was no longer in effect.*

*In 1846 the United States had 5,000 miles of railway in operation. The idea of a transcontinental railroad—from Lake Michigan to the
Columbia River—had been proposed even before the war. Survey parties in the 1850s set out to determine the best route to the coast.
Their findings inspired the Gadsden Purchase. It acquired a route that Missouri Senator Thomas Hart Benton described as
"so utterly desolate, desert, and God-forsaken that Kit Carson says a wolf could not make its living on it." After the Civil War,
four transcontinental railroad lines, along northern, central, and southern routes, were built across the country.*

In 1857, the Warren party produced the first accurate map of the new U.S. territory west of the Mississippi. The Emory expedition mapped the new borderlands. In the 1870s, the Wheeler party surveyed much of the Southwest, traveling through Nevada, across Death Valley, and to the Grand Canyon to prepare the "United States Geographical Surveys West of the One Hundredth Meridian." Wheeler hoped to advance his army career by his surveys, but many other survey parties had the same goal. By 1878, the area had been thoroughly explored, and the teams of adventurers were replaced by a governmental agency, the U.S. Geological Survey.

BORDERLAND RESIDENTS

As U.S. citizens moved into former Mexican provinces, they encountered the peoples and cultures already in place: Native Americans and Hispanics who had settled in New Mexico and California.

DEVASTATION OF THE NATIVE INHABITANTS

This encounter marked a profound change for the inhabitants, notes R. David Edmunds:

Mexico's control [of these territories] had not been very pervasive. Mexico's political hegemony over the region had been limited by the country's limited resources, and by the Mexican government's focus upon other issues. Moreover, during Mexico's occupation of the region there had been little actual Mexican immigration into the region. Native American people in modern Arizona, New Mexico, and the interior of California had remained relatively untouched by Mexican political control. . . .

With the coming of the Americans and their government, all this changed. First, the region was overrun by miners seeking gold, silver, and other minerals. Unlike the Mexican population, the miners traveled into every corner of the Southwest, and they were very disruptive to the Native American population. Almost all miners wanted to "get rich quick" and, unlike farmers, really had no intention of "settling down" in the region and developing any ties with the people who lived there. Mining camps were notorious for their racism, exploitation of women, and lawlessness, and most of the "Indian Wars" in the West following 1850 resulted from clashes between miners and Native Americans. Soon innocent civilians on both sides had become victims.

Once the wars started, the American military was forced to intervene, and unlike the forces at the disposal of the Mexican government, the American troops were more numerous, better equipped, and a more formidable opponent. Consequently, the transfer of the Southwest to the United States was the death knell for Native American political autonomy in the region. Wars were conducted against the Navajos, Comanches, Kiowas, Apaches, and others. The Native American population in California dropped from about 90,000 in 1850 (as the Gold Rush was starting), to around 35,000 in 1860, and by 1890 it was 18,000. Other regions did not suffer such precipitous declines, but Native American populations throughout the Southwest did fall considerably. Native Americans were confined to reservations, and the federal government, supported by religious and benevolent organizations, launched ill-advised programs designed to eradicate Native American cultures.

Last Indian choir at the Mission San Buenaventura.

"[It] was the death knell for Native American political autonomy in the region. Wars were conducted against the Navajos, Comanches, Kiowas, Apaches, and others."

"Aboriginal Life Among the Navajoe Indians Near Old Fort Defiance, N.M."
This photograph was taken during the 1873 Wheeler Survey of the American Southwest.

Under the Treaty of Guadalupe Hidalgo, Hispanic borderland residents could choose to stay and retain their Mexican citizenship, become U.S. citizens, or they could return to Mexico. Although "Mexico was very interested in repatriating them," says David J. Weber, "very few left. This was, after all, their country, their *patria chica*." Despite the treaty's guarantee of all of the rights of citizens, says Weber, "many of them found that they were second-class citizens, that the treaty of Guadalupe Hidalgo was not enforced well, that they lost their lands, that in the courts they didn't receive an equal shake."

Chicana poet Gloria Anzaldúa concurs. In *Borderlands/La Frontera*, she writes: "The land established by the treaty as belonging to Mexicans was soon swindled away from its owners. The treaty was never honored and restitution, to this day, has never been made."

The "Conquered Generation"

Mario T. García calls the Mexican residents of the annexed lands the "Conquered Generation" in Hispanic history. Refuting the popular notion that Mexicans are "one of the last groups of immigrants to the United States," he notes that these first people were residents who were acquired by treaty. Mexicans living in the conquered territories in 1848 numbered perhaps 75,000.

Creation of the Chicano

Chicanos have created a vibrant border culture that draws strength from both the United States and Mexico. "One thing Chicanos have contributed to humanity," says Alfred Arteaga, "is a sense of border. . . . My poems are interlingual poems . . . playing in the linguistic terrain characteristic of the zones of international frontiers."

In his essay "The Motherland," José Antonio Burciaga writes:

Mexico, land that my parents left so long long ago. Their memory lingers in Agustín Lara songs—*Farolito, Solamente Una Vez, Noche de Ronda*—and in the familiar sounds of the Spanish language.

I overhear conversations. I'm home, I'm not a stranger though I was not born in Mexico. But I'm no longer Mexican . . . I think . . . I pause with indecision. I don't know. Mexico has grabbed me back—*Mexico lindo y querido*—"My beautiful and beloved Mexico"; but so had my good ole U. S. of A.

On a radio interview I am asked, "Pardon the question, but do you write as a Mexicano, or . . . what?" Eager for the question that I have anticipated for years, I answer, "I write as a Mexicano and I write as a gringo. I am a

Mexican ranch hand and his family at Rose Ranch in the late 1870s. From that time forward, political and economic upheavals impelled thousands of Mexicans to immigrate to Texas, California, and elsewhere in the Southwest. For decades since, the agricultural wealth of the region has depended on these farmworkers.

"For too many years we have been treated as the lowest of the low," said César Chávez, as he began to organize a

movement for decent wages and working conditions for agricultural laborers in the 1960s. His movement, La Causa, inspired a growing demand for Chicano rights throughout the country.

It is ironic that Mexico's failure to populate its northern territories contributed to the loss of those lands, while today Hispanic peoples are on the verge of becoming the region's most populous ethnic group.

"The U.S.–Mexican border es una herida abierta [an open wound] where the Third World grates against the first and bleeds."

Indians and Mexicans assembled for work in Pasadena in the 1870s. With a growing population, Los Angeles suffered increasing class and racial tension after the war. Andrés Pico led an anti-"greaser" vigilante committee in the mid-1850s. Outlaw activity was followed by lynchings and the passage of anti-Hispanic laws..

Mexicano and I am a gringo!" I say it with pride and conviction, for what else is a Chicano?

THE NEED TO REMEMBER

For Chicanos, the war is not forgotten. Historian Deena González says, "Perhaps New Englanders or other U.S. citizens have forgotten the event, but most Chicanos in the Southwest, and Mexicanos in Mexico, recall it very well; the most informally educated person on both sides

of the border has much to say about the war." In González's view, the conflict must not be forgotten. "Ignorance about Mexicans was a prerequisite for war—just as the invisibility of Native people was a prerequisite for continental expansion across the centuries." Only through knowledge of each other and our different cultures and histories can we achieve the mutual respect and understanding, the sense of equality despite differences, that are necessary for peace, cooperation, and creative growth.

FINAL WORDS

The eleven historians who served as advisers to this project provided crucial insights at every stage of the production of the KERA documentary. The producers acknowledge their contributions with gratitude. We asked if they would each say a few words about what they felt the legacy of the war has meant for both countries and their peoples—eleven did so. When they and other project participants speak of the legacy of the U.S.–Mexican War, they often search for words to help heal the 150-year-old wounds dividing the two countries. Their comments, if any, follow.

R. DAVID EDMUNDS
ANNE STARK WATSON AND CHESTER WATSON PROFESSOR OF AMERICAN HISTORY, UNIVERSITY OF TEXAS AT DALLAS

For Native Americans, the aftermath of the war proved disastrous. The treaty of Guadalupe Hidalgo opened up the Southwest to Anglo-American miners who swarmed into the region. Interested primarily in "striking it rich," the miners viewed Native Americans primarily as obstacles to their advancement. Native Americans were subjected to violence and wars of extermination, much of their political autonomy was lost, and the survivors were forcibly moved to barren regions deemed undesirable by Anglo-Americans. Native people have endured, but they have been hard-pressed to preserve their communities.

DEENA GONZÁLEZ
ASSOCIATE PROFESSOR OF HISTORY OF CHICANO/A STUDIES, POMONA COLLEGE

Those of us whose ancestors' lands slipped into the United States today call ourselves by various names: Chicano, Chicana, Mexican or Mexican-American, Hispanic, Latino, Latina. We understand that matters of loyalty, citizenship, language, and land rights are all tied together, and that we are an "in-between" people, people of several languages, histories, and ideologies. Perhaps for us this is the best legacy of the U.S.–Mexican War: it tells us many stories about ourselves, some tragic, some full of hope for a better future. Like these lands' native peoples, we survived the imposition of institutions and ideas that were not our own. Our survival does not deny the legacy of takeover, but it reminds us that we are here to stay. Finally, we can say: We did not come to the U.S., it came to us.

RICHARD GRISWOLD DEL CASTILLO
PROFESSOR OF HISTORY, MEXICAN AMERICAN STUDIES DEPARTMENT AT SAN DIEGO STATE UNIVERSITY

The U.S.–Mexican War and the Treaty of Guadalupe Hidalgo mark the birth of the Chicano people. They were a creation of war and conquest and as such share a distinctive American heritage with Native Americans and African Americans. The hundred thousand Mexicans who were "acquired" by the United States have not forgotten that their lands were once part of Mexico and that they are native to this region of the country. Despite calls by some to "go back to Mexico," they have persisted and endured as Americans for 150 years.

SAM W. HAYNES
ASSISTANT PROFESSOR OF HISTORY AT THE UNIVERSITY OF TEXAS AT ARLINGTON

For Americans, the U.S.–Mexican War raised some very basic questions about the kind of nation they wanted the United States to be. Americans had always pointed proudly to their republic as a beacon of liberty, a shining example for others to follow. But the war against Mexico—and the spirit of aggressive expansionism that led to it—exposed a far less uplifting aspect of the American character, one that seemed jarringly inconsistent with the ideals upon which the country had been founded. Little wonder, then, that Americans have tended to view the war with mixed emotions. The conflict with Mexico transformed the United States into a continental empire, but at the cost of its claims of moral stewardship. Again and again in the twentieth century, the United States has struggled with its contradictory urges to be a "good" nation and a "great" one.

ROBERT W. JOHANNSEN
J. G. RANDALL DISTINGUISHED PROFESSOR OF HISTORY AT THE UNIVERSITY OF ILLINOIS AT URBANA-CHAMPAIGN

The U.S.–Mexican War was one of the most significant episodes in American history, yet it was so overshadowed by the Civil War just over a decade later that it has become America's forgotten war. In its time, it signaled a new era in the nation's growth, fulfilling the vision of countless Americans—even many of those who had opposed the war—of an "ocean-bound republic." The war gained new prestige and influence not only for the United States, but for democratic government as well. It marked, as many of the nation's literary spokesmen said, America's coming of age.

ROBERT RYAL MILLER
PROFESSOR EMERITUS OF HISTORY AT CALIFORNIA STATE UNIVERSITY, HAYWARD

In the United States, the exhilarating effect of a series of military triumphs and the acquisition of half a million square miles of land partially offset some negative aspects of the war: the number of dead and wounded soldiers, the huge financial outlay, and the increased tensions over slavery that ensued. Because the war was fought on Mexican soil, many of that country's buildings, roads, and port facilities suffered extensive damage. But more important, the thousands of military and civilian casualties, the loss of battles and territory, and the humiliation of having its cities occupied by the enemy all had long-lasting psychological impact.

DAVID PLETCHER
PROFESSOR EMERITUS OF HISTORY AT INDIANA UNIVERSITY

What can we learn from the study of this war? Perhaps the necessity of examining our reasons for each war as we approach it. Requiring a generation of young men to risk their lives requires a worthwhile goal. If the Mexican War was fought to achieve something that might have been achieved without fighting, that is a grave indictment of leadership of the time—however courageous or daring that leadership.

MIGUEL SOTO
PROFESSOR OF HISTORY OF THE SCHOOL OF PHILOSOPHY AND LETTERS AT UNIVERSIDAD NACIONAL AUTÓNOMA DE MÉXICO

It appears to me that the war with the United States has been oversimplified for a long time in public discourse in Mexico.

To believe that such symbolic figures as the *Niños Héroes* were the ones who determined the outcome is to fail to confront the degrees of complexity and fragmentation that Mexico experienced during this time. To me it is crucial to recognize the real conditions of the war.

JOSEFINA ZORAIDA VÁZQUEZ
PROFESSOR OF HISTORY AND CHAIR OF THE CENTER FOR HISTORICAL STUDIES AT EL COLEGIO DE MÉXICO

For the Mexicans, the loss of territory and life was a painful legacy of the war. But there were positive sides to the legacy, too: Mexico survived its neighbor's intention of total annexation; its political parties refined their intentions; and Mexican nationality was strengthened through this violent contact with the country that had served as its model. In the longer term, it is unfortunate that the efforts of the Americans to justify an unjust war, and their racial prejudice, have created a heritage of negative attitude toward Mexicans, which hinders our relations to this day.

JESÚS VELASCO-MÁRQUEZ
PROFESSOR OF INTERNATIONAL STUDIES AT THE INSTITUTO TECNOLÓGICO AUTÓNOMO DE MÉXICO

The fear of ceasing to be an independent nation was what impelled the Mexican people to consolidate a national plan and to define the type of country and government they would have. In other words, we lost territory but we gained in political consciousness and in means to unite the nation. I believe that for Mexicans this is the greatest effect of the war.

DAVID J. WEBER
ROBERT AND NANCY DEDMAN PROFESSOR OF HISTORY AT SOUTHERN METHODIST UNIVERSITY

The U.S. and Mexico went to war despite the fact that neither side wanted a war. To promote American economic growth and security, the Polk administration wanted territory and hoped to buy it or bully it from Mexico. When Mexico would not surrender, Polk drummed up a war. Boasting of the superiority of their institutions, Americans went to war against a people many regarded as inferior, and over the next two years Mexicans and Americans fought among one another as well as against one another. Like many other historical events, the U.S.–Mexico War reveals stunning ironies and contradictions.

TIMELINE

MEXICAN GOVERNMENT	EVENTS IN NORTHEASTERN AND CENTRAL MEXICO	EVENTS IN CALIFORNIA AND NEW MEXICO	U.S. GOVERNMENT
1821			
Mexico wins independence from Spain. Some in United States consider that this voids Adams–Onis Treaty of 1819, which established borders of New Spain's northern frontier with United States.			
1836			
July: Mexico notifies United States it will not honor Velasco agreement (signed by Santa Anna under duress from Texas rebels).	Mar.: Texas declares independence from Mexico. Apr. 21: Texas rebels defeat Mexican forces at Battle of San Jacinto. May 14: Velasco peace agreement signed. Oct.: Texas asks to be annexed to United States.	Alta California threatens secession from Mexico.	Congress puts off recognition of Republic of Texas until next year.
1841			
Mexico is assessed $2 million in claims for damages to U.S. citizens. Mexican payments lapse after less than 20 percent paid.			
1845			
Mar.: Mexico breaks diplomatic relations with United States over annexation of Texas. Oct.–Dec.: President Herrera agrees to talk to U.S. negotiator about loss of Texas if naval blockade is lifted. U.S. minister John Slidell travels to Mexico. Herrera refuses to receive him.	July 4: Texas votes to accept U.S. statehood. U.S. troops move into disputed Texas territory, just past Nueces River. Oct.–Dec.: U.S. army assembles at Corpus Christi, Mexican army at Matamoros.	July: U.S. Pacific Squadron is ordered to occupy California ports if war between United States and Mexico is declared over annexation of Texas.	Mar.: President Tyler signs joint resolution to annex Texas a few days before inauguration of new president, Polk. Dec. 29: Texas admitted to Union.
1846			
Jan. 4: Mariano Paredes takes oath as president, vows to fight to regain Texas to Sabine River.	Jan.: U.S. Gulf blockade reestablished; it stays in place throughout war.	Jan.: U.S. explorer John Frémont leads party of armed men to Monterey, California.	Jan. 12: News of Slidell's failure to begin negotiations reaches Washington. Jan. 13: Polk orders U.S. troop advance.
Mar. 21: U.S. Minister Slidell officially rejected.	Mar. 8: U.S. army begins march to Rio Grande (disputed territory).	Mar. 4–8: Frémont flies U.S. flag at Gavilan Mountain. Mar. 9: Frémont leaves California, goes to Oregon.	Polk is preoccupied with Oregon question; United States refuses British proposal to divide territory.
Apr.: Paredes sends more troops to Matamoros and announces "defensive war."	Apr. 25: Skirmish between U.S. and Mexican troops near Fort Texas (now Brownsville).	Apr. 17–May 9: Polk's agent bearing secret instructions follows Frémont to Oregon.	Apr.: Congress votes to end joint occupation with Britain of Oregon.

MEXICAN GOVERNMENT	EVENTS IN NORTHEASTERN AND CENTRAL MEXICO	EVENTS IN CALIFORNIA AND NEW MEXICO	U.S. GOVERNMENT
1846			
May 12: Revolt against Paredes in Guadalajara.	May 8: Battle of Palo Alto. May 9: Battle of Fresaca de La Palma. May 17–18: U.S. troops cross Rio Grande and occupy Matamoros.	May 15: Army of the West ordered to occupy New Mexico and California; army leaves Fort Leavenworth, Kansas, less than three weeks later.	May 9: News of April 25 casualties arrives in Washington. May 11: Polk sends war message to Congress. May 12–13: War declared with appropriations and request for volunteers.
June: Paredes elected president.	June: U.S. volunteers mass in Matamoros.	June 14: Frémont and Bear Flaggers declare California an independent republic.	June 15: Oregon Treaty signed with Britain.
July: Protest against Paredes grows.	July 6: U.S. army advances from Matamoros to Camargo.	July 7: Navy raises U.S. flag over Monterrey, California.	
Aug.: Paredes overthrown as Santa Anna returns from exile.	Aug. 19: U.S. army begins march to Monterrey.	Aug. 12: U.S. forces occupy Los Angeles. Aug. 15: Army of the West claims New Mexico. Aug. 18: Kearny's troops occupy Santa Fe.	Aug.: Polk's second war appropriation bill filibustered to death after anti-slavery amendment is added.
Sept.: 14: Santa Anna arrives in Mexico City. Sept. 28: Santa Anna marches north to lead Mexican army.	Sept. 20–24: Battle of Monterrey. U.S. army captures city.	Sept. 22–23: Los Angeles Californios rebel. Sept. 25: Kearny's dragoons leave Santa Fe for California. Sept. 30: Californios reclaim Los Angeles.	
	Sept. 24–Nov. 13: Eight-week armistice.		
Nov.: Santa Anna in San Luis Potosí (northern Mexico) training troops.	Nov. 14: U.S. navy in Tampico. Nov. 16: U.S. army in Saltillo and Monterrey.	Nov. 20: Doniphan begins march toward Chihuahua from New Mexico.	Nov.: Whigs win majority in House. Nov. 18–19: Polk names General Scott to lead attack on Mexico City.
Dec. 6: Santa Anna elected president but remains in San Luis Potosí with army.	Dec.: U.S. navy in Laguna. U.S. army along 500-mile Saltillo line.	Dec. 6: Battle of San Pascual, California. Three weeks later, U.S. army and navy unite to march to Los Angeles.	Dec.: Whigs in Congress criticize war.
1847			
Jan.: Acting President Gómez Farías approves unpopular scheme for church property to be sold to pay for war.	Jan. 3: Scott takes almost half of Taylor's troops for campaign against Mexico City. Taylor's troops pull back to Monterrey. Jan. 28: Santa Anna begins advance toward Taylor's position.	Jan. 8: Battle of San Gabriel, California. Jan. 9: Battle of La Mesa, California. Jan. 10: Los Angeles is reoccupied by United States. Jan. 13: Treaty of Cahuenga ends California conflict.	Jan.: Whig party informed that General Taylor is willing to accept nomination for president.
Feb.: Polkos Revolt pits church defenders in civil guard against government.	Feb.: Taylor's troops retreat to Buena Vista as Santa Anna's troops approach. Feb. 22–23: Battle of Buena Vista. Santa Anna retreats after this last major battle in NE Mexico.	Feb. 5: Taos surrenders to U.S. troops, ending Santa Fe revolt against U.S. occupation. Feb. 28: Battle of Sacramento, near Chihuahua.	

MEXICAN GOVERNMENT	EVENTS IN NORTHEASTERN AND CENTRAL MEXICO	EVENTS IN CALIFORNIA AND NEW MEXICO	U.S. GOVERNMENT
1847			
Mar. 21: Santa Anna ends Polkos Revolt, enters Mexico City to be sworn in as president.	Mar. 5: U.S. troops, massing off Gulf Coast, move toward Veracruz. Mar. 9: Scott's forces land at Veracruz. Mar. 26–29: Battle of Veracruz.	Mar. 1–Apr. 28: U.S. troops under Doniphan occupy Chihuahua. Mar. 29: U.S. navy occupies San José and San Lucas in Baja California.	
Apr. 1: Anaya becomes acting president. Apr. 20: Mexican Congress expands its powers, prohibits treating with United States.	Apr. 8: U.S. troops advance on road to Mexico City. Apr. 18: Battle of Cerro Gordo.	Apr. 13: U.S. navy occupies La Paz, Baja California.	Apr. 15: Polk appoints Trist to negotiate treaty with Mexico.
May 22: Santa Anna resumes presidency. May–July: Behind-the-scenes treaty efforts in Mexico City.	May: United States controls northeastern Mexico. Gulf Squadron holds several Gulf Coast towns. May 15: Scott occupies Puebla.	May: United States controls California and New Mexico; reinforcements arrive. May 31: Military governor arrives in California. May–July: Pacific Squadron holds several Baja California towns.	

Aug. 7: U.S. army begins march from Puebla to Valley of Mexico.
Aug. 19: Battle of Contreras.   Aug. 20: Battle of Churubusco.
Aug. 24: Armistice of Tacubaya.
Sept. 6: Armistice/negotiations terminated.   Sept. 8: Battle of Molino del Rey.
Sept. 13: Battle of Chapultepec; Battles at Mexico City Gates.
Sept. 14: United States occupies Mexico City.

MEXICAN GOVERNMENT	EVENTS IN NORTHEASTERN AND CENTRAL MEXICO	EVENTS IN CALIFORNIA AND NEW MEXICO	U.S. GOVERNMENT
Oct. 7: Santa Anna ordered relieved of command. Oct.–Dec.: Querétaro made temporary capital, Congress assembled, treaty commissioners appointed.	Oct. 12: End of monthlong Mexican siege of U.S. troops occupying Puebla.	Oct.: U.S. navy occupies Guaymas and Mazatlán.	Oct.: Polk orders Trist home, but Trist stays in Mexico to negotiate with treaty commission.
Nov. 11: Anaya elected interim president.	Nov. 25: Taylor is relieved of command, returns to United States.		
	Dec.: U.S. reinforcements arrive in northern and central Mexico.	Dec.: Reinforcements continue to arrive in California.	
1848			
Jan. 2: Negotiations begin. Jan. 8: Peña y Peña becomes acting president.			Jan. 13: Polk orders Scott relieved of command.
Feb. 2: Treaty of Guadalupe Hidalgo signed.	Feb. 29: Military armistice.	Feb. 29: Military armistice not received, and U.S. troops attack in Chihuahua and Baja California.	Feb. 23: Polk submits treaty to Senate.

Mar. 10: U.S. Senate modifies and ratifies treaty.   May 25: Mexican Congress ratifies treaty modified by U.S. Senate.
May 30: Treaty formally exchanged.   June–July 15: U.S. troops leave Mexico.

1854

James Gadsden negotiates purchase of lands south of Gila River (southern Arizona) from Mexico, which is again governed by Santa Anna.

BIBLIOGRAPHY

I. CONTEMPORANEOUS SOURCES

Adams, John Quincy. *Memoirs, Comprising Portions of His Diary from 1795 to 1848.* 12 vols. Edited by Charles Frances Adams. 1875–77; reprint ed., Freeport, N.Y.: Books for Libraries Press, 1969.

Alamán, Lucas. *Historia de Méjico: Desde los Primeros Movimientos que Prepararon Su Independencia en el Año de 1808 hasta la Epoca Presente.* 5 vols. Mexico City: J. M. Lara, 1849–52.

Alcaraz, Ramón; Alejo Barreiro; José María Castillo; Félix María Escalante; José María Iglesias; Manuel Muñoz; Ramón Ortiz; Manuel Payno y Flores; Guillermo Prieto; Ignacio Ramírez; Napoleón Saborio; Francisco Schiafino; Francisco Segura; Pablo María Torrescano; Urquidi. *Apuntes para la Historia de la Guerra entre México y los Estados-Unidos.* Edited by Josefina Zoraida Vázquez. 1848; reprint ed., Mexico City: Consejo Nacional para la Cultura y las Artes, 1991.

———. *The Other Side: Notes for the History of the War between Mexico and the United States.* Translated by Albert C. Ramsey. 1850; reprint ed., New York: Burt Franklin, 1970.

Anderson, Robert. *An Artillery Officer in Mexico, 1846–7: Letters of Robert Anderson.* New York: Putnam, 1911.

Balbontín, Manuel. *La Invasión Americana, 1846 a 1848: Apuntes del Subteniente de la Artilleria Manuel Balbontín.* Mexico City: G. A. Esteva, 1883.

———. *Memorias del Coronel Manuel Balbontín.* Mexico City: Editorial "Elede," 1958.

Ballentine, George. *Autobiography of an English Soldier in the United States Army.* Edited by William H. Goetzmann. Chicago: Lakeside Press, 1986.

Bancroft, Hubert Howe. *The Works of Hubert Howe Bancroft.* Vols. 18–21: *History of California, History of Arizona and New Mexico, History of the North Mexican States and Texas.* San Francisco: History Company, 1884–90.

Bayard, Samuel John. *Sketch of the Life of Commodore Robert F. Stockton.* New York: Derby and Jackson, 1856.

Benton, Thomas Hart. *Thirty Years' View: A History of the Working of the American Government for Thirty Years, from 1820 to 1850.* 2 vols. New York: Appleton, 1854–56.

Brooks, N. C. *A Complete History of the Mexican War: Its Causes, Conduct, and Consequences: Comprising an Account of the Various Military and Naval Operations, from Its Commencement to the Treaty of Peace.* Philadelphia: Grigg, Elliot, 1849.

Calderón de la Barca, Frances. *Life in Mexico, during a Residence of Two Years in That Country.* 1843; reprint ed., Berkeley: University of California Press, 1982.

Carson, Kit. *Kit Carson's Autobiography.* Lincoln: University of Nebraska Press, 1966.

Chamberlain, Samuel E. *My Confession: The Recollections of a Rogue.* Introduction and postscript by Roger Butterfield. New York: Harper, 1956.

———. *My Confession: Recollections of a Rogue.* Unexpurgated and annotated ed. Edited by William H. Goetzmann. Austin: Texas State Historical Association, 1996.

Cooke, Philip St. George. *The Conquest of New Mexico and California.* 1878; reprint ed., Albuquerque: Horn and Wallace, 1964.

Dana, Napoleon Jackson Tecumseh. *Monterrey Is Ours! The Mexican War Letters of Lieutenant Dana, 1845–47.* Edited by Robert H. Ferrell. Lexington: University of Kentucky, 1990.

Douglass, Frederick. *Narrative of the Life of Frederick Douglass, an American Slave.* Edited by H. Baker. New York: Viking, Penguin, 1982.

Emory, William H. *Notes of a Military Reconnaissance.* Washington, D.C.: Wendell and Van Benthuysen, 1848.

Frémont, John Charles. *Memoirs of My Life.* Chicago: Belford, Clarke, 1887.

French, Samuel Gibbs. *Two Wars: An Autobiography.* Nashville: Confederate Veteran, 1901.

Giddings, Luther. *Sketches of the Campaign in North Mexico in 1846 and 1847.* New York: Putnam, 1853.

Grant, Ulysses S. *Personal Memoirs of U. S. Grant.* 2 vols. New York: Webster, 1885, 1886.

Gregg, Josiah. *Commerce of the Prairies.* 2 vols. 1844–45; reprint ed., New York: Lippincott, 1962.

Henry, William Seaton. *Campaign Sketches of the War with Mexico.* New York: Harper, 1847.

Hitchcock, Ethan Allen. *Fifty Years in Camp and Field: Diary of Ethan Allen Hitchcock, U.S.A.* Edited by W. A. Croffut. New York: Putnam, 1909.

Hughes, John T. *Doniphan's Expedition: Containing an Account of the Conquest of New Mexico.* Cincinnati: James, 1848.

Kendall, George Wilkins. *Narrative of the Texan Santa Fe Expedition.* 2 vols. New York: Harper, 1844.

———. *The War between the United States and Mexico.* Illustrated by Carl Nebel. 1851; reprint ed., Austin: Texas State Historical Association, 1994.

Kirkham, Ralph W. *The Mexican War Journal and Letters of Ralph W. Kirkham.* Edited by Robert Ryal Miller. College Station: Texas A&M University Press, 1991.

Lee, Robert E., Jr. *Recollections and Letters of Gen. Robert E. Lee.* New York: Doubleday, 1904.

Lewis, Oscar, series ed. *The United States Conquest of California.* Introduction by Carlos E. Cortes. New York: Arno, 1976.

Magoffin, Susan Shelby. *Down the Santa Fe Trail and into Mexico: The Diary of Susan Shelby Magoffin.* Edited by Stella M. Drumm. 1926; reprint ed., New Haven, Conn.: Yale University Press, 1962.

Mansfield, Edward D. *The Mexican War: History of Its Origin.* New York: A. S. Barnes and Co., 1848.

McNierney, Michael, ed. *Taos 1847: The Revolt in Contemporary Accounts.* Boulder, Colo.: Johnson Publishing Co., 1980.

Myers, William Starr, ed. *Mexican War: The Diary of George B. McClellan.* Princeton, N.J.: Princeton University Press, 1917.

Nunnis, Doyce B. *From Mexican Days to the Gold Rush: Memoirs of James Wilson Marshall and Edward Gould Buffum Who Grew up with California.* Chicago: Lakeside Press, 1993.

Polk, James Knox. *Diary of James K. Polk.* Edited by Milo Quaife. 4 vols. Chicago: A. C. McLurg and Co., 1910.

Pourade, F. Richard. *The Sign of the Eagle: Letters of Lieutenant John James Peck.* San Diego,: Union-Tribune, 1970.

Prescott, William H. *History of the Conquest of Mexico.* 3 vols. New York: Random House, 1844–1845.

Prieto, Guillermo. *Memorias de Mis Tiempos, 1828–1853.* 2 vols. 1906; reprint ed., Mexico City: Libreria de la Vda. de C. Bouret, 1948.

Ramírez, José Fernando. *Mexico during the War with the United States: Letters to Durango.* Edited by Walter Scholes, translated by Elliott Scherr. Columbia: University of Missouri Studies, 1950.

Reid, Samuel C. *Scouting Expeditions of McCullough's Texas Rangers.* Freeport, N.Y.: Books for Libraries Press, 1970.

Roa Bárcena, José María. *Recuerdos de la Invasión Norte-Americana (1846–1848).* 1883; reprint ed., Mexico City: Editorial Porrua, 1947.

Santa Anna, Antonio López de. *The Eagle: The Autobiography of Santa Anna.* Edited by Ann Fears Crawford. Austin, Tex.: State House Press, 1988.

Scott, Winfield. *Memoirs of Lieutenant-General Scott: Written by Himself.* New York: Sheldon and Co., 1864.

Semmes, Raphael. *Service Afloat and Ashore during the Mexican War.* Cincinnati: W. H. Moore, 1851.

Simpson, George. *Narrative of a Journey Round the World during the Years 1841 and 1842.* 2 vols. London: H. Colburn, 1847.

Smith, E. Kirby. *To Mexico with Scott: Letters of Captain E. Kirby Smith to His Wife.* Cambridge, Mass.: Harvard University Press, 1917.

Smith, George W., and Charles Judah. *Chronicles of the Gringos: The U.S. Army in the Mexican War, 1846–1848.* Albuquerque: University of New Mexico Press, 1968.

Taylor, Zachary. *Letters . . . from the Battlefields of the Mexican War.* Edited by William H. Samson. Rochester, N.Y.: Genesee, 1908.

Tornel y Mendivil, José María. *Breve Reseña Histórica de los Acontecimientos Más Notables de la Nación Mexicana desde el Año de 1821 hasta Nuestros Días.* 1852; reprint ed., Mexico City: Comisión Nacional para las Celebraciónes del Aniversario de la Revolución Mexicana, 1985.

Twitchell, Ralph Emerson. *The Spanish Archives of New Mexico.* Cedar Rapids, Iowa: Torch, 1914.

Vallejo, Mariano Guadalupe. "Recuerdos Históricos y Personales Tocantes a la Alta California, 1769–1849." Manuscript; microfilm at library of the University of California, Berkeley.

Weber, David J., ed. *Foreigners in Their Native Land: Historical Roots of the Mexican Americans.* Albuquerque: University of New Mexico Press, 1973.

Webster, Daniel. *Works of Daniel Webster.* 6 vols. Boston: Little and Brown, 1852.

II. GENERAL BOOKS ABOUT THE WAR

American Heritage. *Texas and the War with Mexico.* Narrative by Fairfax Downey. New York: American Heritage, 1961.

Bauer, K. Jack. *The Mexican War, 1846–1848.* New York: Macmillan, 1974.

———. *Surfboats and Horse Marines: U.S. Naval Operations in the Mexican War, 1846–48.* Annapolis, Md.: U.S. Naval Institute, 1969.

Bill, Alfred Hoyt. *Rehearsal for Conflict: The Story of Our War with Mexico, 1846–1848.* New York: History Book Club, 1947.

Caruso, A. Brooke. *Mexican Spy Company: The United States Covert Operations in Mexico, 1845–1848.* Jefferson, N.C.: McFarland and Co., 1991.

Chalfant, William Y. *Dangerous Passage: The Santa Fe Trail and the Mexican War.* Norman: University of Oklahoma Press, 1994.

Chidsey, Donald Barr. *War with Mexico.* New York: Crown, 1968.

Connor, Seymour V., and Odie B. Faulk. *North America Divided: The Mexican War, 1846–1848.* New York: Oxford University Press, 1971.

Cutler, Wayne. *Essays on the Mexican War.* Edited by Douglas W. Richmond. College Station: Texas A&M University Press, 1986.

Eisenhower, John S. D. *So Far from God: The U.S. War with Mexico, 1846–1848.* New York: Random House, 1989.

Frazier, Donald S., ed. *The United States and Mexico at War: Nineteenth-Century Expansionism and Conflict.* New York: Macmillan, 1998.

Harlow, Neal. *California Conquered: War and Peace on the Pacific, 1846–1850.* Berkeley: University of California Press, 1982.

Henry, Robert Selph. *The Story of the Mexican War.* New York: Frederick Ungar, 1950.

Johannsen, Robert. *To the Halls of the Montezumas: The Mexican War in the American Imagination.* New York: Oxford University Press, 1985.

Martínez, Orlando. *Great Landgrab: The Mexican-American War, 1846–1848.* London: Quartet Books, 1975.

Martínez Caraza, Leopoldo. *La Intervención Norteamericana en México, 1846–1848: Historia Político-Militar de la Pérdida de Gran Parte del Territorio Mexicano.* Mexico City: Panorama Editorial, 1989.

May, Robert E. "Invisible Men: Blacks and the U.S. Army in the Mexican War." *The Historian* 49 (Aug. 1987).

Meltzer, Milton. *Bound for the Rio Grande: The Mexican Struggle, 1845–1850.* New York: Knopf, 1974.

Miller, Robert Ryal. *Shamrock and Sword: The Saint Patrick's Battalion in the U.S.–Mexican War.* Norman: University of Oklahoma Press, 1989.

Nardo, Don. *The Mexican-American War.* San Diego, Calif.: Lucent Books, 1991.

Nevin, David. *The Mexican War.* The Old West Series. Alexandria, Va.: Time-Life Books, 1978.

Rives, George Lockhart. *The United States and Mexico, 1821–1848: A History of the Relations between the Two Countries from the Independence of Mexico to the Close of the War with the United States.* 2 vols. New York: Scribner's, 1913.

Robinson, Cecil, trans. and ed. *The View from Chapultepec: Mexican Writers on the Mexican-American War.* Tucson: University of Arizona Press, 1989.

Singletary, Otis A. *The Mexican War.* Chicago: University of Chicago Press, 1960.

Soto, Miguel. *The Monarchist Conspiracy and the Mexican War.* Essays on the Mexican War: The Walter Prescott Webb Lectures. College Station: Texas A&M University/University of Texas at Arlington, 1986.

Velasco-Márquez, Jesús. *La Guerra del 47 y La Opinión Pública (1845–1848).* Mexico City: Secretaría de Educación Pública, 1975.

Weems, John Edward. *To Conquer a Peace: The War between the United States and Mexico.* New York: Doubleday, 1974.

Winders, Richard Bruce. *Mr. Polk's Army: The American Military Experience in the Mexican War.* College Station: Texas A&M University Press, 1997.

III. U.S. AND MEXICAN HISTORY

Barr, Alwyn. *Texans in Revolt: The Battle for San Antonio, 1835.* Austin: University of Texas Press, 1990.

Bergeron, Paul H. *The Presidency of James K. Polk.* Lawrence: University Press of Kansas, 1987.

Billington, Ray Allen. *Far Western Frontier, 1830–1860.* New York: Harper and Row, 1956.

Boorstin, Daniel J. *Hidden History.* New York: Harper and Row, 1987.

Brack, Gene. *Mexico Views Manifest Destiny.* Albuquerque: University of New Mexico Press, 1975.

Callcott, Wilfrid Hardy. *Santa Anna: The Story of an Enigma Who Once Was Mexico.* New York: Archon Books, 1964.

Christman, Margaret C. S. *1846: Portrait of the Nation.* Washington, D.C.: Smithsonian Institution Press, 1996.

Clarke, Dwight L. *Stephen Watts Kearny: Soldier of the West.* Norman: University of Oklahoma Press, 1961.

Clarke, Mary Whatley. *Chief Bowles and the Texas Cherokees.* Norman: University of Oklahoma Press, 1971.

Copeland, Fayette. *Kendall of the* Picayune. Norman: University of Oklahoma Press, 1943.

Cozzens, Samuel Woodworth. *Explorations and Adventures in Arizona and New Mexico.* Secaucus, N.Y.: Castle, 1988.

De Palo, William A., Jr. *The Mexican National Army, 1822–1852.* College Station: Texas A&M University Press, 1977.

Eisenhower, John S. D. *Agent of Destiny: The Life and Times of General Winfield Scott.* New York: Free Press, 1997.

Encyclopaedia Britannica editors. *Annals of America: The Manifest Destiny.* Vol. 7: 1841–1849. Chicago: Encyclopaedia Britannica, 1968.

Fuentes, Carlos. *Buried Mirror: Reflections on Spain and the New World.* Boston: Houghton Mifflin, 1992.

Gibson, A. M. *The Kickapoos: Lords of the Middle Border.* Norman: University of Oklahoma Press, 1963.

Hawgood, John A. *First and Last Consul: Thomas O. Larkin and the Americanization of California.* Palo Alto, Calif.: Pacific Books, 1970.

Haynes, Sam W. *James K. Polk and the Expansionist Impulse.* Edited by Oscar Handlin. Library of American Biography. New York: Longman, 1997.

Hietala, Thomas R. *Manifest Design: Anxious Aggrandizement in Late Jacksonian America.* Ithaca, N.Y.: Cornell University Press, 1985.

Jackson, Sheldon G. *A British Ranchero in Old California: The Life and Times of Henry Dalton and the Rancho Azusa.* Glendale, Calif.: A. H. Clark Co., 1977.

Johannsen, Robert W. *Manifest Destiny and Empire: American Antebellum Expansionism.* Edited by Sam W. Haynes and Christopher Morris. College Station: Texas A&M University Press, 1997.

Jones, Oakah. *Santa Anna.* New York: Twayne Publishers, 1968.

Kilgore, Dan. *How Did Davy Die?* College Station: Texas A&M University, 1978.

Krause, Enrique. *Mexico: Biography of Power.* Translated by Hank Heifetz. New York: Harper Collins, 1997.

Lavender, David. *Bent's Fort.* Lincoln: University of Nebraska Press, 1954.

Mares, E. A., et al. *Padre Martínez: New Perspectives from Taos.* Taos, N.M.: Millicent Rogers Museum, 1988.

McHenry, J. Patrick. *A Short History of Mexico.* Garden City, N.Y.: Dolphin Books, Doubleday, 1962.

McKittrick, Myrtle M. *Vallejo: Son of California.* Portland, Ore.: Binfords and Mort, Publishers, 1944.

Merk, Frederick, and Lois Bannister. *Manifest Destiny and Mission in American History: A Reinterpretation.* New York: Knopf, 1970.

Olavarría y Ferrari, Enrique. *México a Traves de los Siglos. Vol 4: México Independiente, 1821–1855.* Mexico City: Editorial Cumbre, 1958.

Olivera, Ruth R., and Liliane Crété. *Life in Mexico under Santa Anna, 1822–1855.* Norman: University of Oklahoma Press, 1991.

Pletcher, David M. *The Diplomacy of Annexation: Texas, Oregon, and the Mexican War.* Columbia: University of Missouri Press, 1973.

Rosenus, Alan. *General M. G. Vallejo and the Advent of the Americans: A Biography.* Albuquerque: University of New Mexico Press, 1995.

Sears, Louis Martin. *John Slidell.* Durham, N.C.: Duke University Press, 1925.

Sierra, Justo. *Political Evolution of the Mexican People.* Austin: University of Texas, 1969.

Smith, Justin H. *Annexation of Texas.* New York: Baker and Taylor, 1911.
———. *The War with Mexico.* New York: Macmillan Co., 1919.

Stephenson, Nathaniel W. *Texas and the Mexican War: A Chronicle of the Winning of the Southwest.* New Haven, Conn.: Yale University Press, 1921.

Time-Life Books editors. *The Spanish West.* The Old West Series. New York: Time-Life Books, 1976.

Turner, Frederick Jackson. *The United States, 1830–1850: The Nation and Its Sections.* 1935; reprint ed., New York: Norton, 1965.

Vázquez, Josefina Zoraida. *De la Rebelión de Texas a la Guerra del 47: Interpretaciónes de la Historia de México.* Mexico City: Nueva Imagen, 1994.

———. *Don Antonio López de Santa Anna: Mito y Enigma.* Mexico City: Centro de Estudias de la Historia de México Condumex, 1987.

———. *México Frente a Estados Unidos: Un Ensayo Histórico, 1776–1988.* Mexico City: Colegio de México, 1982.

Vázquez, Josefina Zoraida, and Lorenzo Meyer. *The United States and Mexico.* Chicago: University of Chicago Press, 1985.

Weber, David J. *The Mexican Frontier, 1821–1846: The American Southwest under Mexico.* Albuquerque: University of New Mexico Press, 1982.

———. *The Spanish Frontier in North America.* New Haven, Conn.: Yale University Press, 1992.

Zavala, Lorenzo de. *Obras: Viaje a los Estados Unidos del Norte de America.* Mexico City: Editorial Porrúa, 1976.

IV. IMAGES

Goetzmann, William H. *Sam Chamberlain's Mexican War: The San Jacinto Museum of History Paintings.* Austin: Texas State Historical Association, 1993.

Sandweiss, Martha A., Rick Stewart, and Ben W. Huseman. *Eyewitness to War: Prints and Daguerreotypes of the Mexican War, 1846–1848.* Washington, D.C.: Smithsonian Institution Press, 1989.

Tyler, Ronnie C. *The Mexican War: A Lithographic Record.* Austin: Texas State Historical Association, 1973.

V. CHICANO/CHICANA LEGACY

Anzaldúa, Gloria. *Borderlands/La Frontera: The New Mestiza.* San Francisco: Aunt Lute Books, 1987.

Arteaga, Alfred. *The House with the Blue Bed.* San Francisco: Mercury House, 1997.

Burciaga, José Antonio. *Drink Cultura: Chicanismo.* Santa Barbara, Calif.: Joshua Odell Editions, 1993.

———. *In Few Words/En Pocas Palabras: A Compendium of Latino Folk Wit and Wisdom.* San Francisco: Mercury House, 1996.

DeMarco, Gordon. *A Short History of Los Angeles.* San Francisco: Lexikos, 1988.

García, Mario T. *Mexican Americans: Leadership, Ideology and Identity, 1930–1960.* Yale Western Americana Series 36. New Haven, Conn.: Yale University Press, 1989.

González, Deena J. "The Spanish-Mexican Women of Santa Fe: Patterns of Their Resistance and Accommodation." Ph.D. diss., University of California, Berkeley, 1985.

Griswold Del Castillo, Richard. *Treaty of Guadalupe Hidalgo: A Legacy of Conflict.* Norman: University of Oklahoma Press, 1990.

Lamb, Ruth S. *Mexican Americans: Sons of the Southwest.* Claremont, Calif.: Ocelot Press, 1970.

McWilliams, Carey. *North from Mexico: The Spanish-Speaking People of the Southwest.* 1948; reprint ed., New York: Greenwood Press, 1968.

Monroy, Douglas. *Thrown among Strangers: The Making of Mexican Culture in Frontier California.* Berkeley: University of California Press, 1990.

Moquin, Wayne. *A Documentary History of the Mexican Americans.* New York: Bantam, 1971.

Ornelas, Michael R. *Between the Conquests: Readings in Early Chicano History.* Dubuque, Iowa: Kendall/Hunt, 1991.

Pitt, Leonard. *The Decline of the Californios: A Social History of the Spanish-Speaking Californians, 1846–1890.* Berkeley: University of California Press, 1970.

Saldívar, José David. *Border Matters: Remapping American Cultural Studies.* Berkeley: University of California Press, 1997.

Viola, Herman J. *Exploring the West.* Washington, D.C.: Smithsonian Books, 1987.

VI. POETRY AND ESSAYS

Galeano, Eduardo. *Memory of Fire: Faces and Masks.* Translated by Cedric Belfrage. New York: Pantheon Books, 1987.

Paz, Octavio. *The Labyrinth of Solitude* and *The Other Mexico.* Translated by Lysander Kemp, Yara Milos, and Rachel P. Belash. New York: Grove Weidenfeld, 1985.

Snyder, Gary. *Turtle Island.* New York: New Directions, 1969.

Thoreau, Henry David. *Civil Disobedience and Other Essays.* 1906; reprint ed., New York: Dover Publications, 1993.

White, Randy. *Motherlode/La Veta Madre.* Newcastle, Calif.: Blue Oak, 1977.

IMAGE CREDITS

FRONT MATTER

i   Library of Congress, LC-USZ C2-2108

ii-iii   Amon Carter Museum, Fort Worth, Texas, 1976.33.6, J. Vollmering and Francis D'Avignon after Henry Walke, "The Landing of the Naval Expedition, Against Tabasco. (Mexico) Comore. M. C. Perry in Command," 1848, toned lithograph (hand-colored)

vi   Graham Pilecki Collection

vii   Graham Pilecki Collection

viii-ix   1987.91, "Siege of Puebla, Began Sept. 13th. ended Oct. 12th. 1847," James T. Shannon, chromolithograph, 1850. Amon Carter Museum, Fort Worth, Texas

PART ONE

xxi   Amon Carter Museum, Fort Worth, Texas, 1972.186.12, Adolfe-Jean-Baptiste Bayot after Carl Nebel, "Gen'l Scott's Entrance into Mexico," 1851, toned lithograph (hand-colored)

CHAPTER 1

7   Corbis-Bettmann

8   Declaration of Independence 4 July 1776, by Trumbull, Library of Congress

9   Institute of Texan Cultures, San Antonio, Texas

10   Corbis-Bettmann

11   INAH/Coordinación Nacional de Difusión/Proyecto México

12   Courtesy American Antiquarian Society

13t   Nettie Lee Benson Latin American Collection, General Libraries, University of Texas at Austin

13b   "Fandango" by T. Gentilz, Gift of the Yanaguana Soc., Daughters of the Republic of Texas Library

14   Courtesy of the John Carter Brown Library at Brown University

CHAPTER 2

15   Nettie Lee Benson Latin American Collection, General Libraries, University of Texas at Austin

17   Texas Memorial Museum CN02318, The Center for American History, The University of Texas at Austin

18   Institute of Texan Cultures, San Antonio, Texas

20   INAH/Coordinacion Nacional de Difusion/Proyecto México/del Archivo de la Fototeca de Pachuca of Texas

21l   Texas Memorial Museum CN 02318, The Center for American History, The University of Texas at Austin

21r   Nettie Lee Benson Latin American Collection, General Libraries, University of Texas at Austin

22   Alamo Images, Colln #A86.1392:341:036, DeGolyer Library, Southern Methodist University, Dallas, Texas

23   Library of Congress, LC-USZ62-54014

24   Courtesy of the R. W. Norton Art Gallery, Shreveport, Louisiana

26   Prints & Photographs Collection, CN01255, The Center for American History, The University of Texas at Austin

27t   Texas Memorial Museum, acc # 1776-1, The Center for American History, The University of Texas at Austin

27b   Missouri Historical Society, St. Louis

CHAPTER 3

29   Prints & Photographs Collection, CN01255, The Center for American History, The University of Texas at Austin

30   Institute of Texan Cultures, San Antonio, Texas

31   National Archives

32   The Beinecke Rare Book & Manuscript Library, Yale University

33t   Courtesy, Special Collections Division, the University of Texas at Arlington Libraries

33b   The Metropolitan Museum of Art, Gift of I. N. Phelps Stokes, Edward S. Hawes, Alice Mary Hawes, Marion Augusta Hawes, 1937 (37.14.2)

34   Library of Congress, LC-US Z62-20058

35   Courtesy American Antiquarian Society

36   Courtesy American Antiquarian Society

37   Courtesy American Antiquarian Society

38   National Archives

39   Collection of the James K. Polk Memorial Association, Columbia, Tennessee

40   University of North Carolina, Chapel Hill, NC

41   California Historical Society

42t   Corbis-Bettmann

42b   Corbis-Bettmann

43   Corbis-Bettmann

PART TWO

44   Amon Carter Museum, Fort Worth, Texas, 1974.2.1, Charles R. Parsons after Daniel Powers Whiting, "Birds-Eye View of the Camp of the Army of Occupation, Commanded by Genl. Taylor. Near Corpus Christi, Texas, (From the North) Oct. 1845," 1847, toned lithograph (hand-colored).

CHAPTER 4

47   INAH/Coordinación Nacional de Difusión/Proyecto México/Pedro Gualdi, Foto. del Archivo del Museo Nacional de Historia

48   INAH/Coordinación Nacional de Difusión/Proyecto México/Foto. del Archivo de la Fototeca de Pachuca

50   Corbis-Bettmann

52   Courtesy U.S. Army Center of Military History

53   Hemeroteca Nacional de México, Claudio Linati

54   INAH/Coordinación Nacional de Difusión/Proyecto México/autor desconocido, Foto: M. Zabé

55t   Courtesy American Antiquarian Society

55b   Nettie Lee Benson Latin American Collection, General Libraries, University of Texas at Austin

CHAPTER 5

56   Courtesy American Antiquarian Society

58   Courtesy, Special Collections Division, the University of Texas at Arlington Libraries

59   Courtesy, Special Collections Division, the University of Texas at Arlington Libraries

60   The San Jacinto Museum of History, Houston, Texas

61   Hemeroteca Nacional de México

156 Amon Carter Museum, Fort Worth, Texas, 1971.48, Frances Flora Bond Palmer after Joseph H. Eaton, "Battle of Buena Vista. View of the Battle-Ground of 'the Angostura' fought Near Buena Vista, Mexico February 23rd, 1847 (Lookin S. West)," 1847, toned lithograph (hand-colored)

157 Graham Pilecki Collection

159 Corbis-Bettmann

PART FIVE

162 INAH, Coordinación Nacional de Difusión/Proyecto México

164 Courtesy, Special Collections Division, the University of Texas at Arlington Libraries

165 Courtesy, Special Collections Division, the University of Texas at Arlington Libraries

CHAPTER 12

166 Print Collection Neg# 24,940 California State Library

168 Nettie Lee Benson Latin American Collection, General Libraries, University of Texas at Austin

169 Beverly R. Robinson Collection, U.S. Naval Academy Museum

171 Missouri Historical Society, St. Louis

172 Amon Carter Museum, Fort Worth, Texas, 1978.9, Unknown artist, "Scene in Vera Cruz during the Bombardment, March 25th 1847," lithograph (hand-colored)

173 Weir, The Valentine Museum

174 © Collection of the New-York Historical Society

176 INAH/Coordinación Nacional de Difusión/Proyecto México

CHAPTER 13

177 Amon Carter Museum, Fort Worth, Texas, 1972.40, James Cameron, "Battle of Cerro Gordo April 18th, 1847," 1847, lithograph (hand-colored)

178 Nettie Lee Benson Latin American Collection, General Libraries, University of Texas at Austin

181t Amon Carter Museum, Fort Worth, Texas, 1978.8, Francisco Bastin, "Defense de Cerro Gordo Contra el Ejercito Norte Americano el 18 Abril 1847," ca. 1850, lithograph (hand-colored)

181b Amon Carter Museum, Fort Worth, Texas, 1972.119, H. Mendez, "View of Cerro Gordo with Genl. Twiggs' Division Storming the Main Heights 18th April 1847," 1847, lithograph (hand-colored)

183 Amon Carter Museum, Fort Worth, Texas, 1971.64, Unknown artist, "Battle of Sierra [sic] Gordo, April 17th & 18th, 1847, Between Genl. Scott and Santa Anna," ca. 1847, lithograph (hand-colored)

184 Hemeroteca Nacional de México

CHAPTER 14

185 INAH/Coordinación Nacional de Difusión/Proyecto México/Autor José Inés Tovilla, Foto del Archivo del Museo Nacional de Historia

187 Courtesy, Special Collections Division, the University of Texas at Arlington Libraries

188l Neg#25,043 California State Library

188r Library of Congress, LC-USZ62-35464

190 (public domain)

191l Concord Free Public Library

191r The Bancroft Library, University of California, Berkeley, California

193 © Collection of the New-York Historical Society

195 Nettie Lee Benson Latin American Collection, General Libraries, University of Texas at Austin

CHAPTER 15

198 Courtesy U.S. Army Center of Military History

201t (public domain)

201b Amon Carter Museum, Fort Worth, Texas, 1975.31, Joaquin Heredia, "Battle of Contreras. Mexico. August 19 and 20. 1847/Battalla de Contreras. Mexico Agosto. Dias 19 al 20 de 1847," ca. 1847–1848, lithograph

204 West Point Museum Collections, U.S. Military Academy

207t Nettie Lee Benson Latin American Collection, General Libraries, University of Texas at Austin

207b Library of Congress, LC-USZ62-15513

208 Graham Pilecki Collection

209 Corbis-Bettmann

210 © Collection of the New-York Historical Society

211t Museo de las Intervenciones

211b Courtesy American Antiquarian Society

PART SIX

212 The Huntington Library, San Marino, California, "Caballeros at Plaza Fiesta, Los Angeles. 1901." CL Pierce 01185

214 Courtesy American Antiquarian Society

215 (public domain)

217 Courtesy American Antiquarian Society

220 © Collection of the New-York Historical Society

221 The National Archive

222t Library of Congress, LC-USZ62-28312 DLC

222b Courtesy American Antiquarian Society

223tr Library of Congress, LC-B8172-6371 DLC

223tl Courtesy, Special Collections Division, the University of Texas at Arlington Libraries

223b Corbis-Bettmann

224 Nettie Lee Benson Latin American Collection, General Libraries, University of Texas at Austin

229 The Bancroft Library, University of California, Berkeley, California

225t Hemeroteca Nacional de México

225b Museo de las Intervenciones

226 Wheeler Photographic Survey of the American West, 1871–1873, 5(I,5)

227 The Andrew J. Russell Collection, plate 78, Courtesy The Oakland Museum of California

228 Seaver Center for Western History Research, Los Angeles County Museum of Natural History

229 Library of Congress, LC-USZ62-8561

230 The Huntington Library, San Marino, California, "Rancheria at Sunny Slope, L.J., Rose Residence, ca. 1880," CL 0156 vol 1 (27)

231 Security Pacific National Bank Photo. Collection, Los Angeles Public Library

COLOR SECTIONS

c1t,1b Franklin D. Roosevelt Library

c2,c3,c4 Courtesy, The Summerlee Foundation and the Texas State Historical Association

c5t Album Pinteresco, Vault Folio 2F 1213.L45, DeGolyer Library, Southern Methodist University, Dallas, Texas

c5b Courtesy, The Summerlee Foundation and the Texas State Historical Association

c6,c7,c8 Courtesy, The Summerlee Foundation and the Texas State Historical Association

c9 Amon Carter Museum, Fort Worth, Texas, 1976.33.5, Henry Walke, "The Naval Expedition under Comre. Perry, Ascending the Tabasco River at the Devils Bend June 15th. 1847," 1848, toned lithograph (hand-colored)

c10 Amon Carter Museum, Fort Worth, Texas, 1976.33.8, Gustavus Pfau after Henry Walke, "The U.S. Naval Battery During the Bombardment of Vera Cruz on the 24 and 25 of March 1847," 1848, toned lithograph (hand-colored)

c11 Nettie Lee Benson Latin American Collection, General Libraries, University of Texas at Austin

c12 Courtesy U.S. Army Center of Military History

c13 Nettie Lee Benson Latin American Collection, General Libraries, University of Texas at Austin

c14 Courtesy U.S. Army Center of Military History

c15 Amon Carter Museum, Fort Worth, Texas, 1972.186.11, Bayot and Bichebois after Carl Nebel, "Storming of Chapultepec-Quitman's Attack," 1851, toned lithograph (hand-colored)

c16 Album Pintoresco, Vault Folio 2 F1213.L45, DeGolyer Library, Southern Methodist University, Dallas, Texas

Index

The U.S.–Mexican War, 1846–1848 was originally produced for PBS by KERA-TV, Dallas/Fort Worth/Denton. The documentary series and its accompanying educational materials were made possible by grants from the following:

National Endowment for the Humanities

The John D. and Catherine T. MacArthur Foundation

Meadows Foundation

Corporation for Public Broadcasting

Public Broadcasting Service

Arthur Vining Davis Foundations

Summerlee Foundation

California Council for the Humanities,
a state program of the National Endowment for the Humanities

Texas Council for the Humanities,
a state program of the National Endowment for the Humanities

Priddy Foundation Fund of Communities Foundation of Texas

Summerfield G. Roberts Foundation

Houston Endowment Inc.

The U.S.–Mexico Fund for Culture sponsored
by the Bancomer Cultural Foundation, The Rockefeller Foundation,
and Mexico's National Fund for Culture and the Arts

The Cecil and Ida Green Foundation

Carl B. and Florence E. King Foundation

Still Water Foundation

Dr. & Mrs. Francis McGinnis

Nevada Humanities Committee,
a state program of the National Endowment for the Humanities

Mr. & Mrs. Jenkins Garrett

J. A. "Tony" Canales

KERA

KERA, a major public television producer and a leading community-based
radio and television institution, serves viewers and listeners throughout
North Texas with high-quality projects and services.